The Monarch Butterfly: International Traveler

FRED A. URQUHART

The Monarch Butterfly: International Traveler

NELSON-HALL nh CHICAGO

Edited by Dorothy Anderson
Designed by Charlotte D'Almaine
Set in Bembo and Bembo Italic by Pam Frye Typesetting, Inc.

Illustrations on the following pages are from F. A. Urquhart, *The Monarch Butterfly* (University of Toronto Press, 1960) and are used with the permission of the University of Toronto Press: 21, 23, 29, 32, 44, 48, 50, 59, 61, 64, 75, 103, 105, 106, 109, 125, 132, 135, and PLATES 9, 19, 22, and 23.

Library of Congress Cataloging-in-Publication Data

Urquhart, Fred A.
    The monarch butterfly.

    Bibliography: p.
    Includes index.
    1. Monarch butterfly.   I. Title.
QL561.D3U78   1987   595.78′9   86-8704
ISBN 0-8304-1039-2

Manufactured in the United States of America

10   9   8   7   6   5   4   3   2   1

The paper used in this book meets the minimum requirements of American National Standard for Information Sciences—Permanence of Paper for Printed Library Materials, ANSI Z39.48-1984.

*Dedicated to my wife, Norah, without
whose constant interest and assistance
in the studies of the monarch butterfly
this book could not have been written.*

Contents

Preface

I suppose I have spent my life working up to the preparation of this book, bringing together all of the data I have amassed over the years concerning the development and habits of that most remarkable monarch butterfly. As a child I was endowed with a natural curiosity about animals and their manners of living. I spent countless hours watching their activities, especially those six-legged animals, the insects.

It started back in 1916 when, as a child of five years, I began learning about the world of insects. My family lived in a small frame house that was located close to a railway line. Along the steel tracks, over which freight trains rumbled back and forth, there were acres of weedy fields that, to my young eyes, were acres of beautiful sweet-smelling flowers. Of these wild-flowers, I have a most vivid memory of the yellow and white sweet clover, which attracted a multitude of busy, buzzing insects, all actively engaged in collecting nectar and pollen. How well I remember one very painful experience: I was attracted to a large, fuzzy bumblebee and, thinking that it resembled a miniature furry kitten, I caught it in my hand. The shock as the bee thrust its sharp stinger into my flesh brought tears to my eyes. I ran home to my mother, who dried my tears, applied a paste of baking soda upon the rapidly swelling welt, and explained that, in order to protect itself from little boys, a bumblebee possesses a stinging apparatus at the tip of its body. I remember my mother ending her explanation with the following statement: "I am certain you will not catch another bumblebee in your bare hands." This was my first introduction into how insects protect themselves from predators, and thus began my initiation into the fascinating realm of insects, later to become my profession.

I spent many happy hours during the warm summer months browsing through my railroad garden of wild plants, watching and listening to the multitude of insects flying with set determination from one flower to another. I caught some insects in a glass pickle jar by holding the mouth of the jar over them while they were busily sucking nectar from flowers and then snapping the lid over the opening. I took these little insect treasures home to be examined at leisure. Eventually, the insects in the jars died and I placed the little inert bodies in small cardboard boxes. I knew nothing about how to prepare insects for a collection—by thrusting pins into their lifeless bodies and arranging them in cork-lined boxes or trays with glass lids. This discovery was to come many years later.

By the time I was eight years old, I had learned a great deal about insects. I watched the small, brightly colored andrenid bees making their nests in small holes in the cedar posts that supported our garden fence. After the bees had deposited a rolled up leaf into the opening and filled it with a supply of bright yellow pollen, I would empty the hole of its contents with a nail and then watch to see what the bees would do when they returned. A rather childish prank, but I later read a book by a French naturalist, Jean Henri Fabre, and was pleased to learn that he had done something similar, but on a much more scientific basis.

Being of a musical turn of mind—music was supposed to be my eventual career—I listened to the orchestration of singing and chirping grasshoppers and crickets. I watched black male field crickets scraping their front wings together and observed that the chirping was quite different if a female were present than when they were calling for mates. I observed small short-horned grasshoppers that resembled miniature violinists as they bowed their slender legs up and down against their parchmentlike front wings; and I also listened to the large, leaflike long-horned grasshoppers make their characteristic "zip-zip-zip," like muffled castanets. When I later came to learn the names of these little musicians, it was possible for me to identify them without having to capture them. My interest in the music of the grasshoppers and crickets led eventually to a master's degree and finally a doctorate in a study of the morphology and ecology of the Orthoptera, the order to which the grasshoppers and crickets belong.

But my fascination for butterflies and moths continued. My collections of these insects grew rapidly, especially the moths which I collected during the hours of darkness as they fluttered about street lights—large luna moths with delicate, pale green wings and long swallowtails and brown cecropia and polyphemus moths with their purple and pink markings and large round spots that closely resembled the eyes of an owl (according to some naturalists, these spots evolved to frighten would-be night-prowling predators). I painted a sweet, sticky solution of rotted apples and molasses on the trunks of trees to attract night-flying moths. Armed with a flashlight and a cyanide jar, I went from tree to tree collecting moths of all shapes, sizes, and coloration. I can still remember the tremendous feeling of pleasure mingled with surprise when I collected my first underwing—those magnificent catocala moths that have barklike front wings, matching the color and texture of the tree, and brilliant red or orange underwings. I spent many pleasant hours examining a night's catch, placing the new acquisitions on spreading boards and finally identifying and arranging them in neat rows in my permanent collection.

Not far from my home was a public library. The children's section was tended by one of the most delightful persons I have ever met. Every Saturday morning throughout the winter months, children would gather there to listen to stories. We would sit on the floor in front of an open fireplace in which huge logs burned with a snapping, crackling sound and clusters of bright yellow and orange flames and filled the room with the delightful odor of wood smoke. The librarian, Miss MacIntosh, had a mass of black hair tied in a knot at the back of her head — I thought it the most beautiful hair I had ever seen. She was slight of build and usually wore a black dress adorned with a necklace of bright, white pearls. Her quiet, well-modulated voice brought to life all the characters that lived between the covers of the books. She would imitate the voices of animals or, in hushed tones, bring to light dangerous situations, such as the advent of a wolf or weasel.

We were allowed to suggest books we wanted read to us and, of course, I suggested books from the shelf headed, with a bright white label, "Natural History." One particular visit was to begin a new chapter in my interest in animal life and eventually a career in the study of insects, especially the monarch butterfly. It was a dark, gloomy Saturday morning; a fine, drizzly rain descended from a sombre sky as I wended my way to the library. Miss MacIntosh had chosen to read a section from a book dealing with an ancient civilization. I listened for a short time, but I felt bored and not too comfortable in my damp clothing, so I decided not to continue with the group but to return to my favorite section to find a natural history book that I had not as yet read. But, to my considerable disappointment, there were none.

When the reading session was over, the librarian spoke to me in words I cannot now recall with any degree of certainty but that were to this effect: "You have read all the books in the section on natural history. I think that perhaps it is time for you to advance to the senior library." With that, she gave me a yellow card upon which she had written a note for the senior librarian.

As I climbed the stairs that led from the children's section in the lower floor to the upper floor where the adult library was located, I felt as if I were in a dream and that the stairs were taking me to some mysterious place where only very serious adults were allowed. I entered a large room filled on all sides with row upon row of books. A few adults were moving noiselessly about the room examining the rows of books, stopping every now and then to remove one from the shelf and peruse it with fixed expression. The librarian, who was thin and wore her light brown hair parted in the middle and pulled back over her ears, peered at me through rimless glasses perched precariously on her nose, as if she were accustomed to looking over them rather than through them. She smiled with a smile that lit up her face and, with a curt nod of her head, beckoned me to approach, which I did, holding out my yellow card. "What can I do for you, dear?" she asked in a hushed voice. Not knowing just what to say, I simply handed her my yellow card. She glanced at it, smiled, and then removed a white card from a wooden box that was placed near the front edge of her desk. Having asked me my name, address and age, she then presented me with the white card that made me a member of the senior library, a card that I cherished for many years.

"I hope you will find many books in our collection to interest you; I have been told by the junior librarian that you have read all of the natural history books in the junior library." She then rose from her seat behind her large, dark brown desk. I was surprised to find that she was quite short and not nearly as old as I had first concluded. She took me by the hand and led me to the natural sciences section and then, with a smile, returned to her thronelike chair.

Thus began my journey into the marvelous world of living creatures. Many of the books I examined were far beyond my understanding and appreciation. A man named Charles Darwin described the origin of the different kinds of animals inhabiting our earth and recounted a voyage he took on a ship named the *Beagle*. A French scientist described his experiments with insects; his name was Jean Fabre. There were many books with beautiful illustrations of different kinds of animals from around the world. What a wonderful world was revealed to my young mind.

I must admit that my interest in animals and plants interfered with my school work. You see, the primary school that I attended was located next to a large cattail marsh that was surrounded by a field of flowering plants and tall grasses. In the spring and early summer the marsh resounded with all sorts of interesting sounds: frogs grunting, toads singing, redwing blackbirds calling "och-a-ree," marsh wrens trilling. Turtles were resting on floating logs. For me to ignore this beautiful marsh on my way to school was, at times, quite impossible. So I lingered, not wanting to enter the stuffy, prisonlike classroom, with the result that I was quite often late. In these early days there was no such subject as natural science taught in the primary schools, and the teachers were not interested in the "creepy, crawly things" that I often brought into the classroom. Quite a different situation exists in the schools today.

I never did become acclimatized to confinement in a primary school class. Finally, the time came when I was released to proceed to a "higher education" in a secondary school. And what a fantastic change this was! I did not have one teacher for all subjects; I had a number of teachers during the year, each one a specialist in his or her chosen subject. Mr. Taylor taught biology and was interested in my mania for the study of animals. He was in charge of the biology room, a place with a number of aquaria containing exotic fish. There was a small, cement pool in the center of the room containing different kinds of turtles. Mounted birds sat on perches peering at me through glassy eyes. Glass-topped trays were filled with rows of insects, including a number of monarch butterflies. At last I had arrived in the world of natural science. And this is when my interest in the monarch butterfly began.

Acknowledgments

It would take many pages to thank all those who have contributed to my research on the monarch butterfly; of these, however, the following warrant special mention.

To Dr. Claude Bissell, past president of the University of Toronto, I owe a sincere debt of gratitude for his intervention on my behalf that made it possible for me to become a member of the Faculty of Arts and Sciences, where research facilities were made available to me, thus leading to many of the advances in our knowledge of the monarch butterfly as presented in this book.

When I first became interested in the monarch butterfly in 1927, I wrote to the late Dr. C. B. Williams, the leading authority on insect migration, asking him whether or not he considered this butterfly to be a migrant. Over the years Dr. Williams became a very dear friend and colleague and a most helpful critic of my studies. My visit with him, to discuss the manuscript of my previous book, in his retirement home in Kincraig, Scotland, was the most fruitful experience of my life.

Over four thousand individuals, residing in various parts of the United States, Canada, Mexico, Guatemala, Central America, Australia, New Zealand, and islands of the South Atlantic and the Caribbean, have contributed much over the past many years by alar tagging migrants and submitting observations dealing with flight directions and population densities. Their kindness, generosity, and most friendly cooperation have been astonishing. The efforts of these individuals, some of whom have been associates for over thirty years, have been basic to the research; without their assistance the overwintering site in Mexico (the terminus of a long migratory flight of the Eastern Population) would not have been discovered. Not only did these associates work with me, but they also donated most generously to the financial support of the research, establishing a fund held in trust by the University of Toronto. In addition, the associates presented lectures to various organizations on television and radio, and held press interviews, thus bringing the project to the attention of the public.

Much of the success of field investigations depends upon the enthusiasm of field assistants, and in this I have been most fortunate. Had it not been for the close cooperation between myself and Cathy and Ken Brugger, it might have taken many more years to discover the loci of the overwintering site in Mexico. I will always remember this relationship with very deep feelings. In our field studies of the monarch butterflies in Yucatan, I was most fortunate to obtain the assistance of Señora Barbara De Montes, resulting in our being able to follow the aberrant migration to Guatemala. My son, Douglas, and his wife, Judith, carried out an extensive field research program in New Zealand, which forms the basis of my discussion in the present work dealing with the monarch butterflies in the islands of the South Pacific. Dr. C. N. Smithers, of the Department of Entomology of the Australia Museum of Natural History, carried out an intensive alar-tagging program based upon the methods I was using in North America and submitted the results of his efforts to me; these reports were most valuable in understanding the movements of the introduced monarch butterfly in Australia as well as allowing me to compare the results with those in New Zealand and other islands of the Pacific.

Through the generosity of Dr. Bogusch, former chairman of the Department of Biology of Texas A & I University in Kingsville, Norah and I were given office and laboratory space during the winter of 1969, while I was on sabbatical leave from the University of Toronto. With this as our headquarters, we carried out intensive field investigations along the Rio Grande and Mexico, with a final odometer reading for the period of 22,530 kilometers.

Universities, colleges, and museums in Canada, the United States, and Mexico were most generous in making research collections of butterflies and milkweed species available to me, as well as taking part in many fruitful discussions. I am particularly grateful to the American Museum of Natural History in New York for the loan of specimens of various species of New World Danaidae, which allowed me to make an intensive study of the various species and their distribution.

Without financial assistance, the long-term project recorded here could not have been carried out. I have been most fortunate in obtaining generous research grants from the Committee on Research and Exploration of the National Geographic Society of the United States, the National Research Council of Canada, and donations from our associates.

When one is attempting to follow the movements of a particular animal, be it a bird or insect, it is necessary to bring the project to the attention of the lay public so that they may take part. I have had considerable cooperation in the form of notices in books, magazines, and newspapers, and on radio and television programs. For example, my article published in the August 1976 issue of the *National Geographic Magazine* brought the project to the attention of many thousands of members of the National Geographic Society. As the result of an article Norah and I wrote that appeared in the *Mexico City News*, February 25, 1973, we made contact with Kenneth Brugger. After reading the article, he offered his assistance in the attempt to locate the overwintering site in the mountains of Mexico.

Without adequate research facilities, no scientific project can be successfully carried out. At the Scarborough Campus of the University of Toronto, research equipment and laboratory space were made available to me, and, in addition, I had the help of graduate students and laboratory assistants. The Graphics Department worked closely with me in the preparation of many illustrations that have appeared in my research papers and that are also included in this book.

To all those who have given so generously of their time, effort, and financial support over the past many years, I offer my most sincere thanks. I trust that this book will act as a monument to our combined efforts.

Introduction

Why was this particular species of butterfly given the name "monarch"? The early settlers who came to North America from Europe, particularly those from England and Holland, were impressed by the sight of such a magnificent butterfly, and so they named it "monarch" after King William, prince of Orange, stateholder of Holland, and later king of England—its orange color no doubt suggesting the name. From "William" we get the vernacular "Billy," and hence the name "King Billy," which has also been applied to this butterfly.

I have often been asked the question, What good is the monarch butterfly? To this I have responded by asking another, What good is man to the monarch butterfly? From my point of view, all living creatures inhabiting our earth—of which man, in his variety of races, is but one—have an equal right to life and were not placed on earth for the aggrandizement of man nor to satisfy his egocentricity. However, the monarch butterfly inadvertently does contribute a great deal to the welfare of the human species and therefore is an insect that is well worth our consideration and study from the following points of view.

1. *The agricultural viewpoint.* The larvae of the monarch butterfly feed on the leaves of various species of milkweed, which is considered a weed. In parts of the United States and Mexico, certain species of milkweed are considered poisonous to cattle and have been given the vernacular name of "loco weed," since they presumably cause a form of insanity among the cattle eating them. Hence, the monarch might be considered of economic importance, and one may class it as a "beneficial insect," since it helps to reduce the abundance of a potentially noxious plant.

2. *The scientific viewpoint.* The monarch butterfly is used in various investigations, such as the functions of lipids, a form of fats, that are the monarch's fuel supply during its long migratory flights; the characteristics of the compound eyes of the adult, the physiological aspects of which can be used to interpret the chemical changes in a human eye; and the manner in which monarch butterflies can find their way across thousands of kilometers from feeding areas to overwintering sites and return, a subject of interest to

students of ornithology, particularly in view of recent research in which the substance magnetite has been found in the heads of monarch butterflies as well as in birds. Monarchs are used in research projects such as studies of environmental factors that control growth and development and studies of disease vectors. For example, the polyhedrosis virus and numerous strains of bacteria are important in the biological control of insects and are found among populations of the monarch butterfly.

3. *The educational viewpoint.* The monarch butterfly is an ideal insect for students in primary and secondary schools who are engaged in the study of basic natural science. The students learn by direct observation the amazing transformation involved in insect metamorphosis, and the importance of conservation can be stressed using the monarch butterfly as an example of the destruction in an area where there is an excess use of insecticides and herbicides. As a result of such studies in schools, areas have been set aside as wildlife sanctuaries, thus protecting not only the monarch butterfly population but also the plants and animals with which it is associated.

The monarch is used by many teachers to introduce students to the discipline of entomology and at the same time to emphasize the important part played by insects in the "web of life." What is most important, the students obtain a knowledge of insect life by direct contact with the living specimen, rather than studying collections of dead insects or learning about them only through textbooks.

One of my associates, a primary school teacher, uses the monarch butterfly not only in her natural science course but also in her geography lessons. The students follow the migratory routes of the monarch in North America as well as its distribution in other parts of the world. Some of the students in her classes have written to students in other lands where the monarch butterfly also occurs and, by means of this common interest, have established lasting friendships.

Many teachers have involved their students in tracing the flight of the monarch butterfly by taking part in my alar-tagging program and by carrying out simple experiments. As a result, such students have received scholarships and awards at science fairs, and some have pursued their interest in biology to the university level and are now occupying teaching and research positions.

4. *The monetary viewpoint.* Each winter countless thousands of migrant monarch butterflies collect upon the pine and eucalyptus trees on the Monterey Peninsula of California. Such masses of butterflies, which in some cases cause the branches of the trees to bend under their combined weight, attract thousands of tourists to these overwintering areas, giving rise to in-

creased annual income for shopkeepers and motel and hotel owners. So important is this annual phenomenon to the citizens that each year children dressed like huge monarch butterflies parade through the streets of Monterey in honor of the arrival of these colorful butterflies. A city ordinance was passed to insure the safety of these butterflies.

CITY OF PACIFIC GROVE   ORDINANCE No. 352

PROTECTION OF BUTTERFLIES
Adopted Nov. 16, 1938
ORDINANCE NO. 352

AN ORDINANCE PROVIDING FOR THE PROTECTION OF THE MONARCH BUTTERFLIES DURING THEIR ANNUAL VISIT TO THE CITY OF PACIFIC GROVE

THE COUNCIL OF THE CITY OF PACIFIC GROVE DO ORDAIN AS FOLLOWS:

SECTION 1. It shall be unlawful, and it is hereby declared to be unlawful for any person to molest or interfere with in any way the peaceful occupancy of the Monarch Butterflies on their annual visit to the City of Pacific Grove, and during the entire time they remain within the corporate limits of said City, in whatever spot they may choose to stop in; provided, however, that if said Butterflies should at any time swarm in upon or near the private dwelling house or other buildings of a citizen of the City of Pacific Grove in such a way as to interfere with the occupancy and use of said dwelling and/or other buildings, that said Butterflies may be removed, if possible to another location upon the application of said citizen to the Chief of Police of this City.

SECTION 2. Any violation of this Ordinance shall be deemed a misdemeanor and shall be punishable by a fine of not more than Five Hundred Dollars ($500.00), or by imprisonment in the County Jail of Monterey County for not more than six (6) months or by both such fine and imprisonment.

SECTION 3. This Ordinance is hereby declared to be urgent, and shall be in effect from and after its final passage. The following is a statement of such urgency: Inasmuch as the Monarch Butterflies are a distinct asset to the City of Pacific Grove, and cause innumerable people to visit said City each year to see the said Butterflies, it is the duty of the citizens of said City to protect the Butterflies in every way possible, from serious harm and possible extinction by brutal and heartless people.

PASSED AND ADOPTED BY THE COUNCIL OF THE CITY OF PACIFIC GROVE, this 16th day of November, 1938, by the following vote:

AYES: COUNCILMEN: (Mayor) Fiddes, Norton, Galbraith, Burton.
NOES: COUNCILMEN: Lee, Matthews.
ABSENT: COUNCILMEN: Solomon.
APPROVED: Nov. 16, 1938.

WILLIAM FIDDES,
Mayor of said City.

ATTEST:
ELGIN C. HURLBERT,
City Clerk.

---

5. *The esthetic viewpoint.* I do not know of any species of insect that has aroused a greater interest among the populace in many parts of the world than the monarch butterfly. Literally thousands of published accounts have appeared in newspapers, popular magazines, naturalists' bulletins, and school papers. In addition, documentary films have been produced. The

English firm Survival Anglia did a film for television audiences based on my research on the monarch's migratory habits that has appeared in ninety-six countries of the world and in several languages. Televisa of Mexico produced a similar documentary film that is shown in all Latin countries; short films have been produced for television in England and Japan. All of the above testify to the popularity of the monarch butterfly.

Over the past many years, Norah and I have received hundreds of letters relating the excitement of observing, for the first time, the amazing transformation that takes place when a black-and-yellow-striped larva changes miraculously into a jade colored pupa studded with golden spots; the final transformation as the adult monarch butterfly emerges with budlike wings that eventually swell to full length as body fluid is pumped into them; and trees festooned with thousands of bright orange butterflies on the overnight roosting sites during the fall migration. Many of our associates have taken the pupae into hospitals so that patients could watch the emergence of the adult butterfly. Children confined to hospital beds have had a spark of pleasure light up their lives as a beautiful butterfly suddenly made its appearance from an apparently lifeless pupa.

It would take a separate book — and I have considered writing it — to relate the many experiences concerning the monarch butterfly that have been related to us over the years.

One of the great pleasures Norah and I have had in our studies of the monarch butterfly has been receiving letters from children and adults alike expressing their delight at being introduced to the study of nature through our program of monarch butterfly research. Many young people who have worked with us, alar tagging and reporting observations, have carried their interest through to the university and have received degrees in biology.

The study of the monarch butterfly has been a source of great happiness for me and Norah. I sincerely trust that I have been able to convey this feeling in my book, which I hope will add greatly to your interest and studies of this most attractive and fascinating insect.

The Monarch Butterfly:
International Traveler

PART 1

Milkweed

A brief consideration of the milkweed plant is important in a discussion of the monarch butterfly, because the life history of the butterfly is closely linked to this plant from the time the small, yellow, conical egg is deposited on a leaf to the complete development of the larva to the pupa stage. The milkweed plant controls the distribution of monarch butterfly populations and regulates their density in any given area. And it is the milkweed plant that is primarily responsible for the amazing long-distance migrations that closely resemble those of migratory birds.

In the course of many years of collecting and studying insects, I have come to associate them with the plants on which they feed in their immature stages. If I wish to collect the larvae of a particular species of moth or butterfly, I first look for the plant on which I know the insect feeds, and then I look for the insect. I have learned that, although many species of insects are confined to a particular species of plant, others are not so choosy and will feed on the foliage of a great variety of plants.

The monarch butterfly restricts its menu to milkweed plants belonging to the family Asclepiadaceae. In North America, wherever I located species of this family of plants, I knew I would also find monarch butterflies, although not always in the same abundance. In Australia and New Zealand there are species of milkweed, and there one also finds the monarch butterfly; in

Hawaii and other islands of the Pacific Ocean, there are species of milkweed, and again one finds the monarch butterfly. Africa and Asia have many species of milkweed and many species of butterflies of the same family as that of the monarch, some belonging to the same genus *(Danaus)*.

As I pursued my interest in the biology of the monarch butterfly, culminating in tracing its migratory flights from breeding grounds in the eastern parts of North America to the overwintering site in Mexico, I became more and more attracted to the study of milkweed plants. In the early days of my studies, I thought that all milkweed plants would more or less resemble the species found in Ontario, Canada—*Asclepias syriaca*, referred to in the literature as the common milkweed—which grows in great abundance in fields, along railway lines, and along roadways. But I was to find out that there are milkweed plants in many parts of the world, representing over 2,400 species and 220 distinct genera. In my travels over North America, I found an amazing variety of them. In Arizona, a vinelike species covers small bushes with slender, creeping stems. Other species that I found in arid deserts of Mexico appear as small spruce trees with needlelike leaves. Some grow in marsh areas of eastern North America and resemble small, woody-stemmed bushes, while still others are found in wooded areas beneath a canopy of deciduous and, in some cases, evergreen forest. One of the most fascinating species I have ever encountered I found growing in hot sand dunes along the northern shore of the Gulf of Mexico in Florida. Had it not been for the presence of the typical milkweed flower, I would never have identified it as a species of this family. It is a small plant, not more than 10 centimeters in height, possessing only a few small, round leaves and having slender, elongate petioles that cause the leaves to lie close to the ground. How remarkable that this apparently tender little plant could survive the extremely high temperature of the sand, a temperature so hot that I could barely touch it. On one visit to these sand dunes I was delighted to observe a female monarch alight upon one of the leaves and deposit an egg on its undersurface.

Over the years I discovered many fascinating species all bearing the same milkweed-type flower but with variations in color and length of the corolla lobes. Other species have been sent to me by my associates. With respect to size, I was amazed to find not only diminutive species, such as that growing on the sand dunes, but also one that resembles a small tree, growing to a height of 3 meters and bearing large, oval, somewhat leathery leaves and extremely large seed pods that look like small green melons. On these treelike species growing in Antigua and Montserrat of the Lesser Antilles, I found many monarch butterfly larvae of the subspecies *megalippe*.

Although my interest in milkweed at first was limited to its relationship to the monarch butterfly, I was surprised to learn that in the past milkweed had been considered of agricultural importance. Years ago, when the early colonists came to New England, chicken feathers were scarce, kapok was unknown, and the age of plastics lay many years in the future. So, these hardy and frugal people made use of what occurred in nature. They collected the fluffy floss from the milkweed pods and used it to stuff cushions and pillows. It proved so successful that Governor John Winthrop sent the seeds to England in the year 1670. From England milkweed was transmitted to the European continent and grew abundantly in France, Corsica, and Italy. By the middle of the nineteenth century, *Asclepias syriaca* and *A. incarnata* were cultivated in many parts of Europe. Attempts were made to bring these plants into full commercial use in England, France, Germany, and Russia but without success.

Milkweed stems possess long, tough fibers that can be removed easily when the soft tissue rots. Hence, some milkweed species have been grown commercially as a source of fibers to replace those of flax and hemp. However, the amount of fiber obtained from the milkweed plant is less than the amount obtained from the same volume of flax and hemp, so milkweed fiber could not compete commercially with flax or hemp, and the project was discontinued. Attempts also were made to replace flax and hemp fibers with those of milkweed stems and pods in the manufacture of high quality paper, but again the enterprise failed.

During World War I, natural rubber was difficult to obtain, since it is cultivated only in tropical latitudes. Numerous attempts were made to remove the latex sap (milk) from various species of milkweed plants, but without success as far as quantity was concerned. It was considered again during World War II. Now, of course, synthetic rubber has almost completely taken over the market for natural rubber.

During World War II, I was a meteorological officer with the Royal Canadian Air Force. I recall going into a section of the supply depot where damaged equipment was stored. I noticed a rather faded yellow life jacket that had been discarded because of a large rip in one of the packed units, and the stuffing attracted my attention. It was exceedingly light, very fluffy, and possessed a noticeable sheen. I took some of it from the jacket and noted that it was the seed fluff from milkweed plants. The jacket was much lighter than those filled with kapok or cork, and I can well imagine that it would possess a quality of high flotation owing to the amount of air trapped in the milkweed fibers.

I do not know of any flower that produces a more appealing aroma than that of certain species of milkweed. A bouquet of milkweed flowers will fill a room with a delightful perfume in a short time. Because of this, milkweed plants are grown in gardens across North America. Even if I did not possess such a strong admiration for milkweed plants because of their relationship to my studies of the monarch butterfly, I would still wish to have them in my flower garden. I enjoy seeing the many species of insects that are attracted to the blossoms. In the fall, I often watch the seeds being carried aloft, hanging from their delicate silken parachutes. And in the winter, Norah and I can still enjoy milkweed plants as they stand erect, capturing little piles of snow, like small white caps, on their open seed pods. In the fall, when we gather various dry weed plants for a winter bouquet, we always add a few milkweed stems bearing pods, as is also commonly done by florists.

Milkweed plants are considered weeds by many agriculturists. Granted, the seeds may be a nuisance when harvesting grain or hay, but it does seem unfortunate that, in some parts of the country, the indiscriminate spraying of herbicides has destroyed thousands of acres of milkweed along roadways, where the possible effects of milkwood plants are not an agricultural problem. One company involved in the manufacture of herbicides has produced a specific "milkweed killer." As I shall discuss later, this destruction of milkweed plants in local breeding areas of the monarch butterfly will undoubtedly have a disastrous effect on monarch populations in the near future. And this is in addition to the direct effects of indiscriminate spraying of insecticides.

There is a widely held belief, particularly in parts of Mexico and the islands of the Caribbean, that all species of milkweed are poisonous to cattle. While carrying out field investigations in Trinidad and Tobago, I heard about the effect of milkweed, termed "locoweed," on cattle. I questioned some of the natives who possessed cattle as to the nature of this sickness, and much to my surprise, although all agreed that it was a "very bad plant," none of them had ever had any cattle affected by it. In fields where the cattle were grazing, I noticed that the grass and small plants had been consumed, but the milkweed plants were untouched. I noted this same situation during other field expeditions in parts of Florida and the islands of the Greater and Lesser Antilles. Obviously, cattle grazing in a field do not eat milkweed plants.

Of the twenty-four hundred species of milkweed in the world, some are undoubtedly poisonous. In fact, some African species are used by natives to poison their arrows. Some natives mix ground-up milkweed roots with grain in order to paralyze birds that eat the mixture. It has also been reported, again in Africa, that large mammals have been killed when eating meat to which ground-up milkweed plants have been added.

On the other hand, it is interesting to note that the seed pods and young plants of *A. syriaca* have been used as food in various parts of North America. Here are two recipes taken from a pioneer cookbook:

Boil the young plants with salt; add spices to taste.

Gather milkweed pods when they are a dusty shade of green and not more than one to one and a half inches in length; boil in salted water for ten minutes; place pods on a hot dish and sprinkle with salt; add pepper and grated cheese; dip the pods in butter as you eat them.

THE COMMON MILKWEED

Throughout the many years I have devoted to the study of the monarch butterfly, the common milkweed *(Asclepias syriaca)* has received most of my attention. I depended on this species over the years for food for the thousands of larvae I reared for biological research. That is why I have chosen this particular species as an example of the family of milkweeds, Asclepiadaceae.

The common milkweed ranges across North America east of the Rocky Mountains and is therefore the species that you are most likely to locate as you look for the larvae of the monarch butterfly. But you will encounter many different species as you travel across the continent; some resemble the common milkweed, while others can be identified only if you are able to obtain the flower.

One of the best ways to locate an unusual species of milkweed is to watch a female monarch as she deposits her eggs upon the leaves of the plant. While visiting one of our associates in Pearsall, Texas, Norah and I were making observations on the presence and abundance of the spring migrants. We happened to notice a female monarch flying close to the ground on a well-kept lawn in front of a church; she paused every now and then to alight upon a small and inconspicuous plant, as if depositing her eggs. On hands and knees we examined the plant and located a number of eggs. Since it was early spring, the plant had no flowers. Had it not been for the ovipositing female we would never have recognized this small, prostrate, inconspicuous plant as a member of the milkweed family.

By far the largest populations of monarch butterflies occur in areas where the common milkweed grows, particularly in northeastern United States and two of the eastern provinces of Canada—Ontario and Quebec. In this area, the greatest preponderance occurs in the vicinity of the Great Lakes, where the common milkweed grows in great abundance in fields and along roadways and railway lines.

Milkweed flowers occur in dense, close, terminal or lateral clusters. The flowers of all species of this family in North America possess the same general characteristics. The flower clusters may be off-white, greenish white, pink, or bright orange. This great variety of color within a species results from hybridization between two closely related species or subspecies. I was led to this conclusion because of the following experience. When I first introduced the common milkweed into my garden, the flower clusters were a fairly uniform light pink in color; but when I later introduced a few new plants with white flowers—which at the time I considered to be a different species—my garden of milkweed plants eventually exhibited the variety of colors noted above.

The greenish, scalelike corolla that covers the parts of the individual flowers is divided into five segments that bend downwards when the buds open. Situated above the corolla segments is a crown of five hooded structures, within which are located the nectar cups and the perfume that attracts nectar-seeking insects.

If you examine one of these flower clusters you will usually find small flies, bees, and other insects with their legs stuck to the hooded structures, their wings beating rapidly as they attempt to escape. Many of these trapped insects fail to escape and remain attached to the milkweed flowers. If you remove one of the trapped insects and examine its legs with a magnifying glass, you will see one or more pairs of small, bright yellow sacs attached to the insect's claws and the hairs of its legs. These small sacs contain milkweed pollen to be carried by the insect to another flower. This is accomplished as follows.

The entire structure attached to the insect's legs is termed a *pollinium* and consists of two completely enclosed packages of pollen. The pollen sacs are connected to a yellow yolklike process called the *retinaculum,* the arms of which are elaborately ringed, or fluted. The arms are joined to a common body termed the *corpusculum,* which is brown in color, in contrast to the yellow pollen sacs, and is of a rather leathery texture. It is somewhat compressed, and the inner surface is smooth and entire, while the outer surface has an elongated slit passing from one end of the corpusculum to the other.

The corpusculum is the mechanism that traps a visiting insect and operates as follows.

When an insect is busily engaged in sucking nectar from a nectar cup, one of its legs slips into the narrow slit of the corpusculum and, as a result, becomes firmly attached to it. If the trapped insect is a powerful flyer, it is able to dislodge the pollinium bearing the two pollen sacs. If, however, the insect is a weak flyer, it will be unable to dislodge the pollinium and, as a result, becomes permanently attached. The strong flyer that succeeds in dislodging the pollinium visits another milkweed flower. The leg bearing the pollen sacs slips into the narrow space between the contiguous wings of the anther of the flower, thus transferring the pollen to its destined chamber.

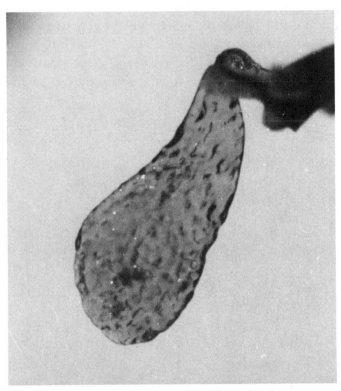

If you remove one of the insects trapped on the flower of a milkweed and examine its legs under a microscope, you will see small yellow structures adhering to them. Each of these structures is called a pollinium. Here, magnified forty times, is a pollinium on the tarsus of a honeybee.

The chamber bearing the *stigma* is composed of the lateral margins of the *anthers* except at the very tip, where a small area of true stigma is exposed. Within a few hours after the pollen sacs have been placed in the stigma chamber, pollen tubes emerge, one from each of the pollen grains in the pollen sacs. The tubes penetrate the stigma and pass through to the cavity of the *carpel*, where the nucleus of the pollen grain unites with the nucleus of the female *ovule*, thus producing a milkweed seed.

As the seeds develop, the characteristic milkweed pod begins to form. At first it is small and shaped like a green glove. Dead or dying flowers (those that were not fertilized) surround the small pod. As the pod develops it assumes an elongate form. In some species the pod is long and slender, but in the common milkweed it is swollen near the central section and elongate and slightly curved at the apical end, somewhat resembling a rather fat bird. (As a young lad I would place two feathers, one on each side of the pod, to represent wings, glass pins for eyes, and small sticks for legs. When completed, the pod had the appearance of a gray swan, and for this reason some species of milkweed have been termed "swan plants.") The outer skin of the pod may be smooth or covered with a number of minute, soft, spinelike processes in addition to larger lumps and irregular striations.

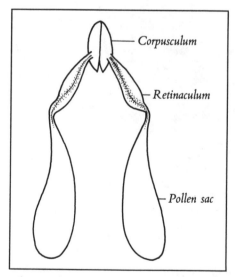

The method used by milkweed species for cross-fertilization involves a structure termed a pollinium. An insect visiting a milkweed flower to obtain nectar may pass its leg into the slit in the corpusculum. When the insect flies away, it pulls the pollinium out of the pocket in the flower and carries the two pollen sacs, attached to a stem termed a retinaculum, to another flower.

Milkweed pods are attractive structures. Housed within the tough outer shell are rows of seeds, each one slightly overlapping its neighbor, giving the impression of fish scales. Each seed is attached to a tuft of fibers that resemble fine strands of silk; before liberation, the silklike tufts are held together to form a single strand. When liberated, the fibers spring apart to form a downlike parachute that carries the seed to a distant place. Often as a child I took the seeds from the pods, threw them into the air, and watched the small parachutes, glistening in the sun. The empty pod, with its central, light-brown, parchmentlike stalk, to which the seeds had been attached, is most attractive and is used extensively by florists in arrangements of dried plants.

There are, apparently, no true rhizomatous species of milkweed in North America (rhizomatous species are those that produce roots from the lower surface and plant shoots from the upper surface). Some species, including the common milkweed, produce long roots with vegetative centers, similar to the eyes found in potatoes, that produce clusters of small plants referred to as *clones.* The clones grow rather slowly throughout the summer months, and it takes three to four years for such clones to reach maturity and produce flowers and seeds.

Female monarch butterflies tend to lay their eggs on clone clusters or on seedlings rather than on the thicker and somewhat tougher leaves of larger and older plants. This preference for smaller and more tender leaves on which to lay eggs will be discussed in part 2.

The ancestral home of the genus *Asclepias* is rather conjectural. As indicated by the list of species for various parts of North America presented in the Appendix, it would appear that, based on the number of species, Mexico might have been the ancestral home. However, if one considers that species of milkweed were present as early as the Cretaceous period, many millions of years ago when the Rocky Mountain area was mostly below sea level, then the ancestral home may have been in the Appalachian and Ozark highlands, which were land areas at that time. With the uplifting of the Rocky Mountains, resulting in the drainage of the Cretaceous seas, the western portions of the United States and Mexico gradually received various species of *Asclepias* from the east, mostly from the Ozarks and Florida (Orange Island). This immigration took place during the Pleistocene epoch, commonly referred to as the Ice Age.

The presence of so many species of milkweed in Mexico, as compared to the rest of the continent, may be due to adaptive radiation as a result of the repeated environmental and ecological changes that culminated in the Pleistocene. The California species may be considered as the culmination of the westward migration.

Although milkweed seeds possess a tuft of downlike hairs that make it possible for such heavy seeds to be transported by wind, they apparently do not travel great distances. Thus, the species *Asclepias nivea* found in the Greater Antilles has not reached the Bahamas or Florida. Also, the continental species have not been found in the Bahamas to any extent. *Asclepias curassavica* is widely distributed in the tropics of both North and South America, but I believe this is due to escapes from gardens, where it has been grown for its attractive color and fragrance, and not to the scattering of the seeds by wind.

During the forty-six years that I have been studying the monarch butterfly, I have witnessed a gradual advancement of the common milkweed from the southern portions of Ontario, Canada, to the more northern regions. This has been brought about by the increase in the number of roadways being built, together with the clearing of hundreds of miles of forest to allow for the erection of power lines. It is interesting to note that the increase in automobile traffic has greatly assisted the milkweed in its northward advancement. As automobiles speed along the highways, they produce strong updrafts that carry the milkweed seeds, clinging to their little parachutes, to greater heights. Seeds also become attached to the radiators of automobiles to be later dislodged in remote places. As a result of this increase in the numbers of milkweed plants, there has been a marked increase in the northern population of the monarch butterfly.

Owing to disease, or in some cases because a plant is growing in an area not suited to its well-being, some plants are noticeably less vigorous in growth than others and hence do not exhibit a luxuriant foliage. The disease is the result of a virus infection that turns the leaves yellow and ultimately causes the death of the plant. Such diseased plants may be found in the same field with healthy plants. However, I have never witnessed the complete destruction by this disease of all milkweed plants in a given field, which would seem to indicate that it is not readily transferred from one plant to another.

Milkweed plants are also host to a number of leaf-eating insects. The most common are the red-spotted milkweed beetle, a species of long-horned beetles of the family Cerambycidae, and a species of woolly bear of the family Arctiidae.

Species of aphids, which overwinter in the soil near milkweed plants, become extremely abundant in mid to late summer, often covering the underside of the leaves or forming dense clusters along the midrib. These leaf-sucking insects produce a sweet, sticky substance, vernacularly referred to as "honeydew," that covers the undersurface of the leaves. Ants that feed on this sweet substance, which is a waste product from the digestive system of the aphids, may be seen crawling up the stems of milkweed plants. This has led to the erroneous conclusion that ants feed upon the larvae of monarch butterflies.

KEY TO SOME COMMON
SPECIES OF MILKWEED

If you wish to make a collection of milkweed plants for your own personal enjoyment or as a classroom project, the following key will assist you in identifying seventeen of the most abundant and widespread species found in the eastern United States, east of the Mississippi drainage, and in Canada. There are also many illustrated regional books dealing with wildflowers that will assist you in identifying the more common species growing in your particular area. Such reference books are available at most libraries.

1. Flowers orange; leaves irregularly arranged
   (not opposite); juice not milky; New
   Hampshire, Ontario, Minnesota, and
   southward   *A. tuberosa*

   Flowers not orange; leaves opposite; juice
   milky   2

2. Flowers bright red or purple; leaves opposite and usually broad   3

   Flowers greenish, yellowish, white,
   or greenish purple; leaves opposite
   or whorled   6

3. Flowers small (7 mm wide, 3 mm long);
   hoods 2–3 mm long and equal to anthers;
   veins ascending; swamps; New Brunswick
   westward and southward   *A. incarnata*

   Flowers large (12 mm wide, 3 mm long);
   hoods 6 mm long and exceeding the anthers; veins of leaves transverse   4

4. Dry ground; underside of leaves pubescent; dark purple flowers; New Hampshire to Ontario and Minnesota and southward   *A. purpurascens*

Wet pine barrens; underside of leaves without pubescence; flowers red or reddish purple   5

5. Flowers red; leaves elongate and tapering toward base and apex; slight petiole; wet, coastal, pine barrens; New Jersey to Florida and west to Texas   *A. lanceolata*

Flowers reddish purple; leaves rounded or heart shaped at the base and tapering to an acutely pointed apex; distribution and habitat similar to *lanceolata*   *A. rubra*

6. Seedpods covered with soft spines and a fine, silky pubescence, or only apex of pod with soft spines   7

Seedpods smooth or slightly pubescent, without soft spines   9

7. Entire plant smooth with slight indication of spines at apex of seedpod; leaves with slightly heart-shaped base; flowers decidedly purple; rich soil; Ontario to Minnesota, Nebraska to Kansas   *A. sullivantii*

Pubescent; base of leaves oval; flowers greenish purple to white; rich soil or margins of streams   8

8. Flowers greenish purple to white; rich and sandy soil; New Brunswick to Saskatchewan and westward   *A. syriaca*

Flowers purplish; margins of streams; Minnesota to Arkansas and westward   *A. speciosa*

9. Stem of seedpod curved downward, but
   seedpod erect or nearly so   10

   Stem of seedpod straight   14

10. Single cluster of flowers on a naked
    terminal stem (peduncle)   11

    More than one cluster of flowers   12

11. Leaves with heart-shaped, clasping base;
    flowers greenish white; sandy woods and
    fields; New Hampshire to Nebraska and
    southward   *A. amplexicaulis*

    Leaves with obtuse base; flowers greenish
    purple; dry ground; Wisconsin, Indiana,
    and Iowa   *A. meadii*

12. Leaves mostly pubescent; hoods of flowers
    two or three times the length of the an-
    thers; prairies and oak openings; Illinois,
    Wisconsin to South Dakota and Manitoba   *A. ovalifolia*

    Leaves mostly smooth; hoods nearly equal
    in length to anthers   13

13. Pedicels (stems of individual flowers) few
    and well separated and equal to length of
    flower-head stem (peduncle); corolla lobes
    greenish; hoods white; moist soil; New
    England to Minnesota and southward to
    Georgia and Arkansas   *A. phytolaccoides*

    Pedicels numerous and crowded together;
    pedicels longer than peduncle; peduncle
    pubescent; corolla lobes white; hoods
    purplish or reddish; dry woods; Long
    Island, New York, to Indiana and
    southward to Florida and westward to
    Louisiana   *A. variegata*

14. Leaves broad   15

    Leaves narrow to filiform   16

15. Flowers pale pink; dry woods and hills;
New Hampshire to Ontario and Minnesota
southward to North Carolina and Arkansas   *A. quadrifolia*

    Flowers white; lowlands; moist soil; In-
diana to Missouri, Florida, and Texas   *A. perennis*

16. Plants 80–90 cm tall; few branches; leaves
arranged in a whorl; prairies and open
woods; Massachusetts to Saskatchewan and
southward   *A. verticillata*

    Plants 10–15 cm tall; many branches from
a woody base; leaves arranged in a spiral;
dry plains; Iowa and Nebraska to California
and New Mexico   *A. pumila*

PART 2

Egg and Larva

The eggs of the monarch butterfly can be found on the underside of the leaves of the milkweed plant. Although you may find the occasional one on large, mature leaves, most are attached to the leaves of the small seedling plants. At first glance, the egg may seem to be a small, yellow object with few distinctive characteristics, but if you examine it with a strong magnifying glass, you will see much more.

When I first examined an egg of the monarch butterfly with the aid of the low power of my microscope, I was amazed to find that this minute and seemingly structureless object was, on the contrary, an exquisitely sculptured object. As I gazed through my microscope, adjusting the mirror for transmitted and reflected light, questions arose in my mind: How much does this minute egg weigh? What are its dimensions? How can I describe such complicated sculpturing?

Employing a finely adjusted torsion balance housed in a cabinet so as to be free from the effect of air currents, I weighed one hundred eggs and found that the average weight was .54 milligrams. Since there was the possibility that the eggs would change in weight with the development of the larval embryo, I used eggs that had been laid during a twenty-four-hour period.

In order to calculate the length and width of the egg, I employed a dissecting microscope that had a millimeter grid inserted in one of the lenses. I measured the length from the base to the conical tip, as if on a plane surface, which is not a completely accurate method since it does not take into account the curvature of the egg. The width was taken, again as if on a plane surface, at the widest point, which occurs at midpoint, since the egg expands in width from the base to this midpoint and then tapers to the conical apex.

When I first started making measurements, I assumed that the eggs would be of uniform size. I was surprised, therefore, to find that there were slight variations. Based on measurements of fifty-five eggs, the average length is 1.20 millimeters and the width, .87 millimeters.

The eggshell is marked by a series of longitudinal and branched ridges, together with numerous small cross-ridges, producing a series of small cells that somewhat resemble those of a honeycomb. Slight variations occur in the number and arrangement of the ridges. On an average, there are twenty-two longitudinal ridges and six branched ridges; and there are approximately thirty-two cells per row delineated by the longitudinal and branched ridges and cross-ridges.

At the apical end of each row of cells there are a number of small irregularly shaped cells, followed by still smaller cells. These finally merge with an indefinite opaque center forming a caplike region referred to as the *micropyle* (Greek: *mikros*, small; *pyle*, a gate or door). This is the region through which the fully developed larva eventually exits.

If you examine a number of eggs using a magnifying glass or microscope, you will find a certain degree of variation in both the arrangement of the ridges and the number of cells. It is possible that there may exist individual variations of the type one finds in the ridge pattern of human fingers.

HATCHING OF THE LARVA

As the embryo develops, the egg changes over a period of three or four days from the creamy yellow of the newly laid egg to dark gray, with a distinct black area in the region of the micropyle. These subtle changes result from the production of cellular tissue that imparts to the egg the dark color of the developing embryo. In the final stage of development, the black head of the young larva is visible through the transparent integument of the micropyle.

As in all stages in the development of the monarch, the higher the temperature (below lethal temperatures), the more rapid the rate. When I placed newly deposited eggs in the laboratory control cabinet set at a

To the unaided eye, the monarch butterfly egg attached to a milkweed leaf looks like a small yellowish object, but when the empty shell is seen through the lenses of a compound microscope, it takes on the appearance of a gemlike object.

temperature of 16.7°C the average development time was 122 hours (5.1 days). At a controlled temperature of 25.5°C, development time was reduced to 106 hours (4.4 days). When I placed the eggs outdoors in the direct rays of the sun, thus increasing the egg temperature due to incident radiation, development time was reduced to an average of 94 hours (3.9 days). I found that it was possible to delay hatching beyond five days by holding the eggs at temperatures between 12° and 16° C. When studying the effect of crossing the monarch butterfly of the Antilles with the monarch of North America, I could delay the development of one of them and speed up the development of the other in order to have mature butterflies available at the same time for crossing. The results of these experiments are discussed in part 7.

When the time for hatching (termed "eclosion" in the scientific literature) approaches, the black head of the larva, clearly apparent through the transparent eggshell, can be seen moving as the larva prepares for its exit. The following observations, taken from my notes, describe this most interesting phase:

12:00 P.M.: First indication of a minute, slitlike opening in the eggshell, near the micropyle.

12:10 P.M.: Continuous chewing movement has produced an elongated slit equal in width to the larval head.

12:20 P.M.: During the past ten minutes, larva remained inactive.

12:25 P.M.: Larval activity commences.

1:30 P.M.: During the past hour, the larva enlarged the opening slightly with frequent moments of inactivity.

2:25 P.M.: Slit now an irregular hole slightly smaller in size than the head of the larva.

2:30 P.M.: Larva now very active enlarging the hole.

2:35 P.M.: Larva emerged.

I have been using the term "larva" when referring to the immature stage of the monarch butterfly. You might be more familiar with the term "caterpillar," which was originally applied only to those immature stages in which the body was covered with hair, as in some species of moths. The word is derived from the Latin *cattus*, meaning cat, and *pilos*, meaning hair. Thus, larvae covered with hair, resembling a cat, were termed caterpillars. Another lay-term is "woolly bear."

On emerging from the egg, the action of the larva may vary from complete immobility to marked activity. During an active period it may consume the entire eggshell or a part of it. In order to estimate the proportion of eggs consumed, I removed some eggs from milkweed leaves by cutting out small sections of the leaves to which the eggs were glued. The eggs were placed separately in small plastic petri dishes so that the emerging larvae would not devour neighboring eggs or eggshells. Of forty-seven eggs thus examined, only nineteen, or approximately 41 percent, were completely devoured.

When I checked my laboratory results with what occurs out of doors, the following results were obtained: eighteen eggshells left intact; eight eggshells partly eaten; and six eggshells completely devoured. Thus, of thirty-two eggs, only six, or 18.7 percent, were completely devoured.

These counts indicate that the larvae do not always consume the entire eggshell, contrary to the conclusions of a number of authors. The low count of eggshells completely consumed in nature is perhaps due to the researchers' difficulty recognizing the minute basal plate, as compared to the more obvious unconsumed or partly consumed eggshells. Also, in nature, larvae are free to wander away from the eggshells after hatching, while in my experiments they were confined.

In order to study the habits of the larvae after they emerged from their eggs, I adopted the following procedure. Eggs that had been deposited on filing cards (see part 3) were placed in petri dishes, and each egg was identified by a file number written beneath it. This method facilitated keeping notes for each egg but also resulted in the destruction of some unhatched eggs, which were partly devoured by the newly hatched larvae from adjacent eggs. (This cannibalistic habit is not likely to occur in nature, since a female monarch usually deposits only one egg on a leaf of a milkweed plant.) Upon hatching, larvae were removed from the petri dishes using a fine, slightly moistened artist's brush and placed on milkweed leaves in other petri dishes. I then recorded the following observations.

Because of their minute size, newly emerged larvae crawl with some difficulty over the fine hairs covering the underside of a milkweed leaf. The first larval meal takes place approximately twenty minutes after emerging and consists of these fine hairs. Over a period of seventy-five minutes, a larva consumes a number of these fine leaf hairs, moving a short distance from one hair cluster to another and producing a series of shallow dimples on the underside of the leaf. The larva then leaves the area, as if satisfied with its first meal of plant hairs, and wanders aimlessly about the leaf. After a few minutes, it returns to the area where it ate the hairs, there to gnaw through the leaf, producing a minute hole, characteristic of the presence of young larvae on milkweed leaves in nature.

After completing the first stage of its development, marked by the shedding of its skin, the more mature larva turns its attention to the leaf margins. There it gnaws at the tissues while moving its head forward and backward, producing a moon-shaped notch in the leaf margin.

LARVAL DEVELOPMENT

As the larva develops, it periodically sheds its skin. The shedding of the skin is referred to in the scientific literature as an "ecdysis (Greek: *ecdysai,* to strip). One might state that a larva "strips off" its old skin, revealing a new, more elastic one that permits further growth. During this process, a fluid termed the *molting fluid* is produced, which disintegrates the old cuticle. The stage between each molt is termed an *instar* (Latin: *instar,* form).

In order to estimate rates of development of the larvae under natural conditions, I set up a number of rearing tubes — glass tubes 45 centimeters in length and 6.3 centimeters in diameter. They were placed in a woodlot so as to protect the tubes from the direct rays of the sun and yet expose them to natural temperatures and daylight periods. One series of tubes tested growth rates during July and the first two weeks of August; a second series tested growth rates during the last two weeks of August and the month of September. I found that, during late summer and early fall, the average development time from first instar to fully formed larva was twenty-one days. The developmental period during July and early August was thirteen days. Differences in the rates of development are correlated with temperature and daylight period; higher temperatures and longer daylight periods in early and midsummer produce a more rapid rate of development as compared to the lower temperatures and shorter daylight periods in late summer and fall.

In order to establish the rate of development under laboratory conditions and compare it with the rate that occurs in nature, larvae were raised at 21°C in growth chambers with light periods and humidity kept constant. Samples of the larvae were removed from the growth chamber at regular intervals and weighed; for the first two instars, a number of larvae were weighed at one time and the average taken. The results obtained are shown in the accompanying table. Note that during the first four days development was slow, followed by an increase in weight after the fourth day and a much more rapid rate after the twelfth day. The larvae entered the pupa stage on the sixteenth day.

Rates of development in nature will vary not only in different parts of the

North American continent but also in different localities of the same area—exposed areas compared to open areas, sandy areas compared to grassy fields, and so on. Incident radiation can increase body temperature markedly, causing a much more rapid growth rate. Weather conditions play a most important part in growth rate—prolonged periods of overcast conditions, especially when accompanied by rain, retard the growth rate, as will periodic fluctuations in temperature.

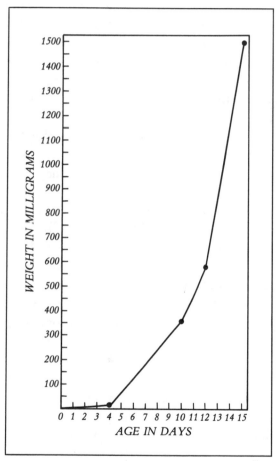

The growth rate of the monarch larva is slow for the first four days after it emerges from the egg. Then its growth increases phenomenally, accompanied by a ravenous appetite. At hatching, the average weight of the larva is approximately .54 mg. At the end of the fifteenth day, the average weight is 1,500 mg, an increase of 1,499.46 mg (or 2,777.8 times the hatchling's weight). If a human baby that weighed 8 lbs at birth grew this rapidly, it would weigh 22,222 lbs after two weeks!

After rearing thousands of larvae under experimental conditions and observing their responses, I realized that there was a decided difference among individuals. Some exhibited hyperactivity and others showed hypoactivity, and those that were hyperactive developed more rapidly than their less active relatives. Some of them came to realize that when I removed the cotton plug from the top of the tube, a fresh supply of food appeared, and they would crawl rapidly to the top and move the front end of their bodies back and forth in anticipation. Some individuals showed such marked differences in response that Norah and I gave them names!

As a larva develops it passes through five instars, each one delineated by a molting process. Between each molt the body characteristics remain constant, changes taking place only after each molt. You can ascertain each instar by locating the cast-off skin. This is done by examining the sides of a glass jar containing a larva with a magnifying lens. However, since the larvae invariably eat their cast-off skins, only very small remnants of it may be still adhering to the sides of the jar.

To follow the changes that take place during development of a larva, descriptions of the successive instars will prove helpful. Reference should be made to my drawings as you examine the various color patterns, arrangement of hairs, and the length of the feelerlike appendages.

The *thoracic region* is that part of the body to which the *true legs,* bearing claws, are attached. It is divided into three segments: the *prothorax,* to which the first pair of legs are attached; the *mesothorax,* to which the second pair of legs are attached; and the *metathorax,* to which the third pair of legs are attached. The *abdominal region* is that portion of the body extending from the rear end of the thorax to the end of the body.

Propping up the elongated abdomen is a series of paired fleshy appendages variously referred to as "false legs," "prop legs," or most frequently as "prolegs" (derived from *prop* and not referring to being in front of, or *pro*). These fleshy structures are unsegmented and possess a ring of spines, termed *crochets,* instead of claws. Finally, at the end of the abdomen there is a pair of large prolegs, termed *anal prolegs,* which play an active part in the suspension of the pupa. (I will discuss this in detail in part 3.)

FIRST INSTAR

On emerging from the egg, the minute larva is light grayish-white in color; the head is shiny black; and there is a light ring around the base of each antenna and a similar light area at the base of the mouth parts.

The prothorax is light in color, except for a pair of small triangular dark spots bearing a cluster of long, fine hairs. The *spiracle* (breathing pore) is

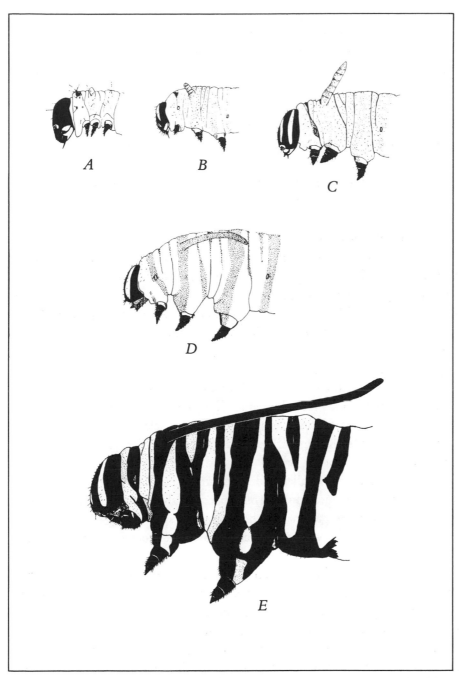

As the larva grows, it passes through five distinct stages, or instars. The hatchling (A) represents the first instar. After shedding its skin (molting), it passes into the second instar (B). The third (C) and fourth (D) instars exhibit marked differences, and finally we see the mature larva (E), the stage best known to both children and adults.

small, round, and light in color. Adjacent to the spiracle is a small, oval, pigmented area that bears two long hairs. The prothorax extends ventrally to form an obvious fleshy process, or tubercle, located ventrally between the head and the first pair of legs.

The mesothorax bears a pair of fleshy, dorsal tubercles that are slightly pigmented; note that these feelerlike appendages, termed *mesothoracic filaments,* become longer with each instar. Situated immediately beneath the filaments are two long hairs surrounded at the base by a V-shaped pigmented area.

The metathorax bears four long hairs, and there is an elongated, slightly pigmented area on each side.

SECOND INSTAR

One of the most noticeable differences between the larva of the second instar and that of the first is the presence of two pairs of elongated, yellow bands that surround a central triangular spot on the head, in contrast to the almost solid black head of the first instar. Immediately beneath this triangular central spot is a transverse light-brown marking that remains constant throughout all following instars.

Larvae of the second instar are decidedly stouter than those of the first instar and very light in color — almost translucent. The triangular spot on the prothorax has become more elongated, and there is a definite indication of a dark band extending beyond the spiracle. The spiracle has a dark border that contrasts with the lighter background. The ventral tubercle is much reduced in size and not so acutely pointed. The first pair of legs tend to become comparatively smaller and to assume a position closer to the head, which position becomes more pronounced in the remaining instars. The large hairs that were present on the triangular spot during the first instar have disappeared, as have the two large hairs that were associated with the spiracle.

The *mesothoracic filaments,* which in the first instar were small and oval in shape, have become more elongated and, when viewed under a microscope or magnifying glass, have the appearance of being segmented. The long hairs that protruded from the mesothoracic filament in the first instar have disappeared. A faint brownish band now extends from the base of the mesothoracic process down to and including the basal segment of the legs. The mesothorax is sparsely covered with a number of very short, fine hairs, together with a sprinkling of small, irregular spots.

The long hairs associated with the metathorax of the first instar have disappeared. A narrow, light-brown band extends from the dorsal surface of the larva down to and including the basal segments of the legs.

The common milkweed (Asclepias syriaca) is found in eastern North America. Owing to its ability to grow in a variety of soil conditions, it enjoys wide distribution. This, together with its habit of forming dense clusters, is responsible for the large population of monarch butterflies in eastern North America, particularly in the vicinity of the Great Lakes and in the New England states.

When a milkweed seedpod is ripe, the leathery case breaks open along a well-defined fracture line. The numerous seeds, packed in regular rows, are carried by the wind, suspended from their individual silken parachutes.

PLATE 1

The perfume of the milkweed flower attracts many species of nectar-feeding insects. If such visitors happen to be trapped by the pollen mechanism and are unable to extract it from the flower, they eventually die. It is common to find a flower cluster festooned with dead and dying insects.

About four days after the female monarch butterfly deposits an egg on a milkweed leaf or flower bud, the larva, now fully developed, gnaws a ragged hole in the shell, thrusts out its black, shiny head, and crawls forth. The hatchling will often consume the eggshell as its first meal, as shown here.

PLATE 2

The larva of the monarch butterfly is surely one of the most distinctive and well-known insects of North America. Its body is about 5 cm long and is strikingly marked with bands of white, black, and yellow. Some larvae have broad black bands, imparting an overall black appearance, while others have narrow black bands and appear much lighter in color.

When the larva is disturbed, it rolls itself into a tight ball and falls to the ground, where it remains inactive for a variable period of time. I term this reaction "playing possum." Eventually, it unrolls and crawls across the ground in search of a milkweed plant.

PLATE 3

The first indication that the pupa is about to emerge from the larval integument, or skin, is a split in the skin (a) immediately behind the head. A peristaltic wave extending from the posterior to the anterior end of the pupa causes the pupa to swell (b), forcing the skin back to the posterior end (c). To free itself from the skin, the pupa oscillates vigorously (d), coming to rest when the skin has been shaken off (e). When the pupa first emerges from the larval skin, it is very soft, and deep fissures occur between various parts of the body (e). I have termed this the "prepupa stage." Finally, the pupa assumes a compact, waxy appearance (f).

PLATE 4

Towards the end of the pupal stage, the developing butterfly can be seen through the transparent pupal shell. The gold spots of the pupa appear to control, in some manner not as yet understood, the deposition of pigment in the scales of the monarch's wings. Microcauterizing the various gold spots results in lack of pigment in the hind and front wings, depending on which of the spots is treated (top left and right, bottom left). As a control, I cauterized a small area close to, but not on, the gold spot; the butterfly indicated no reduction in scale pigmentation (bottom right).

PLATE 5

a. b. c.

d. e. f.

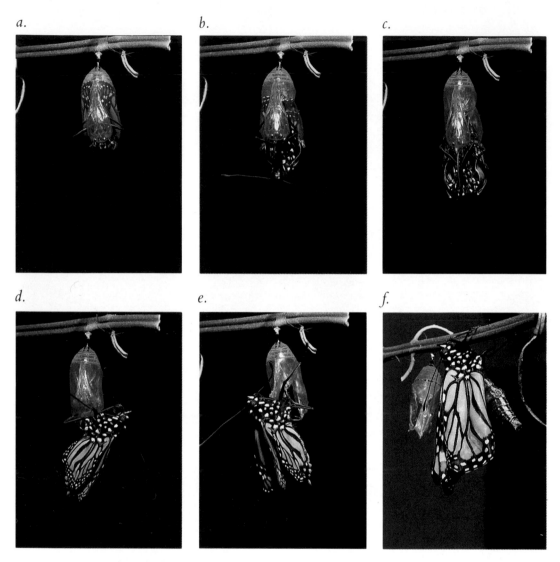

When the butterfly is ready to leave the pupal case a straplike portion of the case breaks away, allowing the legs to emerge and grasp the pupal shell (a, b). Various fractures in the shell then allow the butterfly to emerge (c). At first the butterfly's wings are small, oval in shape, and somewhat swollen. As body fluid is pumped into the space between the upper and lower membranes of the wings, they begin to expand (d, e, f).

PLATE 6

The proboscis, or sucking tube, is coiled like a watchspring and tucked beneath the head when not in use. It is composed of two separate elements, termed maxillae, which are held together when the butterfly is feeding. Notice the large, dark, bulbous compound eyes.

To deposit an egg on a milkweed leaf, the female monarch clings to the margin of the leaf and curves her abdomen so that the egg is placed on the undersurface of the leaf. In nature, usually only one egg is deposited on a leaf. Under artificial, laboratory conditions, however, a number of eggs may be placed on any part of a milkweed plant, as shown in this photograph.

PLATE 7

In addition to its lighter color and finer wing venation, the male monarch butterfly possesses a distinct black spot, the alar gland, on the dorsal surface of each hind wing.

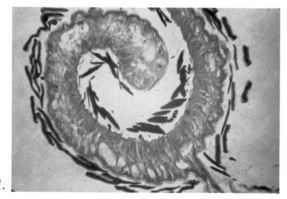

1.

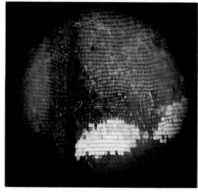

2.

1. *If you make a transverse section through the alar gland, it is seen as a fold of the wing membrane containing on its inner surface numerous cells. Attached to the cells are small, narrow scales. The section in this photograph has been stained to show the structure of the cells.*

2. *When you rub the surface of a butterfly's wing with your finger, a powdery substance is removed, leaving a clear patch of wing membrane. This dustlike substance is composed of hundreds of minute, colored scales that are arranged in regular rows on the wing surface.*

PLATE 8

THIRD INSTAR

In the third instar, the prothorax shows one obvious change—the pigmented triangular area that was present in the first and second instars has now become greatly elongated and extends down in a thin line to a point beyond the spiracle. In addition, the spiracle has assumed an oval rather than round shape and has a very heavy contrasting border. The ventral fleshy tubercle is still present but is now quite small.

The mesothoracic filaments have become more elongated and irregular in outline. If the filament is placed along the back of the larva, it will now extend to a point beyond the front portion of the metathorax. The light-brown band is now more obvious and much darker in color.

Little change has occurred in the characteristics of the metathorax other than its being sparsely covered with minute hairs and irregular, pigmented spots.

FOURTH INSTAR

The broad pigmented band on the prothorax is very obvious in this instar and completely surrounds the spiracle extending from the back of the larva to and including the undersurface near the base of the first pair of legs. The first pair of legs is closer to the head. The ventral tubercle is no longer apparent. There is a slight indication of two secondary pigmented bands on the back associated with creases that in turn are associated with the segmentation of the body.

The mesothoracic filaments have become elongated and extend to a point immediately behind the metathorax. There is still the appearance of segmentation of these filaments, which is obvious when viewed with a magnifying glass or microscope. The pigmented band has become very broad and extends to the base of the legs. In addition, a large secondary pigmented band has appeared near the posterior portion of the metathorax, together with a third pigmented band associated with the intersegmental folds.

With the exception of an additional thin pigmented band, little change has taken place in the metathorax.

FIFTH INSTAR

The fifth instar marks the final growth period of a larva and one in which the final color pattern is established. In the previous instars the bands (with the occasional exception) tend to be light to medium brown in color, and the overall color is definitely pale. In the fifth instar, however, the pigmented bands are very dark in color in comparison with the other instars, and there is also a slight variation in pigmentation from light to dark cream, which imparts a secondary banding effect.

The dark band of the mesothorax has become much broader, and the legs have come close to the base of the head. The mesothoracic filaments, which still indicate segmentation, have become greatly elongated and now extend well beyond the posterior portion of the metathorax. The color bands have become broad, and the two secondary bands, mentioned in the description of the fourth instar, have joined to form a common band that gives the appearance of a dark area surrounding two lighter patches of a paler color. There is also a broadening of the secondary band in the intersegmental fold between the mesothorax and the metathorax.

The amount of pigmentation in the metathorax has increased decidedly. The primary band has become broader and has joined, at its base, the secondary band, which in turn joins ventrally to the bands associated with the first segment of the abdomen.

This final instar displays the characteristics of the monarch butterfly larva with which we are so familiar, alternating dark brown (black) and light cream and yellow bands. You will find considerable variation in the width of the black bands; in some specimens the black bands dominate to the extent that the larva appears to be black. There exist in the islands of the Antilles monarch butterflies with larvae that are almost completely black and give rise to very dark adult butterflies. This dark form has been described in the scientific literature and has been given the name *Danaus plexippus megalippe.* The results I obtained when crossing this dark monarch with our lighter North American species are described in the Appendix.

MOLTING

When one observes the final stages in the molting process, it appears to be rather simple; the larva simply moves out of its skin, much the way one removes a glove. However, the physiological processes involved are complex and from onset to conclusion take a number of hours to complete and require hormones from the central nervous system as well as secretions between the old and new skin. During the process the larva displays a number of interesting activities.

When beginning the process of shedding its skin (integument), the larva becomes lethargic, moving about the milkweed leaf in a leisurely fashion and, at times, leaving the leaf in search of a more suitable location. Finally, it comes to rest, remaining immobile for periods of from one to several hours. This rest period is correlated with complex chemical processes going on within its body. Such processes having been completed, the larva enters a convulsive phase, during which there are marked body contortions, the body swaying back and forth and from side to side, with a few brief inactive periods. Such activity is related to the process of detaching the old skin from the new one beneath it. The larva then loses its bright coloration, and the skin becomes decidedly wrinkled. A split appears in the old skin immediately behind the head. This split is a "fracture point" that is seen again when the pupa appears from the skin of the suspended larva. By a series of rapid contortions and peristaltic waves extending from the hind end of the body to the front end, the old skin is forced back to the rear end of the body and finally discarded.

Having thus divested itself of the old skin the larva remains quiescent. During this period the new skin becomes hardened, especially in the more heavily chitinized head capsule and its attached mouth parts. The larva usually consumes the old skin—for reasons unknown—before moving to its regular diet of milkweed leaves.

Molting is an involved physiological and biochemical process. It commences with the production of secretions from a group of specialized cells located in the larval brain. These biochemical secretions act upon glands that are located in the head and thorax and are referred to as the *ventral glands,* or *thoracic glands.* These, in turn, secrete a hormone termed the *molting hormone,* which causes the epidermal cells of the new skin to become detached from the old one. The new sheet of epidermal cells becomes folded, similar to the folds in a piano accordion, thus allowing for future bodily expansion. At the same time, a new skin, or cuticle, which is also folded, is secreted by the epidermal cells. Once the cuticle has been formed, a molting fluid is produced, which lies between the old and the new cuticle. Its function is to dissolve the inner layers of the old cuticle. Having completed its specialized process, the molting fluid is then absorbed by the cells of the new skin. When the old skin is finally removed there is little fluid remaining. The cast-off skin has the appearance of a thin piece of withered tissue. In order to facilitate the removal of the old skin there are located in the dorsal region of the head and the dorsal region of the thorax behind the head areas of weakness that have been termed molting sutures.

Not only is the old skin of the larva removed, but also the breathing tubes—the tracheal system—that ramify throughout the body, along with portions of the front and hind ends of the intestinal tract. So, what seems at first observation to be a rather simple act is indeed a most complex performance, one that is repeated each time the larva goes from one instar to the next. Finally, when the last larval skin is removed, the pupa is revealed. That process will be discussed in part 3.

PLAYING POSSUM

When you remove a larva from a milkweed leaf, it will curl up, forming a tight little ball. If you hold it in your hand, it will remain in this position, which I have termed "playing possum," for a certain length of time and then unfold and start to crawl again. If you then touch the larva as it attempts to crawl away, it will again play possum, but you will observe that it does not remain in the curled-up position for the same length of time. If, instead of holding the larva in your hand, you simply touched it as it rested upon the leaf of a milkweed plant, it would immediately fall to the ground, there to remain curled up for a variable period of time.

Having witnessed this interesting behavioral characteristic, I thought that perhaps the time the larva remained in the curled-up position varied according to the number of times it had been disturbed. To test out this possibility, I performed the following experiments.

The larvae used in the experiments were stimulated by probing them with the blunt end of a pencil. The "playing possum" time was recorded after each stimulation. Saturation time was reached when, regardless of the number of stimulations given, a larva no longer played possum. The data I obtained from these experiments are presented graphically in the accompanying figure, which shows the results obtained after twenty consecutive stimulations. The first stimulation caused the larva to play possum for over 320 seconds; the second stimulation resulted in a period of only 60 seconds. The duration of inactivity then remained constant at 50 seconds until the fifteenth stimulation, at which time the duration dropped off rapidly, reaching zero—no response—at the twentieth stimulation. From such experimentation I am led to the conclusion that there is a certain store of response in the nervous system that, after repeated stimulations, becomes exhausted or dissipated, resulting in zero response.

You might ask, Of what advantage to the survival of the monarch butterfly is this act of playing possum when alarmed? Is it a defensive action against the attacks of predators? To such questions I offer the following answers.

We know from fossil evidence that insects have inhabited our earth for many millions of years. They flew in abundance over primordial fields of tall grass and massive swamps in which grew the luxuriant vegetation that eventually formed extensive coal deposits; hence the name Carboniferous has been given to this era of earth's history. It was during this era that the amphibians and reptiles arose—including frogs, salamanders, and newts. In response to such predators, insects developed many ways to escape. Some of them evolved to closely resemble living green leaves or small, gnarled, brown twigs, while others came to look like the bark of trees. (Predators also evolved to resemble various parts of plants so that they would not be detected by their prey.) Some butterflies, referred to as "leaf wings," closely resemble dead leaves and perhaps have thus been able to avoid detection by would-be predators. The subject of resemblances and the implications in-

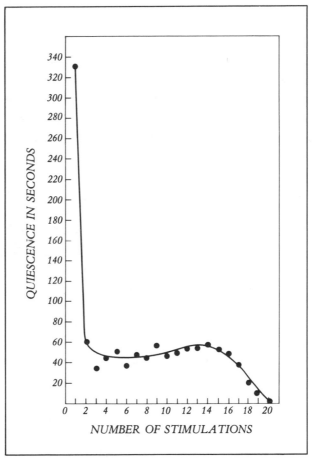

When "playing possum," the larva remains still for about 330 seconds; then it unrolls and crawls away. If you alarm it by picking it up or prodding it with a stick, the larva will curl up once again and remain quiescent, but for a much shorter period of time, about 60 seconds. If you repeat this action a number of times, the quiescent period will last for about 50 seconds. In this experiment, after the fourteenth stimulation, the quiescent period shortened rapidly, reaching zero—that is, no response—at the twentieth stimulation.

volved is vast and one that is rife with anthropomorphism, as in the case of one butterfly "mimicking" another, a subject dealt with in part 7.

I postulate that the larva of the monarch butterfly, when alarmed, falls to the ground, there to remain undetected by its predator. I once thought that when the larva dropped to the ground in the act of playing possum, it would have little difficulty in locating the plant from which it had dropped or a neighboring one. Otherwise, the action would be suicidal. But I had observed on numerous occasions that larvae would disappear from a particular plant, especially if the plant was isolated from other plants, and I was unable to find them again. On a particular day when I was examining a plant upon which there were seven young larvae, my dog, a large Scotch collie with a magnificent bushy tail, came to investigate what I was looking at. As usual, in his friendly style, he wagged his tail back and forth, and in so doing he hit the milkweed plant, causing the larvae to fall to the ground. Not finding anything of interest, the dog then moved off to find more fruitful entertainment, leaving me to gaze at the larvae now curled up on the warm sand beneath the milkweed plant, playing possum. I watched the larvae as they uncurled and started to crawl. I assumed that they would immediately crawl back to the plant from which they had been so rudely dislodged, but to my surprise all but one moved away from the plant and began to crawl to an area where there were no milkweed plants. I followed one of them for a period of an hour and a half, during which time it crawled past a number of milkweed plants, finally disappearing beneath my neighbor's fence and into his garden, where I knew there was no milkweed—my neighbor considered it a weed to be destroyed. For the remainder of the day I thought about what I had witnessed, which seemed to have no survival value. The following day, having given it considerable thought, I decided to carry out an experiment under controlled conditions, giving the larvae freedom to move away from or towards a leaf of a milkweed plant.

My living room floor became my research laboratory. I placed a large sheet of white paper on the floor, and in the center of the paper I placed a freshly picked milkweed leaf. Except for one experiment in which I used a first instar larva, all larvae were in the third or fourth instars. The larvae were not fed for a period of twenty-four hours before the experiment to assure a hunger response. As the larvae moved about the paper, I followed their peregrinations with a lead pencil, making an accurate tracing of their movements. The results obtained are shown in the two accompanying charts on page 32, which have been reduced to approximately one-fifth of the size of the originals.

In experiment A, a first instar larva was placed on the margin of the leaf but oriented away from it. I shone a bright light toward the larva, and it moved toward the source of light. After it had traveled to point x, I moved the light source and again the larva moved toward it. Thus, the first instar larvae seem to have a tendency to move toward increased light intensity.

In experiment B, a larva was placed at a distance of 18 centimeters from the leaf. After traveling a circuitous route, it moved towards the leaf but continued past it and off the test paper.

In C, the larva was placed at a distance of 14 centimeters from the leaf. It wandered aimlessly about the paper, moving toward the leaf, then turning to retrace its track back to the starting point. By a lengthy circuitous route, it finally reached the leaf. Experiment C was repeated using the same larva. After a circuitous route (D) leading towards the leaf, it reversed its direction and moved away from the leaf, finally leaving the test paper.

In the second chart, experiment A was similar to those in the first chart, but in A, three larvae were liberated at one time. Of these, one failed to locate the leaf. The remaining two moved almost directly to the leaf. In experiment B, the larva was placed so that the posterior end of its body touched the margin of the leaf. The larva moved away from the leaf, continuing beyond the test paper. In experiment C, I repeated B, using the same larva; after making a short circuitous route it located the leaf.

I then decided to move my laboratory outdoors, choosing a sandy area with milkweed plants growing here and there. I traced the paths of the larvae using a stick, thus leaving a tracing on the sand, which I then transferred to a sheet of paper (experiments D and E).

In experiment D, four larvae were liberated at a position close to the milkweed plants (indicated by circles). Three larvae, after circuitous routes, located plant 1; the fourth larva moved directly to plant 3.

In experiment E, two larvae were placed equidistant from two milkweed plants (indicated by squares). Both larvae moved toward the plant on the right. One succeeded in locating it, while the other moved away from it and crawled toward the plant on the left without locating it, finally moving to an area where there were no milkweed plants.

It is obvious from the above experiments and from field observations that when a larva, having been alarmed, drops from its host plant, it locates another plant by random movement. There are apparently no scent receptors on the body of the larva that can detect an airborne odor emanating from a milkweed plant.

The question then arises: If the larva does not possess scent receptors that can locate a milkweed plant, how does the larva recognize the leaf of a milkweed? In order to obtain a plausible answer to this question, I performed the following experiment.

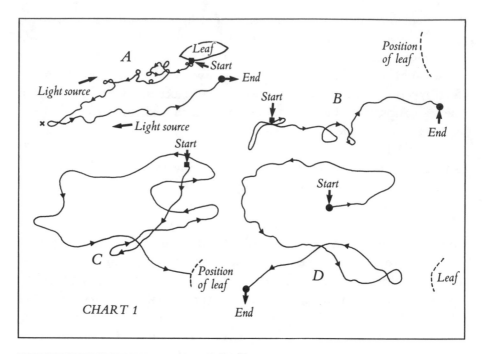

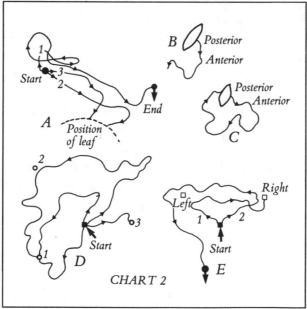

If a larva falls from a milkweed plant, it experiences difficulty finding the same plant or another one. In these two charts, reduced to about one-fifth the original size, I plotted the results of a series of experiments in which a leaf from a milkweed plant was placed near one or more larvae and the movements of the larvae were followed as they attempted to find the leaf. I repeated the experiment outdoors using the whole milkweed plant; the results are shown in Chart 2, D and E.

First, I modified an instrument employed by physicians to remove warts and other skin blemishes. This instrument creates, by use of a spark-gap condenser circuit, a very high frequency damped current of a relatively high voltage but low amperage that can be adjusted to various intensities. I replaced the large, stout electrode supplied with the instrument with a much finer one. (This I accomplished by reducing the diameter of a 29-gauge tungsten wire by heating it and then placing it in powdered sodium nitrate, thus producing a very fine, hairlike wire. I mounted this wire in a small, hollow metal cylinder that fitted over the original electrode of the instrument.)

Since the delicate operation of burning out a few cells on the mouth parts of the larva could not be carried out by manual control alone, I attached the handle bearing the electrode to a micromanipulator, an instrument composed of a set of very fine gears that allow the needle to be raised or lowered or moved from side to side by a set of finely adjusted levers. Thus I was able to bring the tip of the needle to any spot on the mouth parts of the larva, which I placed under a dissecting microscope in the following manner.

During this rather delicate operation, the larva must remain quiet with little or no movement of the mouth parts. I tried using ether and chloroform, but such anesthetizing substances caused the larva to regurgitate a watery green substance that coated the mouth parts, making it impossible to locate the area to be cauterized and at the same time reducing the power of the spark. I tried placing the larva on ice without success. The use of carbon dioxide gas also proved unsuccessful. I then subjected the larva to various low temperatures and found that a temperature of $-2°C$ for four to six hours, depending upon the size of the larva, was most effective.

I placed the cooled larva, ventral side up, on a small block of plasticine in which there was a shallow depression to receive the body of the larva. I used fine insect pins to secure the larva in place on the block, one pin being placed across the midsection of the body and another immediately posterior to the head so that the mouth parts were accessible. I then placed the block on the stage of a dissecting microscope, illuminated it from above, and proceeded to burn off certain cells of the mouth parts.

Of twenty larvae thus treated, fourteen were unable to recognize the milkweed leaf as the source of food, but six others, after a period of time, began to feed upon the leaf. I concluded that not all of the scent receptor cells had been removed from the latter.

As a result of the above experiment I found that the scent receptor cells were located on the *maxillary palpi* (feelers connected with the mouth), which, by contact with a leaf, can distinguish milkweed from any other plant. One might compare this action to that of a human tongue in which contact is necessary for receptor cells to respond. When I described this to a group of my students, one of them remarked, "The larva gives the leaf a lick"—a simple way of expressing it.

LOCAL POPULATION VARIATION

Although species of milkweed are found throughout much of North America, the population density of the monarch butterfly varies considerably. This may be due to the fact that the migratory route is oriented in a southwesterly to northeasterly direction and does not pass through many of the northwestern areas. However, it may be directly correlated with the habits of the various species of milkweed. Some species do not form dense clusters of plants, each plant being widely isolated from its neighbors. Larvae in such areas might find it impossible to locate another plant when dislodged from the one on which they had been feeding. By far the largest populations are found in areas where the species *A. syriaca* grows in profusion, particularly around the Great Lakes. These plants supply an abundance of food for the larvae, and it is also possible for them to travel readily from one plant to another.

PETIOLE NOTCHING

Petiole notching is a most interesting behavior occasionally carried out by some monarch larvae. I have not observed it in any other species of butterflies that I have reared. It takes place when the larva is fully grown, toward the end of the fifth instar. At this stage in development, the larva crawls along the petiole of a leaf to a spot close to the main stem of the plant and there gnaws a shallow notch in the upper surface. This produces a weak point in the petiole, like a logger's notch in a tree to be felled. Having produced the notch, the larva crawls to the far end of the leaf. The leaf falls to a vertical position, due to the weight of the larva, which then commences to feed on the tissues of the leaf from an upside-down position.

What is the function of this peculiar behavior? As an answer to this question, one writer suggested that the milky fluid (latex) would thus be stopped from entering the leaf blade. However, by testing the presence of latex in a leaf that had been notched and comparing it with one that had not been notched, I found that there was no apparent difference. I have come to the following conclusion.

When the mature larva enters the final stage of producing the pupa, it suspends itself in an inverted, or upside-down, position. Thus, the impulse to hang in an inverted position commences before final pupa formation. Gravitational force, due to the inverted position, appears to play a role in the formation of the pupa.

How does a larva "know" that forming a notch in the leaf will cause the leaf to fall to a vertical position? This question can be answered only by stating that it is part of the whole behavioral complex of the developing larva that has evolved over eons of time. Such questions arise whenever we study the behavior of any species of animal. To add to the difficulty in explaining the instinctive action of petiole notching, not all larvae perform this action. It is not clear why some larvae perform petiole notching and others do not. Perhaps further observations and experimentation might supply a plausible answer. Like so many other questions about the life of the monarch butterfly, I must leave these for future investigations.

CANNIBALISM

When eggs are massed together, hatchling larvae will devour adjacent unhatched eggs. Larvae reared in great numbers under crowded conditions and with insufficient food supply will often feed on one another. The attacking larva first commences eating fecal material as it issues from the anal opening of the one being attacked. This leads to devouring the rear portion of the larva and, in some instances, the major part of the body. Larvae, under such conditions, will also consume parts of suspended pupae.

In nature cannibalism does not take place. The ovipositing female rarely deposits more than one egg on a milkweed leaf, so larvae are never found in crowded conditions. In rearing larvae for study purposes, adequate space and a liberal supply of milkweed must be supplied.

INDIVIDUAL RESPONSES

In the course of many years of rearing monarch butterflies, it became obvious to me that there are marked differences in individual responses among the larvae. For example, I have observed that, on hatching from the egg, one larva would tend to be rather sluggish. It would take its time crawling forth from the cramped confines of the egg shell and would have frequent rest periods, elevating the thoracic region of its body and waving it languorously back and forth. Then it would consume a small portion of the egg shell. In contrast, another larva would chew its way out of the egg shell, as if in a hurry to escape its crowded quarters. It would devour the complete shell then crawl rapidly away to begin devouring the hairs on the milkweed leaf. Since the larvae were contained individually in glass observation tubes, I was able to observe their activity and growth periods. The differences, in some cases, were so marked that Norah and I came to look upon our young charges as one would consider children, and we gave them names. Instead of using Greek letters, as one might do in a science report, we had "Mary," "John," and so on. One very active larva I named "Gonzales" after a cartoon character, a little Mexican mouse known as "Speedy Gonzales."

Recording the growth rate of these different individuals under exactly the same environmental conditions, I found that the more active larvae reached maturity as much as six days in advance of their more sluggish relatives. I had often wondered why this happened. The above observations supplied the answer.

We tend to consider "lowly" forms of life, such as wormlike larvae, to be devoid of individual personalities, though we recognize differences among our pet cats and dogs. That such differences exist among larvae of butterflies came as a surprise to me. I am certain that by selective breeding one could eventually produce a "super" monarch butterfly race that would mature at a much faster rate than the average. I believe it is also possible to "train" the larvae to do interesting intelligence "tricks" as those performed by such lowly forms of invertebrate animals as the octopus and planarian worm. If such experiments in insect behavior were carried out, one might eventually find individual responses or, to put a human interpretation upon it, differences in "intelligence."

VARIATIONS IN
INSTAR LARVAL POPULATIONS

At the conclusion of one of my lectures on the order Lepidoptera (butterflies and moths), during which I discussed briefly the migratory habits of the monarch butterfly, one of my students posed the question: If monarch butterflies returned to their breeding grounds from the overwintering site, should there not be one generation, all larvae in the same stage of development, as in the case of migratory birds?

When the overwintering populations from Mexico journey northward, the females, sexually mature and having mated, deposit eggs along the northward migratory routes. This behavior is quite unlike that of birds, which fly directly from their overwintering sites to definite breeding areas, there to deposit their complement of eggs. As a result of the monarch eggs being thus disseminated over a considerable distance from Mexico to the more northern areas, together with the time interval between the first egg laid and the last one, there occur populations of larvae across North America in different stages of development. In the spring and early summer, fifth instar larvae occur in Texas, third and fourth instars in Missouri, and first and second instars in Illinois. As each of these overlapping populations reaches the adult stage, it migrates northward, the females depositing eggs en route. As a result, in various parts of North America one finds a wide variation in the larval instars. Eventually, all populations journey northward, with the result that larvae and adults are absent during the mid- and late-summer period in the more southern regions. As the fall migration takes place, some females deposit eggs, giving rise to larvae in the southern areas where they had not existed during a major part of the summer season.

The survival value of all this is obvious. From early March to late October and November (extending into December in some southern states), the monarch butterfly produces many overlapping generations, resulting in a massive buildup towards the end of the breeding period. Because there are a number of destructive factors that greatly reduce the monarch population, both during the migratory movements and on the overwintering sites, a very large population is necessary for the survival of this butterfly. This is accomplished, in part, by the dissemination of larval populations over a wide geographic area.

PART 3

Pupa

When a larva has reached its full growth, it enters the second and most dramatic stage in its development, the pupa (Latin: a puppet) stage. A pupa is sometimes termed a *chrysalis* (Greek: gold) when referring to butterflies because of the gold spots present in some species. During this stage the final cellular reorganization takes place that changes the wormlike creature into a colorful butterfly. This remarkable transformation never fails to fascinate me even though I have watched it hundreds of times. It is a phenomenon that interests children and adults alike, especially those who have never previously witnessed it. Indeed, many naturalists and biologists were introduced to the study of natural science by having observed as children this remarkable metamorphosis.

LARVAL NOMADISM

At the end of the larval phase, the larva leaves the milkweed plant on which it has been feeding and seeks a suitable place for the suspension of the pupa. Before leaving the plant, the larva consumes enormous quantities of milkweed leaves in a relatively short period of time, resulting in a rapid increase in weight, described in part 2.

The nomadic phase is an active one. For example, if a larva that has left its milkweed plant in quest of a pupa site is picked up, it will wriggle vigorously in an attempt to escape its captor rather than play possum. If it is returned to the milkweed plant, it will crawl rapidly back to the ground and continue on its way. The feeding response is no longer active. The rate at which a larva crawls away from the plant after being returned to it is directly related to the number of times its journey has been forcibly interrupted, the agitation increasing each time it is returned. The reason for this increased activity is that the pupa is rapidly developing within the body of the larva, and a suitable site must be located before the development of the pupa makes crawling impossible. The cellular process of pupal development is strictly geared to a time element.

The distance larvae crawl from their host plants varies, partly because some larvae tend to wander in circles more than others and partly because of physical obstructions. I have collected pupae at distances of 70 meters from the nearest milkweed plant; only on rare occasions have I found a pupa on the underside of a milkweed leaf, undoubtedly on a separate plant from that on which the larva had been feeding.

Pupae may be found in a wide variety of places, including the undersides of logs (those that are not lying flat on the ground but are held up at one end by a branch or some other object), of tree limbs, of leaves of various plants, of horizontal timbers of fences, of eaves and windowsills of buildings, and so on. Almost any object that will give support and shelter may be selected. By being attached to the undersurface of an object, a pupa is protected from the direct rays of the sun (which can cause its body temperature to reach lethal levels) and from rain.

Protection from rain is most important. In my experiments, when it was necessary to remove pupae from their supports I moistened the silk mat that attaches the pupa to its support with water. This loosens the silk, making removal of the pupa possible while it is still attached to the silk button and mat. In nature, if the silk mat becomes saturated with rain, it will lose its adhesive qualities, and the pupa will fall to the ground, where it may become prey to various predators. If it is not detected by predators, the emerging adult is unable to free itself successfully from the pupal skin, resulting in wing distortion, a common occurrence following periods of heavy rain.

In seeking a suitable pupal site, the larva becomes "negatively phototaxic," which means that it seeks areas of reduced illumination. To test this response I carried out the following experiment. I constructed plywood boxes 60 cm by 19 cm by 18 cm completely sealed off from outside illumination. The inside of the box was coated with flat black paint, which would absorb any light reaching the sides of the box from the installed light source. At one end I inserted a small lamp, taken from a dissecting microscope, and sealed the space around the light with adhesive tape so as to exclude any light from outside. Thus, the brightest light was at the end of the box nearest the lamp and the dimmest light was at the farthest end. Larvae that had produced a silk mat were placed in the box through an opening in the top of the box, which was then sealed off. After forty-eight hours the box was opened by removing the entire top section, and the arrangement of the pupae was noted. The following results were obtained based on five such boxes, each box containing twenty larvae: 82 percent were suspended at the rear third of the box, away from the light source; 12 percent were located in the middle third; and only 6 percent were located in the front third nearest the light source.

CONSTRUCTION OF
THE SILK MAT AND BUTTON

Having chosen a suitable site, the larva enters a lethargic period during which it moves more slowly and deliberately than previously. Slowly raising the front portion of its body, it sways back and forth, as if testing the environs for possible objects that might interfere with the final formation of the pupa, a precaution that I later found to be most important to the survival of the pupa. This exploratory period lasts for two or three hours, terminating when the larva commences to lay down a layer of silk on the surface of the supporting object.

The area of the silk mat varies considerably, depending on the nature of the supporting surface. The area covered on a glass surface is much greater than that formed on a rough surface, such as wood or cardboard. The larva appears to be cognizant of the clinging power of various supporting surfaces.

When the larva has completed the silk mat, it begins to pile strands of silk one on top of another, in an irregular pattern, near the center of the mat. This central mat is referred to as a *button*. The strands vary considerably in thickness throughout their length; some are rather flat, which causes them to curl, thus allowing for a very loose weave. The buttons vary in size and height, some being as high as 4 millimeters, while others are less than 2 millimeters. They may be conical or rounded in shape.

LARVAL SUSPENSION

After completing the formation of the button, the larva grasps it with the sharp, curved spines that are arranged in a ring around the anal prolegs. Then it hangs in an inverted position with the front part of its body curved inward to form a J-shape.

On numerous occasions I have observed larvae that have fallen to the bottom of the rearing jar, having been dislodged from the button. In some cases the larvae would crawl back to the top of the jar, form a second button of silk, and again suspend themselves. In other cases the larvae were unable to climb up the side of the jar and entered the pupal stage while lying on the bottom. That invariably led to the formation of badly distorted pupae because the pupa is in a very soft condition when first formed, and the skin can be readily damaged.

I asked myself why some of the larvae were able to go through the process of forming the button of silk a second time while others were not. To answer this question, I interrupted larvae at various times during the process of laying down the silk mat, the formation of the button, and suspension. I found that larvae removed from the silk mat before the button is formed would climb back to the top of the jar and form a new mat. Such an interruption could be repeated from three to six times, the size of each new mat becoming smaller with each interruption. When I removed the larvae after the buttons had been completed, the occasional larva would crawl back to the top of the jar and make a new button on top of the old mat, the button being much reduced in size. Finally, if I removed the larvae from their buttons after they had become suspended, they were unable to return to the top of the jar and completed the formation of the pupae on the bottom of the jar. These actions can be explained as follows:

When a larva has reached its full development, anatomical changes have already taken place within the body. Each of the various phases, from the seeking of a suitable site to final suspension, takes place with the gradual and continuing development of the pupa. Thus, each phase must be completed in a set period of time.

As development proceeds, the thoracic region straightens out and the larva becomes more elongated. Accompanying this elongation is a change in color. The bright yellow bands become more translucent, assuming a blue-green color. This marks the final stage in the metamorphosis from larva to pupa, and at this stage the pupa is fully formed within the larval skin, giving rise to the change in color, as seen through the semitransparent skin.

The following rates of development were obtained at ambient temperatures of 21°–24°C:

Formation of silk mat: 3 hours, 45 minutes
Formation of button: 3 hours
Suspension to appearance of prepupa: 13 hours
Total time period: 19 hours, 45 minutes.

For twelve sets of observations I found that the time taken for the complete sequence varied from sixteen to twenty-three hours depending on air temperature and exposure to the direct rays of the sun.

ISSUING OF PUPA FROM LARVAL INTEGUMENT

The final developmental stage involves the removal of the larval skin, thus exposing the pupa. The larva, which assumed a J-shape while hanging from the button with the front part of the body arched inwards, now hangs limply extended. Within a few minutes of assuming this position, a split appears in the larval skin immediately behind the head. This is the "fracture point," discussed in part 2, that occurs each time the larva sheds its skin as it passes from one instar to another. The split rapidly increases in size as the pupa is forced through the opening by peristaltic action extending from the posterior to the anterior end. The peristaltic waves cause the skin to be moved back towards the posterior end of the pupa while the larva skin remains attached to the button by means of the circle of spines located on the anal prolegs.

It is possible to hold up development by placing the pupa in a cool chamber, such as a household refrigerator, set at temperatures above 2°C for a limited period of time, not to exceed two days. I used this technique to my advantage when taking a sequence of photographs, especially when an adult butterfly was about ready to emerge in the late evening. By placing the specimen in the refrigerator, I could suspend development so as to obtain the necessary photographs the following day. It should be borne in mind, however, that prolonged periods at low temperature will kill a specimen, particularly during the larval state when it is suspended from the button.

FUNCTION OF THE CREMASTER

A larva grasps the button of silk with the spines located on its anal prolegs. As the skin breaks away and is forced to the posterior end of the pupa, the anal prolegs must maintain their hold on the button until the black hornlike

The clublike tip of the pupal cremaster is covered with a number of hooks of various sizes and shapes. Their purpose is to obtain a firm hold on the button of silk by becoming thoroughly enmeshed in the loose fibers.

cremaster of the pupa is withdrawn from the skin and attached, by means of its numerous hooks, to the button. The question occurred to me on observing this feat: How is it possible for the larval skin to maintain a hold on the smooth surface of the pupa while the cremaster is being withdrawn? This is somewhat similar to a person hanging onto a horizontal bar by one gloved hand and releasing his grip to discard the glove while at the same time maintaining a firm hold on the bar. With the use of high-speed photography, I was able to answer this question.

When the larval skin has been pushed to the posterior end of the suspended pupa, it becomes precariously attached to two very smooth, black, round, slightly curved tubercles, which I termed the *exuvial holdfast tubercles* (EHT) (Latin: *exuere*, to strip off), referring to the removal of the larval skin. While the skin is held by the EHT, the stalklike, black cremaster is carefully removed from the wrinkled skin and gently thrust into the button of silk. At the tip, or knob, of the cremaster are a number of variously curved spines of different shapes and sizes that one can observe using a strong magnifying glass. These become enmeshed in the loosely woven silk strands of the button. During this process there is little or no movement of the pupa; if there were the skin would slip from the EHT, and the pupa would fall to the ground. This often happens in rearing containers when larvae that are crawling about accidentally bump into a pupa when it is in this critical state or when the container is inadvertently jarred. The hooked spines maintain an exceedingly firm grasp on the silk button, as shown by the following experiments. Weights were attached to the pupa by means of thread tied over the posterior end at the base of the cremaster by a loose knot; the ends of the thread were brought together beneath the pupa so that various weights could be attached to it. The following is an account of one trial in which the mat and button had been formed on the glass top of one of the rearing jars.

With a weight of 58 grams, the silk mat was torn loose from the lid, but the cremaster remained embedded in the button. (In other trials, when the mat was attached to a rough surface such as cardboard, the weight required was 122 grams.) By twisting the mat to form a compact strand and tying a thread to it, it was possible to suspend the pupa from a clamp so as to test the tensile strength of the button. With a weight of 84 grams, the button was torn from the twisted silk mat. With a weight of 482 grams, the spines of the cremaster were torn loose from the button.

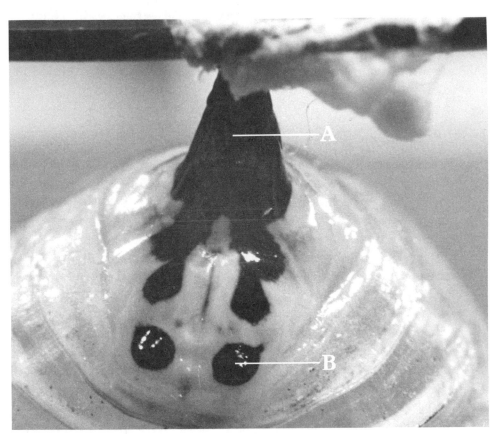

When the larva prepares to enter the pupal stage, it suspends itself by grasping the button of silk with the circle of spines located on the anal prolegs. While suspended, the pupal cremaster (A) is removed and its spines are enmeshed in the fibers of the button. While this process is taking place, the skin of the larva is held by two black, slightly bent, and highly polished tubercles, termed holdfast tubercles (B), located beneath the cremaster. By violently gyrating, the pupa causes the larval skin to slip off the holdfast tubercles.

This gives some idea of the strength of the attachment of the cremaster to the silk button. However, at times the integument of the larva does not remain attached to the EHT long enough to allow the hooks of the cremaster knob to become embedded in the button; the result is that the pupa falls to the bottom of the rearing container. This happens in nature, too, particularly during stormy weather and high winds. In other cases, due to a virus or bacterial infection, the larva may be unable to cling to the button for a sufficient period of time to allow the cremaster hooks to become enmeshed in the silk.

Other factors can weaken the support. For example, moisture in rearing jars weakens the adhesive power of the mat or delays the larva in choosing a suitable site, resulting in an undersized mat. Also, overcrowding in rearing containers causes larvae to interfere with each other during the spinning of the mat and button.

REMOVAL OF THE LARVAL INTEGUMENT

When the skin has been forced back to the posterior end of the body of the pupa and the cremaster has been removed from within the skin and its hooks firmly enmeshed in the silk button, the pupa engages in an active wriggling motion. It has been assumed by entomologists in the past that the purpose of such gyrations was to attach the cremaster more firmly to the button. This explanation, however, seemed doubtful to me, because if the cremaster had not been firmly enmeshed in the button of silk prior to such frantic gyrations, the pupa would most certainly become detached. What then is the explanation for such activity?

A careful examination of the pupa when it first emerges from the larval integument shows it to be very soft and, most important, various parts of the butterfly are delineated and somewhat free from the rest of the body. The thoracic and abdominal segments are distinctly swollen and markedly outlined by deep furrows in the regions of the intersegmental folds. The wing buds are swollen and extend above the surface of the rest of the body. The head, mouth parts, and legs have the appearance of being almost free appendages, similar to the mature pupae of many species of beetles. Since this stage is so unlike the final mature pupa, in which all body parts have become firmly and smoothly amalgamated, I have termed it the *semi-exarate pupa* stage (Latin: *exaratus,* plowed up). One of the most striking features of the semi-exarate pupa is the presence of a deep sulcus (a channel-like depression) located between the two sections of the mouth parts (termed *modified galea*), which unite to form the future sucking tube, or proboscis. The galea are quite obvious when the butterfly first emerges from the pupa. They are seen as two separate units, which later become united into one tube and coiled beneath the head.

Since all of the aforementioned parts of the butterfly are exposed, and with deep fissures between the parts, the free larval skin, if not dislodged, can become embedded in the pupa. In order to test the possibility of this happening and to find out what effect it might have on the mature pupa and emerging butterfly, I carried out the following experiments.

In one series of experiments, the larval skin was prevented from being dislodged from the semi-exarate pupa by a silk thread tied around it. The skin became embedded in the folds of the pupa resulting in a distorted pupa. In a second series, threads were placed around various parts of the body. Wherever the thread crossed any of the exposed appendages or deep folds, it became embedded. Thus, the purpose of the active gyrations of the pupa is to remove the larval skin.

Although some of the adult butterflies in these experiments were able to emerge without apparent injury, particularly those in which the degree of embedding was minimal, many were unable to emerge from the pupal skin, resulting in wing distortion. Occasionally pupae die as a result of the spines penetrating the integument.

When a pupa first emerges and the larval skin is still attached to it, the gyratory motion is intense, gradually becoming less so, until finally there is no further motion. Gyration takes place whether the larval skin has been removed or not. If the skin is removed, the period of gyration is greatly reduced. If I removed the larval skin, causing the motion to be reduced, and then replaced it, or touched the surface of the pupa with a fine brush, the gyratory motion again became intense. After several such stimulations with the brush, the pupa finally failed to respond (similar to the response mechanism described in part 2, the act of the larva playing possum). I am therefore led to the conclusion that the presence of the larval skin touching the sensory receptors on the surface of the semi-exarate pupa produces the wriggling response.

THE FULLY FORMED PUPA

The skin of the semi-exarate pupa gradually becomes firmer; the abdominal segments retract; the wings, legs, antennae, proboscis, and head become less swollen; and the depressions (sulci) between the various structural units become shallower. Finally, the complete, smooth, waxy mature pupa, with its ornament of gold spots, is formed. The process of changing from the semi-exarate stage to the fully formed pupa takes from twelve to nineteen hours to complete.

As pupal development progresses, and particularly in the later stages, the pupa turns from light to dark green, to light brown, and finally to dark

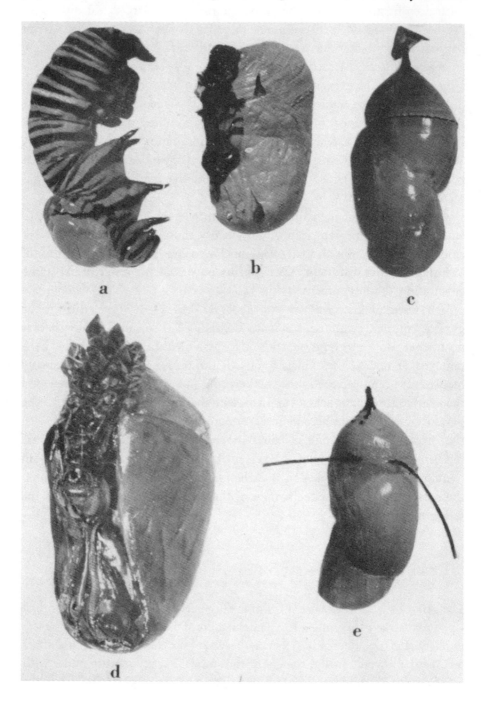

brown. Following this color change, one can see the bright orange wings of the butterfly lying within the transparent skin of the pupa. The time taken for this development, from the first appearance of the mature pupa, varies from nine to fifteen days, depending on temperature and atmospheric conditions.

A pupa has a number of distinct regions. The *appendicular region* (Latin: *pendere*, to hang, referring to the hanging appearance of the limbs) is that area occupied by the head, antennae, legs, and mouth parts. The *alar region* is that area occupied by the wings (note that the second pair of wings appears as small, straplike structures behind the first pair). The *pronatal region* is a small area that appears to be divided into two parts somewhat resembling the shape of the wings of a small moth. It is located immediately behind the head. The *abdominal region* comprises the area between the wings together with the cylindrical, segmented portion extending from the tips of the wings to and including the cremaster.

By placing a pupa with the appendicular region in a downwards position, the following broad regions may be designated: the *ventral region* is that part facing downwards; the *dorsal region* is that part facing upwards; the *lateral regions* are those parts facing to the sides. With the pupa in this position and the head pointing away from the observer, the left side is to the left of the observer and the right side to the right. The following parts may be clearly seen in the appendicular region: the head; the first pair of legs, which are very short and attached to the prothorax; the second pair of legs, which extend to three-quarters the length of the ventral region; the antennae, segments of which are distinct, extending the entire length of the ventral region; and the proboscis, composed of two separate units occupying the central portion.

Immediately following the pronotal region is a large swollen portion to which the front pair of wings is attached. This is the *mesonotum* (Greek: *mesos*, middle). Following this is a narrower segment, the *metanotum* (Greek: *meta*, after), to which the second pair of wings is attached. These wings are only partly visible and appear as a narrow band along the margins

If the larval skin is not removed from the surface of the newly formed pupa (semi-exarate pupa), it might become embedded in the deep folds, causing pupal distortion (b, d). Occasionally, a strand of the silk mat is caught behind the emerging pupa and prevents the removal of the integument (a). If a thread is placed loosely around the newly formed pupa, it causes a distortion (c); when placed in the region of the abdomen, it becomes embedded (e). To prevent injury or distortion, the pupa gyrates rapidly to shake off the larval skin.

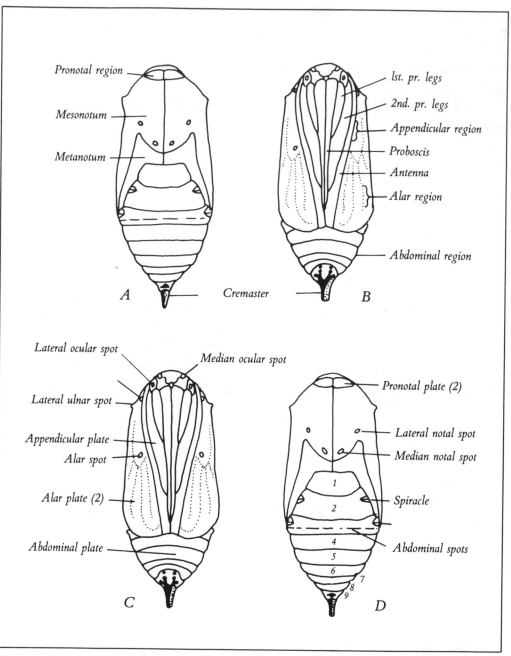

A — Pronotal region, Mesonotum, Metanotum

B — lst. pr. legs, 2nd. pr. legs, Appendicular region, Proboscis, Antenna, Alar region, Abdominal region

Cremaster

C — Lateral ocular spot, Median ocular spot, Lateral ulnar spot, Appendicular plate, Alar spot, Alar plate (2), Abdominal plate

D — Pronotal plate (2), Lateral notal spot, Median notal spot, Spiracle, Abdominal spots

If you examine the pupa, you can identify various parts of the developing butterfly on the dorsal (A) and ventral (B) surfaces. By examining the empty pupal case after the butterfly has emerged, you can identify various segments, termed plates, resulting from the splitting of the pupal case along fracture lines (C). The various gold spots have been given names that designate their position on the pupa (C, D).

of the broad pair of wings. At each side of the pronotum, next to the front margin of the mesonotum, is a *thoracic spiracle,* or breathing pore.

The abdominal region is composed of six well-defined segments (segments 4–9), three incomplete segments located on the dorsal surface between the metanotum, and a distinct line of gold spots. Abdominal segment 4 is hidden in the ventral portion by the wings. Abdominal segments 5, 6, 7, and 8 are ringlike. Segment 9 bears the cremaster as well as two black tubercles on the ventral surface. The *genital orifice* is marked by a slight depression between the two black arms of the cremaster. A pair of well-developed elongate spiracles is located on abdominal segments 4, 5, 6, and 7. On the outside margins of abdominal segments 2 and 3 are pairs of distinct elliptical spiracles that are plainly visible from the dorsal surface.

The cremaster is a blunt, black, spinelike structure located at the posterior end of the pupa that may be conveniently divided into three parts: *knob, shaft,* and *base.* The knob, which is the portion that becomes attached to the button of silk, is slightly larger in diameter than the shaft. Numerous spines, resembling minute buttonhooks, are its most characteristic feature. Some of the spines are broadly curved and possess comparatively large hooks; others are straight and have comparatively small hooks. Still others are slender, straight, and without hooks. Being rounded at the apex, these spines are ideally suited for hooking onto the strands of silk contained in the button. It is therefore a simple procedure for the pupa to thrust the spines into the mass of loose silk and, by gently rotating, to cause each spine to become entangled. The shaft of the cremaster is roughly 2 millimeters in length; it is narrowest immediately behind the knob and gradually becomes broader toward the base. It is heavily chitinized, giving it considerable strength, and shiny black in color. The base is broad, somewhat resembling an inverted wine glass. Attached to the base is a pair of pigmented black bars that I have termed the *arms of the cremaster.* The cremaster is confluent with the rounded base of the pupa.

GOLD SPOTS AND THEIR FUNCTION

Among the most attractive features of the mature pupa are the shiny, gold spots. In scientific publications the gold spots are referred to as *prismatic pigmented maculae* (PPM). I have given them names according to their position in relation to various parts of the pupa as follows.

The two pairs associated with the compound eyes are termed the *ocular spots* (Latin: *oculus,* an eye). The pair located on the inside margin of the eye are the *lateral ocular spots,* and the pair on the outside margin of the eye are the *median ocular spots.* The large pair located at the junction of the first pair of wings to the body are the *ulnar spots;* the small adjacent pair are the *median ulnar spots;* and the pair located on the wings are the *alar spots.* There are two pairs of gold spots on the mesonotum: one pair near the center, the *median notal spots* (Greek: *noton,* back), and one pair near the outside margin, the *lateral notal spots.* On the posterior margin of the third abdominal segment is a row of rounded tubercles joined by a band of gold spots. Each tubercle has a dark, central pigment spot joined to a dark, anterior band. There are twenty-two to twenty-six such tubercles of various sizes. These conspicuous spots are termed *abdominal spots.*

The following simple procedure will demonstrate why these spots have a shining, goldlike luster. Using an instrument with a fine, sharp point, cut away one of the larger gold spots and place it in a shallow vessel containing enough water to cover it. Examine the spot by means of a strong magnifying glass or microscope, turning the spot so that the inner surface is uppermost. Using a fine pin or needle to hold the spot in place, scratch away the tissue with a second pin. You will observe that there is a yellow pigment layer followed by a series of platelike scales, each of which, when scratched away, glistens in the water like a diamond. Thus, light falling on the pupal spot passes through the plates to the pigment and is reflected back again, imparting the golden luster to the spot.

A more exact method to examine the structure of these spots is as follows: The excised spot is placed in a fixative solution that hardens the cells. The tissues thus fixed can then be placed in wax, after passing through different concentrations of alcohol. With an instrument called a microtome, which has a very sharp knife, the wax block containing the tissue is cut into very thin slices, similar to cutting slices of bacon. The resulting sections of tissue can be placed on a microscope slide and examined after the wax has been removed by a solvent. The tissue can then be stained by using various kinds of dyes so as to distinguish the various cells.

As a result of this procedure, one finds that there are many types of cells involved in the formation of the spot. Some of them are broad and cone shaped; others are elongated; still others resemble spindles and flasks.

The question arises as to the possible function of these gold spots. At one time I had concluded that they acted as light receptors that delayed emergence of the adult during periods of inclement weather and allowed for a more rapid development during periods of warm, sunny weather. To test this possibility, I covered the spots with opaque black enamel to prevent light from reaching the pigmented area. The results of numerous such trials proved negative; development time and effects on the emergence of the adult were the same as that of the controls, the spots of which had not been so treated.

To test the possible function of a particular organ in a living organism, the most expedient and often the most successful method is to remove it and then observe the results. By using a microcauterizer, described in part 2, I cauterized various gold spots so that any active tissue would be destroyed. I did this procedure most carefully under microscopic examination so that I would not damage any of the tissue surrounding a particular spot. In control specimens, I cauterized an area close to but not touching the spot. The following results were obtained.

Cauterizing the lateral ulnar and lateral notal spots caused the front wings of the emerging adult butterfly to lose much of their coloration, many of the scales being without pigment. When I cauterized the median notal spot, all four wings of the adult lost some pigmentation. Cauterizing the alar spots resulted in loss of pigment on the tips of the front pair of wings. Cauterizing the abdominal spots resulted in a marked reduction in the number of abdominal scales, but no reduction in pigmentation of the remaining scales. When I cauterized the median ocular spots, there was a reduction in scales and hairs with, as in the case of the abdominal scales, no loss of pigmentation in the remaining scales.

I concluded that the spots of the pupa, in some manner as yet unknown, are associated with the pigmentation of the scales and with the presence of scales on the abdomen and head.

PART 4

Adult

The adult state of the monarch butterfly is familiar to almost everyone living in North America and in many other parts of the world where it occurs. As a child, you may have watched these butterflies flying leisurely over fields of wildflowers. Perhaps you captured one to inspect it more closely. As it fluttered in an attempt to escape from your grasp, you held it more firmly by the wings and, in doing so, tiny colored particles, resembling fine dust, came off the wings and stuck to your fingers. You may have observed that, where the "dust" came off the wing, there remained a shiny bald spot—the wing membrane to which the dustlike particles were attached. You may have wondered if after the particles had been removed from the wings the butterfly would be able to fly. And you were pleased that, on being released, it flew away, apparently unharmed.

Certain questions may have occurred to you: What is the nature of these dustlike particles that cover the butterfly's wings? How are they formed? Where did the butterfly come from, and where was it going when you captured it? You observed that in late summer and fall there were a great many monarch butterflies, whereas there were only a few in early summer. Where did they spend the winter?

Other questions may have occurred to you concerning the structure of this seemingly frail creature: Does it have a brain? Does it have internal organs similar to those of humans—a stomach, intestines, kidneys, and lungs?

In this part and the next, I will attempt to answer these questions and many others. If such questions have not occurred to you, perhaps this part will arouse your interest in the habits and structure of this monarch of butterflies and, in addition, give you an appreciation of the amazing world of insects that are so wrongly condemned because of the few unwanted members we have termed "pests."

EMERGENCE FROM THE PUPA

The emergence of a monarch from its pupa case is a dramatic phase in the life of this butterfly. In part 3, I described the changes that transform it from a wormlike larva into a beautiful, jade-green, gold-studded pupa. Now we witness the final and most inspiring transformation that, by intricate and complex biological processes, produces the colorful adult.

While writing this, I am watching the changes that take place from the time I first saw the appearance of the orange wings of the butterfly through the transparent cuticle of the pupa until the emergence of the adult. To do this, I suspended a twig to which a pupa was attached from the metal vise of my tripod. I focused my camera on the pupa, so that as changes took place I would have a complete record in color to include in this book. I hope you have a chance to witness this dramatic episode yourself in real life; it will be an experience you will never forget.

When I first observed the emergence of a monarch butterfly from its pupa, I was a young lad interested in collecting butterflies and moths. I then considered it a rather haphazard process, like tearing a paper bag apart, in which the cuticle of the pupa simply split to allow the butterfly to emerge. It was not until many years later that, with the aid of a camera and after a close examination of the pupal shell, I discovered how well-defined fracture lines opened the shell, like so many small zippers, to allow the butterfly to emerge. I also discovered that the fracture lines split apart in an orderly sequence.

To describe the process as accurately as possible, I must use the names of the various parts of the pupal cuticle. I have followed the same terminology that I used when describing the completely formed pupa in part 3. Thus, the appendicular region is that part occupied by the head, the antenna, the mouth parts, and the legs; the alar region is the part associated with the wings; the pronotal region applies to the pronotum; and the abdominal region is made up of the segments of the abdomen.

Referring to my drawing of the pupa on page 50, you can see the following: An elongate, triangular plate covers the appendicular region; this is termed the *appendicular plate*. Two small quadrangular plates cover the pronotal region; these are termed the *pronotal plates*. Two quadrangular plates, termed the *alar plates*, cover the alar region, and a cylindrical plate covers the abdominal region and is appropriately termed the *abdominal plate*.

It is difficult to follow the lines of fracture by examining the empty pupal shell, because the alar plates roll back and secondary folding takes place as the shell becomes dry. It is much easier to follow the lines of fracture by examining a pupa at the moment the butterfly is emerging rather than examining the dry pupal shell. The sequence is as follows: The first fracture occurs in the center of the pronotal region and divides this small plate into two separate plates. This constitutes the *first line of fracture*. The next fracture occurs in the center of the mesonotum and metanotum and is called the *second line of fracture*. This is followed immediately by fractures on each side of the appendicular region, which, considered separately, constitute the *third and fourth lines of fracture*. Fractures now occur at the anterior and posterior ends of the pronotal plates (the *fifth and sixth lines of fracture*), freeing the plates from the rest of the pupal shell. At this point, a leg or the antennae will appear outside of the pupal shell. In most cases, it is one of the mesothoracic legs that waves about as if seeking contact with some support outside of the pupal shell. This is followed by the second mesothoracic leg. Concurrently, the head appears through the opening, and the butterfly, with frequent rest periods, attempts to extricate itself from the pupal shell. Finally, a *seventh line of fracture* appears extending from the posterior end of the median line of fracture of the mesonotum and metanotum, along the anterior margin of the first abdominal segment (to the right and left of the median line), and then posteriorly along the outside margin of the mesothoracic wings to the posterior margin of the third abdominal segment near the line of gold spots.

When the seventh line of fracture is complete, the butterfly will have succeeded in grasping the sides of the pupal shell with the sharp sicklelike claws of its mesothoracic legs. The alar plates, reduced to two slender, partly rolled, somewhat shrivelled, skinlike structures, assist the butterfly in obtaining a firm grasp on the pupal shell. The butterfly then pulls its thorax and abdomen free and remains suspended clinging to the now empty pupal shell.

The time taken for the butterfly to emerge from the pupal shell, from the first fracture, varies from three minutes to as rapid as thirty seconds. Based upon the observation of twenty specimens, the average was one minute and twenty seconds. Hence, if you wish to record this process, you must have your camera focused and the shutter ready to be released.

In the course of rearing thousands of monarch butterflies, I became aware that emergence from the pupa usually occurred during daylight hours, particularly around noon. In order to investigate the emergence times, I carried out the following observations.

Each day I removed the adults from the rearing cage, leaving a number of unhatched pupae. In the early morning I found only a few adults; by noon there were a great many. Alar tagging for migration studies was done in the afternoon, so that the cages were nearly emptied of butterflies, except for a few that had emerged so recently that their wings were too soft to handle. In late afternoon relatively few butterflies emerged. I recorded the numbers emerging at specific times of day and plotted the results, as shown in the accompanying figure. Emergence tended to take place between 6:00 A.M. and 3:00 P.M., with a maximum between 7:00 A.M. and 1:00 P.M.

Before I carried out the observations, I had expected that maximum emergence would take place during midday, because incident radiation and higher air temperatures would hasten development. During the night, when temperatures were lower and incident radiation was absent, development would be much slower. With rapid development taking place during the day, I expected to have a number of butterflies emerging during the night, having almost completed development during the previous day. I also believed that there was some sort of light-receptor mechanism operating so that butterflies ready to emerge from the pupa would not do so during periods of darkness or during periods of cloudy, inclement weather. I came to the following conclusion: monarch butterflies will not fly during periods of darkness (described in part 5), a characteristic common to most species of butterflies as distinct from moths. Perhaps, when development within the pupa shell has advanced to the stage when the compound eyes of the butterfly have been completely formed and respond to light, nerve impulses would be sent to the brain causing the butterfly to remain in a quiescent state, awaiting the return of light. This suggestion could be tested by confining pupae in which the butterfly is ready to emerge in total darkness and comparing the results with pupae exposed to light. A second suggestion would be to cover the eye region of some pupae with opaque black paint, the control being pupae with the black paint placed in some other part of the body. I leave this little experiment for some future monarch butterfly researcher, naturalist, teacher, or student.

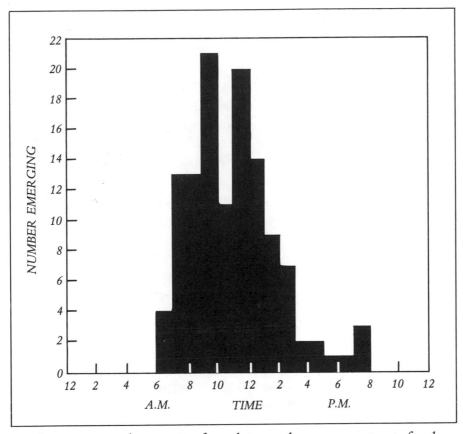

By observing monarchs emerging from their pupal cases over a twenty-four-hour period, I found that the peak of emergence occurred between 6:00 A.M. and 2:00 P.M. Emergence rarely took place from 8:00 P.M. to 6:00 A.M. The advantages of emerging during the daylight hours, particularly during the warmest part of the day, are discussed in the text.

More rapid development during periods of bright sunshine and warm temperature is advantageous to a butterfly. When it emerges from the pupa, a butterfly is a rather helpless creature. Its wings are soft, and flight is impossible, so it is unable to avoid attacks by predatory animals. Strong winds might dislodge it from its support, and once it falls to the ground, its wings would fail to unfold properly. The wings must develop as rapidly as possible, which can be accomplished only in bright, warm conditions.

I have observed that monarch butterflies rarely emerge during periods of inclement weather. This is important since their wings would take longer to dry, and the gusty winds and heavy rains would dislodge the butterfly from its hold on the pupal shell. I once thought that delayed emergence was directly related to lower temperatures and the absence of incident radiation. However, on numerous occasions when the sky was overcast and the air temperature was high, relatively few butterflies emerged. One of my colleagues who was interested in the effects of inclement weather on the rate of pupal development applied a thin spray of water on the pupae and noted the number emerging. After thirty-six hours of continuous spraying with water, none of the butterflies emerged. Immediately after the water treatment was discontinued all of the test butterflies emerged "in a matter of a few moments." I conclude that some factor or factors operate to retard emergence during periods of unfavorable weather conditions. Failure to emerge under such conditions may be compared to the activity of other species of butterflies, which, in the adult stage, are not active during periods of inclement weather.

Depending on weather conditions, the monarch butterfly clings to the pupal shell for two to seventeen hours. Specimens kept in rearing cages, however, attempt flight when alarmed within two or three hours after emergence.

It is during this formative period that the wings become twisted or misshapen if they are not allowed to hang in a vertical position (one pair of wings may be perfectly formed and the other pair distorted). Shrews and mice may attack the butterfly, particularly if the pupa is situated close to the ground, so that the wings become frayed and torn at the margins. When such damage takes place during the emergence period, the wings take on a glazed appearance due to the exudation of body fluid in the vicinity of the torn parts. This can be demonstrated by rupturing a wing of a newly emerged monarch butterfly with a pair of forceps. The glazed appearance does not result if the wing is torn once the wings have become dry.

For many years I had observed that far more butterflies with distorted wings occurred in the late fall than during the summer and early fall and that such damaged specimens were more abundant after a severe frost. I concluded that cold temperatures were responsible, but during the summer of 1956, when I was involved in a great number of rearing experiments, I discovered the true explanation for such distortions. With the advent of low temperatures, particularly freezing temperatures, leaves fall from the various plants in the area where the monarch butterflies have been breeding. Pupae fastened to such leaves fall to the ground, resulting in wing distortion when the adult emerges. As evidence of this conclusion, I collected, on numerous occasions, pupae attached to leaves that had fallen to the ground, as well as many distorted specimens.

In order to expand its wings after emerging from the pupa case, the monarch pumps fluid from its body into the space between the upper and lower wing membranes. The presence of this body fluid in the wings can be demonstrated by cutting a piece from the hind edge of the wing. Yellowish droplets of body fluid form along the edge of the cut.

WING DEVELOPMENT

The newly emerged monarch butterfly has small, rather fleshy wings. On observing the softness of the wing and the fact that if the wing is bruised a fluid blister will form, I thought that perhaps the wing expands when fluid is forced through the wing veins. To test this possibility, I cut the wing along the margin with a pair of scissors shortly after the butterfly had emerged from the pupa. Drops of a clear, yellowish-green body fluid formed along the entire cut edge. This illustrates that body fluid is forced from the body into the space between the upper and lower membranes of the wing, producing the hydrostatic force that causes wing expansion. The body fluid drops become increasingly large as the body of the butterfly pulsates, indicating that this action pumps the fluid into the wing space between the membranes. Those who have reared monarch butterflies know that if you squeeze the wing when it is still in the soft condition, a watery blister will result. This is referred to as "bruising." If you insert a needle into this blister, body fluid will exude. By rupturing the wing membrane in this manner, the upper membrane can be peeled away from the lower one. In approximately fifteen minutes after the butterfly emerges from the pupa, the wings reach their maximum size, although the pumping action continues, accompanied by a back and forth movement of the wings.

Shortly after the butterfly emerges, it discharges a drop of dark, brownish-red fluid from the tip of the abdomen. This is waste material that has accumulated during the development of the pupa.

The metamorphosis of an insect involves an extremely complicated series of developments. Of the many changes that must take place to transform a wormlike larva that feeds on the leaves of plants into a winged creature that feeds on the nectar of flowers, the development of the wings is most spectacular. The wings begin their development within the body of the larva when it is only 5 or 6 millimeters in length. By the time the larva has reached a length of 2 or 3 centimeters, the structures that eventually produce the wings may be seen by carefully removing one side of the outer wall of the body of the larva. The first pair of wings is located in the region occupied by the second pair of legs (mesothorax), and the second pair of wings is located in the region occupied by the third pair of legs (metathorax).

The entire body cavity of the larva is lined with a row of cells located just beneath the hard outer skin (exoskeleton). This layer of cells is termed the *hypodermis,* or *hypodermal layer* (Greek: *hypo,* beneath; Latin: *dermis,* skin). Hypodermal cells are the body cells from which the wing buds are derived.

Wing buds may be compared to the four fingers of a glove, the main part of the glove being the body of the larva and the four fingers the two pairs of wing buds, one pair located on each side of the body. If a section of a wing bud is cut away so that you can examine the inside of it, it would look like that shown in the figure on page 64. Note that very little space separates the upper and lower layers of cells in a developing wing bud. This is the condition that exists before the larva enters the pupal stage.

Development of the wing buds, as well as other morphological changes, takes place rapidly during the mature larval stage and the larva's final suspension. When the larva changes into a pupa, the wings expand to approximately sixty times their former area. If a section of the wing bud of a pupa is cut away, the hypodermal cells are found to be more elongate than columnar, and each cell has an elongated process that is attached to a fine membrane known as the *basal membrane.* The cavity in the center is filled with body fluid *(hemolymph).* The figure is diagrammatic, drawn to show the cellular structure more clearly. Actually, the front pair of wing buds lie above the second pair, and in cutting through one wing bud you would, of necessity, cut through the one beneath it. In the illustration note that there is a thick layer of chitin, the cuticula, in the pupa that is absent in the early stages of development.

As development proceeds, certain cells of the hypodermis become modified, increase in size, and project above the other cells. The projections bend toward the outer edge of the wing. At the same time, a space filled with body fluid develops between the chitinous cuticula and the hypodermal layer.

At a later stage, the walls separating each of the hypodermal cells appear to break down; they can be distinguished one from the other only by the presence of the nuclei of the cells as seen under the microscope. With further development of the projections and apparent disappearance of the cell walls, the hypodermis becomes folded. The hypodermal cells with the elongated projections (that are later to become scales) are located on the crest of each fold. Hypodermal cells secrete a chitinous cover that eventually forms the wing membrane, and the projections on the crest of each fold secrete a chitinous cover that will form the scales. Thus, each row of scales represents a ridge, or crest.

The next step in wing development is the formation of bundles of fibers that extend from the upper to the lower membrane of the wing and from the trough of the upper surface to the trough of the lower surface. When the butterfly first emerges from the pupa, body fluid is pumped into the wing between the upper and lower membranes, forcing the wing to expand. But this expansion process is not due to the stretching of the membrane of the wing, as when one blows up a balloon; rather, it is due to the flattening out of the ridges, somewhat like the expansion of the air chamber in an accordion. If the wing did not possess the bundles of hypodermal fibers that hold the upper and lower surfaces of the wing together, then the wing would expand like a plastic bag filled with water. If you squeeze the wing soon after the butterfly emerges from the pupa, the hypodermal fibers become damaged, thus forming a watery blister.

Once the wing scales have formed over the hypodermal projections, the protoplasm of the wing-scale cells withdraws and leaves behind a series of chitinous pillars. These pillars hold the two surfaces of the scale together. When a wing scale is filled with fluid, it appears to be transparent; when the fluid withdraws, its place is taken by air, and the wing scale becomes white. The chitin on the outer surface of the scale (that is, the surface that is away from the wing membrane) develops well-marked striations, whereas the lower surface is usually unstriated and flat. The presence of these striations in some species of butterflies imparts beautiful iridescent colors to the

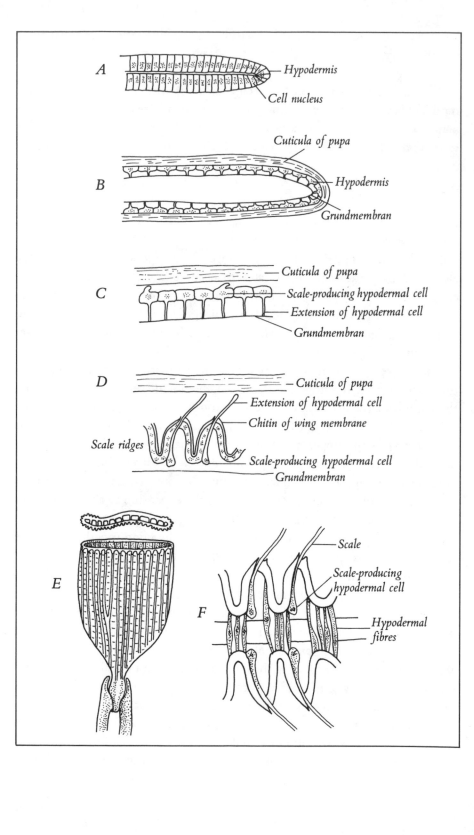

A — Hypodermis
— Cell nucleus

B — Cuticula of pupa
— Hypodermis
— Grundmembran

C — Cuticula of pupa
— Scale-producing hypodermal cell
— Extension of hypodermal cell
— Grundmembran

D — Cuticula of pupa
— Extension of hypodermal cell
— Chitin of wing membrane
Scale ridges
— Scale-producing hypodermal cell
— Grundmembran

E

F — Scale
— Scale-producing hypodermal cell
— Hypodermal fibres

wing by light diffraction. Those scales that are destined to be white are now fully formed and will undergo no further changes. Scales destined to become pigmented are filled with body fluid. Chemical changes, which in the monarch butterfly appear to be related to the gold spots of the pupa, produce the variety of colors found on the wing. In the case of the monarch, the colors vary from dark brown (black), through various lighter stages, to buff and reddish brown. The presence of various chemical compounds and their interactions with each other bring about the variety of colorful patterns found in various species of butterflies throughout the world.

SCALES

If you examine the wing surface of a monarch butterfly with the aid of a strong magnifying glass or a microscope, you will see hundreds of tiny scales arranged in regular rows, like minute shingles. These scales completely cover the upper and lower surfaces of the wings, the abdomen, the thorax, the legs, and the head. As I gazed at these tiny scales under my microscope, the question occurred to me: How many scales are there on the wings of a monarch butterfly? It would be impossible to count each one, so I estimated the number of scales by using the following method.

I chose certain parts of the upper and lower surfaces of both the front and hind wings, then placed the selected portions under the lens of my dissecting microscope, with a bright light illuminating the surface. On top of the wing portion I placed a millimeter scale etched on a microscope slide (referred to as a micrometer) and counted the number of scales along one millimeter's length. After counting the scales in different areas of a number

By careful dissection of the larva when it is in the early stages of development, one can see fingerlike projections (A) that are the beginnings of the butterfly's wings. As the space between the two layers of hypodermal cells increases, the cells produce projections that are attached to a thin membrane (grundmembran) and, at the same time, produce the cuticular substance of the eventual pupa stage (B). At a still later stage, small peglike projections (C) are produced by some of the hypodermal cells; these projections eventually form rows of scales, each one fitting into a hypodermal pocket along scale ridges (D). The final scale (E) is a hollow, ridged structure with a peglike projection that fits into the former hypodermal pocket. Hypodermal fibers form to hold the upper and lower membranes of the wing together (F).

of butterfly wings, I found that the average number was 5.29 scales, a total of 28 scales to a square millimeter, regardless of the size of the specimen involved.

The next step was to estimate the area of the wings. This I did with an instrument termed a compensating polar planimeter equipped with a tracer lens and a vernier rotating scale. I found that the area of the front and hind wings was the same. (I had previously thought that the area of the front wings was much larger than that of the hind wings, a misconception due to the configuration of the wings.) The smallest specimen in my collection had a wing area of 500 square millimeters; the largest had an area of 830 square millimeters.

From this procedure I was able to obtain the following results; bear in mind that even with such a method carried out as accurately as possible, the results can be considered only approximations. For the smallest specimen, I found each wing surface was covered with 112,500 scales, giving a total of 900,000 scales for all wing surfaces (8 × 112,500). For the largest specimen, each wing surface was covered with 186,750 scales, giving a total of 1,494,000 (8 × 186,750) scales for all wing surfaces. The above figures apply only to scales located on the plane surfaces of the wings; they do not take into account the number of small scales covering the veins of the wings or the number of elongated scales along the wing margins. I had assumed, before carrying out the above calculations, that the smaller butterflies would have smaller scales; hence the total number of scales would be the same, regardless of size. However, I found out that the scale size remains constant, while the total number is variable.

The entire body of the monarch butterfly, with the exception of the large compound eyes, is covered with an array of different kinds of scales and hairs. Each part of the body—wings, thorax, abdomen, and head—possesses distinctive scales. If you remove a few scales from various parts of the body by scraping the surface gently with a knife or razor blade and place the scales on a sheet of white paper or in a drop of water on a glass slide, you can examine them with a microscope or a strong magnifying glass. As illustrated in the photographs on page 67, the following are associated with various parts of the body.

Plane surface of the wing. Some scales are elongated, narrow, and bear two teeth; others are broader with two teeth; still others are oval and possess three or four teeth. Some of the teeth are sharply pointed, while others are blunt.

Marginal areas of the wing. All scales are elongated and lack teeth. Some are almost hairlike, while others resemble spears. The hairlike scales form

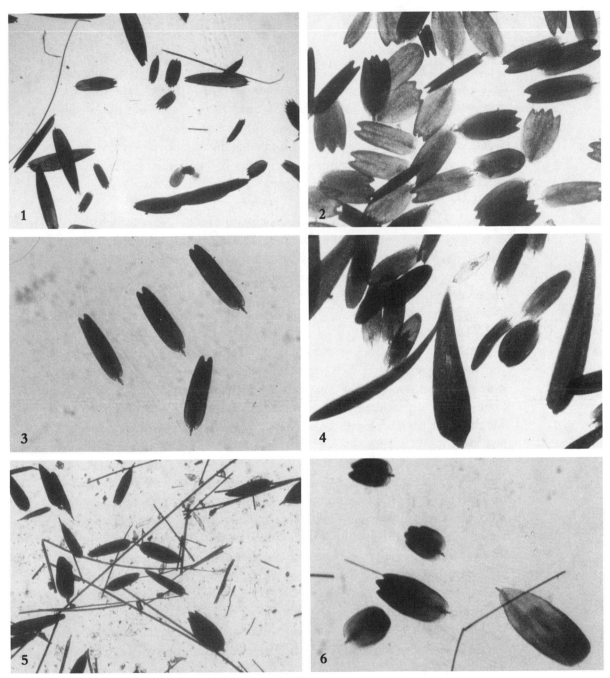

Although the dustlike scales are more obvious on the surface of the wings, they also cover the entire body of the butterfly. The color, size, shape, and configuration of the scales vary depending on where they occur. These photographs show scales from the (1) head, (2) wing surface, (3) legs, (4) wing margins, (5) thorax, and (6) abdomen.

the rather fuzzy margins of the wings and are referred to as the *wing fringe*. Interspersed among the fringe scales are oval or elongated scales without teeth.

Thorax. This area is covered with long hairs interspersed with elongated scales, some of which approach the configuration of hairs, indicating the relationship between scales and hairs. Some of the scales possess two small, blunt teeth, but the majority are spearlike and without teeth. The occasional oval scale with three teeth is located along the dorsal surface.

Abdomen. This part is covered with scales of variable size. The smaller ones possess two or three teeth—or occasionally no teeth—while the larger scales are elongated and lack teeth.

Head. The head is covered with scales of varying sizes, some of which are oval in shape and possess six sharply pointed teeth, while others are narrow and possess two or three teeth of variable size; still others are larger and more elongated and bear two or three teeth. In addition to the scales there are hairs of different lengths.

Legs. The legs possess scales of uniform size and shape that are elongated and possess two blunt teeth.

Minisculate scales. While examining my collection of scales taken from the various parts of the body at magnification 40x to 100x, I noticed a number of minute particles among the scales taken from the thorax. At 200x magnification, these minute specks resembled small seeds. They occur, for the most part, on the thorax. They are oval in shape, possess no teeth, and are without *scale stocks*—the part that attaches the scale to the integument. The absence of the stocks poses the question: How are they attached, if at all, to the integument? One might suggest that they had been picked up by the monarch butterfly as it visited flowers and that they are perhaps pollen grains. However, all my scale samples were taken from butterflies reared in cages and that had not been in contact with flowers. I still have no idea where they lie on the surface of the abdomen or whether they are attached to the hairs or are loosely interspersed among the scales and hairs. I have given the name minusculate scales to these peculiar particles because of their minuscule size.

Scale sockets. If you examine the membrane of a wing after you have removed the scales, you will see orderly rows of small pits, or sockets, into which the stocks of the scales fit.

This description of the scales and hairs found on various parts of the body of the monarch butterfly is far from complete. After examining many thousands of scales taken from numerous specimens, I came to the conclusion that there are at least thirty different types of scales and hairs on the

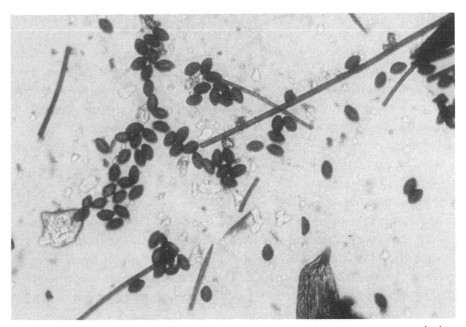

Scattered among the scales of the thoracic region are a great many minute bodies (here magnified 400 ×) that resemble seeds. They do not possess stalks and hence are not attached to the butterfly in the manner of scales. Because of their minuscule size, I termed them "minusculate scales." Their attachment to and arrangement on the integument are unknown.

body and wings of a monarch. And it is highly probable that, by the use of enlarged photographs of scales taken from many parts of the body, twice as many types as here described could be found.

Thus, what appear as small particles of colored dust are really minute scales exhibiting an amazing variety of shapes and sizes, each group playing its particular role. Some possess a sensory function; others produce a scent; still others impart a specific color to the butterfly; and all act as a waterproof coating. In addition, the scales and hairs are hollow structures, and along with the hollow veins and air sacs within the body, they add to buoyancy in flight—"golden feathers floating aimlessly on a warm summer's breeze."

FLIGHT

At first glance, one might conclude that the flight of the monarch butterfly is aimless, lacking in control, and determined by the vagaries of the wind.

One entomologist who was of this opinion came to the conclusion that the movements of all insects depended on the wind. However, after many years of observing and recording the flight of the monarch, I came to realize that, far from being aimless, it is most definitely under the control of the butterfly and varies considerably depending on the circumstances encountered. The monarch butterfly in flight seems to "know" where it is going and how to get there regardless of the wind, which at times acts as a deterrent. I have categorized some of the flight characteristics and the stimuli involved, each one being distinct and purposeful, as follows.

GLIDING FLIGHT

The broad wings of the monarch, like those of a hawk and an albatross, allow it to take advantage of vertical air currents in order to maintain height and to glide effortlessly. This pattern of flight is carried out by all monarch butterflies when they are close to the ground seeking nectar-bearing flowers and by females that are searching for milkweed plants on which to deposit eggs. It is also carried out at heights above 200 meters, which occurs most frequently during the fall migration, when migrants may be seen gliding over tall city buildings and wooded areas. It is most obvious on calm days when there is little or no wind.

CRUISING FLIGHT

In cruising flight, the wings pass through approximately 30 degrees of arc. This is a leisurely flight, interrupted by gliding. It is seen mostly when the butterflies are feeding, passing from one flowering plant to another, and during migration. The speed of this type of flight (based on numerous observations compared with the speed of an automobile) is, on average, 17 kilometers per hour. This type of flight is common when conditions necessitate leisurely movement from one location to another in the absence of any stimulation.

SPEED FLIGHT

The wings of the monarch are capable of considerable vertical movement, from completely closed and held above the body to 30 degrees of vertical beneath the body. In addition, the apical portion of the front pair is capable of bending slightly as the air presses against the broad plane of the wing, thus increasing the forward speed as well as allowing for considerable maneuverability. One can readily demonstrate the flexibility of the tip of the wing by holding the wing at right angles to the butterfly's body and pressing on the apical end. This flexible action of the wing tip is obvious when flight is viewed by high-speed photography.

If you alarm a monarch butterfly, as when you attempt to capture a specimen while it is feeding on a flower, it will take off rapidly in a pattern of flight that I have termed speed flight. Under such conditions, the wings beat rapidly, passing through a vertical arc of 120 degrees. This rapid flight pattern, displaying considerable wing displacement, can be readily observed when a monarch flutters against a windowpane while attempting to escape—the rapidly beating wings show as a blurred image.

It is rather difficult to determine with any degree of accuracy the speed of the monarch butterfly during speed flight, since an alarmed specimen rarely travels in a straight line as it moves away from the source of alarm. I have taken numerous observations on speed flight over very short distances by comparing the speed of the flight with that of my car. As I kept pace with the monarch flying along a roadway, Norah would record the speed shown on the car's speedometer. The average for such observations was found to be 37 km/hr. I am of the opinion that speed flights of 48 km/hr are possible. When assisted by a tail wind of, say, 32 km/hr, the combined speed could be in excess of 80 km/hr, depending upon the speed of the wind.

SOCIAL FLIGHT

Of all the flight patterns I have discussed, none is more fascinating to observe than what I term "social flight." Using a combination of gliding and cruising flights, two or more monarch butterflies will follow each other in a wide circle, executed in a horizontal plane. I have observed such social flights mostly during the fall migration, carried out at a height of over 30 meters. As the butterflies follow each other in this leisurely circular pattern, they drift with the prevailing wind in a manner similar to that of herring gulls returning to the ocean from some distant daytime feeding areas. Monarch butterflies that have been held for a few hours in a rearing cage and then released will often ascend by speed flight to a height of 30 meters or more and then engage in social flight with other released prisoners. It is because of this resemblance to a social gathering that I have termed the activity "social flight." One might consider such a designation purely anthropomorphic, but the butterflies are undoubtedly attracted one to the other, whether males or females, as a social response devoid of sexual attraction, since most fall migrants are in reproductive dormancy. Monarch butterflies are somewhat gregarious during the fall migration, as evidenced by their clustering on overnight roosting trees and when arriving at the overwintering sites. One is struck by the similarities between the migratory flight of monarchs and the behavior of migrating birds, which act individually on the breeding grounds but come together in flocks on roosting and overwintering sites. Under gusty and turbulent wind conditions, however, the monarch butterflies tend to be blown off course. This is important during migration and will be discussed in part 5.

PRENUPTIAL FLIGHT

When a female monarch enters an area patrolled by a male, he will pursue the female by speed flight. If the female is not ready for mating, she will avoid the male by speed flight while executing a zigzag, or dodging, course. If the female is prepared to mate, she will fly in an ascending spiral, which I refer to as a "prenuptial flight," pursued by the male. The vertical distance to which the pair may rise varies considerably. At times the female will break away from the prenuptial flight and elude the male by speed flight. Occasionally, a male will enter another male's territory resulting in a prenuptial flight of short duration. In this case the flight is much more rapid and erratic, each male attempting to get in front of the other and each finally dropping to the ground again.

SEX RATIO

I have found that among the thousands of butterflies I have reared from eggs, the sex ratio remains the same—half males and half females. This is to be expected, since there is an equal chance of the sex chromosomes uniting to form either males or females. However, when collecting adults in nature, I have, at times, noticed marked discrepancies in this sex ratio and have received numerous reports of similar observations from my colleagues in various parts of North America. Some of these observations may be explained as follows.

During the breeding season, I have made counts of the ratio of males to females collected in the field and noted that, when specimens were captured in areas where there was an abundance of nectar-producing composite flowers, I collected far more males than females. On the other hand, in areas devoid of such plants, I collected far more females than males. The reason for this discrepancy is that males tend to remain in areas of flowering plants awaiting the arrival of females. The females, except when they visit nectar-producing flowers, tend to confine their attention to areas where there is an abundant supply of milkweed plants on which to deposit their eggs.

During the spring migration, there is a marked discrepancy in the ratio of males to females in various parts of North America. In Texas, along the Mexican border, one may collect far more males than females in some areas, and the reverse occurs in other regions. While collecting in areas near Laredo, Texas, I found a preponderance of males flying about trees that were in bloom; in adjacent areas, however, only females were collected, and these were flying close to the ground and heading in a northeastward direction. This is explained as follows.

After mating has taken place at the overwintering site, or during the flight through Mexico, the males, for the most part, do not continue northward. Rarely does one collect male specimens at long distances from the overwintering sites during the spring migration. Hence, during the spring migration there is a marked tendency to observe or collect more females than males, the discrepancy being more marked the farther north collections or observations are made.

During the fall migration, some monarch butterflies are in a state of sexual dormancy, or sexual diapause, the reproductive organs being in an inactive condition, such as occurs in the fall migration of birds. I term these members of the migrating population "true migrants." However, some migrants are sexually mature and mate, and the females deposit eggs on the milkweed plants along the migratory routes. As a result, if one collects specimens in the field during the fall, there will be more females than males in areas where milkweed is growing. However, even in these areas, specimens taken from the overnight roosting trees show a fifty-fifty ratio of males to females.

There are, however, some anomalies for which I can offer no plausible explanation. For example, while carrying out field investigations along the north shore of Florida, I encountered a great preponderance of males. These migrants were in a most deplorable condition; their wings were badly tattered and some had sufficient wing membrane remaining to allow for only short flights. The week prior to this incident, violent storms had occurred, with strong winds and heavy rains. The migrants caught in the storms had been dashed against bushes and tall grasses along the shore, thus damaging their wings. But why were there far more males than females? Perhaps males were able to survive the effects of the storms better than the females. Or perhaps, as some of my colleagues have suggested, males had preceded the females during migration.

There are undoubtedly many environmental factors contributing to the marked differences in the numbers of males and females in certain parts of North America at various times of the year. Future observations recorded throughout the year—during migration, on the breeding grounds, and on the overwintering sites—may eventually provide explanations for such occurrences.

MATING HABITS

Of the many fields containing milkweed and flowering plants where I have watched and recorded the habits of the monarch butterfly, one field in particular proved most productive. A small, meandering creek threaded its way through this field, and along its banks grew a tangle of tall grasses, sedges, and flowering plants. The creek divided the field into two roughly equal sections, one of tall grass and flowering plants and one of short grass (the latter resulting from being cut during haying operations). Small seedling milkweed plants grew in profusion in the mowed field. Females, especially during the morning period, confined their attention to the field containing the milkweed. Two males inhabited the area of flowering plants and flew from one plant to another as if patrolling a particular area. As a result of this spatial division of males and females, I was able to record the following mating behavior.

Females, after depositing eggs on the milkweed plants for some period of time, would fly to the area where there were nectar-producing plants on which to feed. A male that had been resting with wings partly spread apart on a broad leaf of one of the hawthorn bushes would immediately give chase. At times, a female, wishing to continue egg-laying in some other field, would increase her flight speed and thus, on a zigzag course, elude her pursuer. At other times, she would fly vertically, executing small circles, closely followed by the male, who also flew in small circles. This flight would continue for a few seconds, the pair flying higher and higher. Eventually, the male would fly in front of the female. With my field glasses, I could see a yellow structure extruded from the tip of the abdomen of the male. This structure is referred to as the *anal gland;* it is covered with long hairs forming what I have termed the *plume,* which disseminates a secretion from the anal gland. The odor of this secretion, to the human sense of smell, closely resembles that of flowers, hence its attraction to the female seeking a nectar-producing flower.

Having completed the courtship flight, the male would fly to a nearby hawthorn leaf, followed by the female. There the pair came to rest. The female, with wings closed or slightly open, would occasionally extend her proboscis in the manner of feeding, perhaps in response to the flowerlike odor from the male gland. The male, his wings moving gently up and down, as if to waft the odor in the female's direction, would strut beside the female and, at times, in front of her. Finally, the male, with anal gland withdrawn, would bend his abdomen in a lateral direction to bring the tip of it into contact with that of the female, whose wings remained closed.

Using his well-developed, jawlike abdominal claspers, the male was then able to grasp the female, his hold so strong that, when alarmed, he would be able to fly carrying the female suspended beneath him.

While holding the female firmly by means of his abdominal claspers, the male inserted his long, needlelike penis, or *aedeagus* (Greek: *aidoice,* genitals) into the reproductive channel *(ductus copulatrix)* of the female and deposited a *spermatophore* (Greek: *sperme,* seed; *pherein,* to bear) into a cavity termed the *bursa copulatrix* (Latin: *bursa,* purse). There it remained until the sperm were needed for fertilizing the eggs as they passed down the oviduct.

Occasionally, after a pair came to rest side by side, the female would display a negative reaction. When the male attempted to grasp the tip of the female's abdomen, the female would avoid further advances by snapping her wings together and at the same time raising her abdomen vertically out of reach of the probing abdomen of the male. It would appear that some other stimulus is necessary to bring about final copulation, which may be explained as follows.

When a male has enticed a female to a trysting place, the anal gland, with its large featherlike plume, must be retracted inside the abdomen to allow for the jawlike claspers to secure a firm hold on the female. As a result, the

Using his jawlike claspers, the male obtains a firm grasp on the tip of the female's abdomen. His hold is so strong that, when alarmed, he is able to fly, carrying the female suspended beneath him. During the mating process, which lasts an hour or more, the male sperm cells are transmitted to the bursa of the female.

aroma from the gland is cut off. Perhaps at this point the alar glands play a significant role by fanning the aroma toward the female. In addition, there appears to exist a contact substance produced by cells located at the tip of the male abdomen that, when brought into contact with receptor cells of the female, causes her to allow the male to grasp her abdomen and at the same time insert the penis. You can demonstrate the existence of this response by holding a female in one hand, her abdomen exposed, and bringing the tip of the male abdomen into contact with that of the female. When you do so, you will see that the male claspers will open, as if having received a stimulus from the tip of the abdomen of the female. I have used this method, which I term "forced mating," on numerous occasions to bring about copulation of caged specimens.

MALE ALAR GLANDS

The two black spots located one on each of the hind wings of the male and referred to as *alar glands* may play an important role in the mating process. If you examine an alar gland with the aid of a strong magnifying glass, you will observe that it is not simply a patch of black scales; rather it is a distinctly swollen area, and the wing vein *(cubitus)* next to it is also slightly swollen. If you cut through this structure and examine the cut surface using a strong magnifying glass or a microscope, you will see that it is not simply a swollen area of the wing but a distinct fold of the wing membrane.

When the adult monarch butterfly first emerges from the pupa, the space between the upper and lower membranes of the wing contains body fluid, and there is a layer of cells present on the inside surfaces. When the wings have become fully expanded and the body fluid reabsorbed or evaporated, the cellular lining of the membranes breaks down and finally disappears, except in the areas of the male hind wings that give rise to the alar glands and the adjacent portion of the cubitus vein.

What is the structure of the alar glands? To answer this question, I made very thin sections, using the paraffin histological technique, stained the sections with certain red and purple dyes, and then examined the prepared sections under the compound microscope. I found that the inside surface of the gland was lined with numerous minute black scales, some of which were narrow and threadlike, while others were much broader, resembling tiny black feathers. I also noticed that these scales were associated with two kinds of cells. One kind had a raised margin, and when viewed from above it resembled a cup. I gave this kind of cell the name *posculum* (Latin: cup or goblet). The other cell type, when viewed from above, resembled a minute saucer, so I gave it the name *patella* (Latin: saucer or small dish). Thus, associated with the alar gland are these two types of cells: the *posculate cell,* with its associated *posculate scale,* and the *patellate cell,* with its associated *patellate scale.* Other researchers have applied other terms, such as "scent cups," "scent pits," and "papillae" to these cells.

Since these minute black scales within the alar gland resemble dust particles to the unaided eye, entomologists have given to them the name *androconia* (Greek: *aner,* male; *konie,* dust). This term is applied to all such modified scales that are associated with a glandular function and, it is believed, diffuse the scent from the glands or, perhaps, actually take up the scent, like a straw, from the cell producing it.

The patellate scale can be divided into three regions: the *blade* (the broad portion); the *stalk* (the narrow portion immediately above the cell); and the *tube* (the rather transparent portion penetrating the cell).

The posculate scale can be divided into two regions: a *blade,* which is much narrower than that of the patellate scale, and a *stalk,* which is very thin and hairlike. In the patellate scale, the tube is either absent or indistinct.

Certain questions arise: Is the alar gland a true gland? Does it produce some kind of secretion? In animal tissues of a glandular nature, the cells contain bodies known as *mitochondria* and *ribosomes* that can be seen only under very high magnification. If the alar gland is functional and producing some kind of biochemical substance, then these cellular bodies should be present. When I examined sections of the cells at 20,000× magnification with an electron microscope, I found that the cells did indeed possess an abundance of both of these cellular bodies. Hence I concluded that the alar glands are true glands.

What is the function of the alar glands in the mating process? To this question I offer the following answer. When the male anal gland is retracted within the body so that only a small portion of the plume remains extruded, the hairs of the plume form a cluster held closely together and referred to as the "pencil," because of its resemblance to the tip of a lead pencil. I hypothesized that the pencil of the male was inserted into the opening to the alar gland, since the glands are situated on the hind wings in a position that could readily be reached by the tip of the male abdomen. I had noticed a bare spot (one devoid of scales) at the opening to the alar gland; the scales could have been removed by the action of the male inserting the hair pencil into it. At times, I thought I had observed such an action in the field; a male at rest sometimes appeared to move the tip of its abdomen toward one of its alar glands. This action had been reported by other researchers for various species belonging to the same genus as the monarch

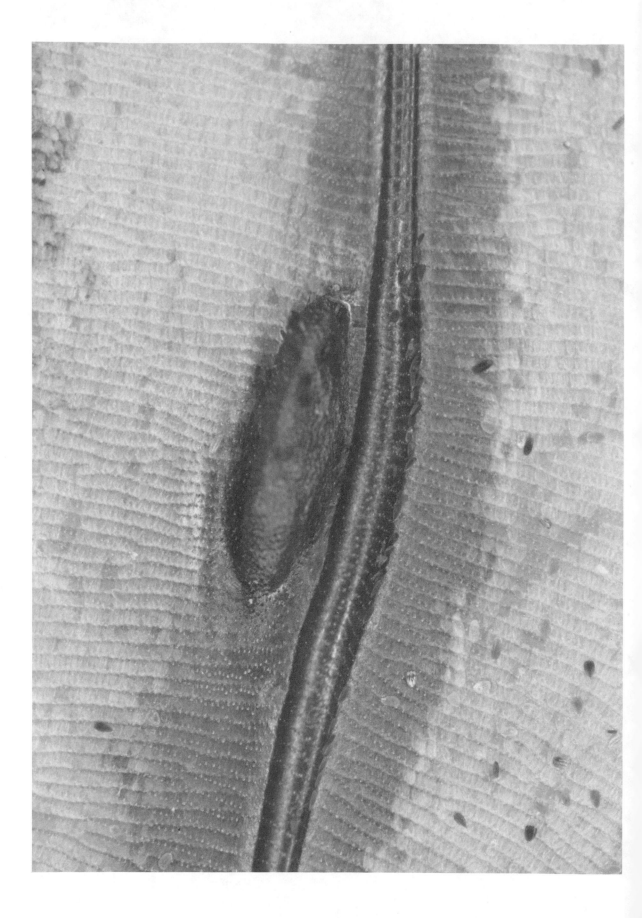

butterfly. Other researchers have reported finding androconia on the hairs of the hair plumes of the male anal gland; these androconia could have been removed from the interior of the gland when the pencil was inserted into it. However, I examined five hundred specimens of male plumes and was unable to detect any androconia scales on the hairs. If there is such a relationship between the hair pencil and the alar gland, then perhaps the male transfers a secretion from the anal gland into the alar gland. Investigating this possibility, one researcher came to the conclusion that the secretions from the anal glands of the male contained a number of chemical elements referred to by the researcher as a "bouquet" and that such substances were contained on "cuticular particles" that are passed to the female during courtship. It was further suggested that it was necessary for such cuticular particles to be placed within the alar gland in order to produce a pheromone compound called "danaidone," a word derived from the family name of the monarch butterfly, Danaidae. This researcher also suggested that this substance is obtained by the monarch when it feeds on the nectar of various Compositae plants, particularly those of the Asteraceae, from which a biochemical substance strikingly similar to danaidone has been obtained.

That there may be some kind of secretion from the male alar gland is, at the present time, purely speculative. Until such a secretion has been isolated, it is not possible to determine its function, as has been accomplished with secretions (pheromones) occurring in other species of insects. However, I offer the following description of the mating process without biochemical formulations.

When the male monarch butterfly pursues a female in flight, the first task is that of bringing the female to rest so as to permit copulation to take place. This is accomplished by the extrusion of the anal gland and the dissemination of a substance, or substances, that act as an attractant to the female. Field observations show that the males tend to remain close to where flowering plants are in abundance, awaiting the arrival of females in search of nectar. By presenting a substance that even to the human olfactory organs closely resembles that emitted by flowering plants, a male can lead a female to a trysting place. In order for the male to grasp the female's abdomen and insert his penis, he must first withdraw the large anal gland, with the result that the perfumelike substance is no longer liberated. Careful observations show that, once the alar gland has been retracted, the male

By removing the scales from the surface of the alar gland and the adjacent vein, we see the gland as an oval, dark, swollen area. The vein next to the gland is also swollen.

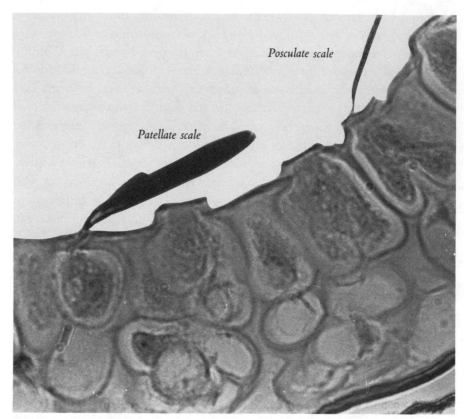

Posculate scale

Patellate scale

Under high magnification (800 ×), one can see two kinds of cells in the alar gland: one kind has a raised margin to which is attached a hairlike scale, and the other lacks the raised margin and has a broad, featherlike scale attached to it. Each type of scale may be divided into the following parts: the blade (the broad portion), the stalk (the narrow part immediately above the cell), and the tube (the portion that penetrates the cell). (Picture reduced to 57.5% of original.)

struts in front of the female, raising and lowering his wings. He then attempts copulation. Failing to do so, he resumes his fanning and strutting. Finally, copulation takes place, but only on the acquiescence of the female, which I believe is due to a substance produced by the alar gland.

Under caged conditions, males will approach females, as in the final stages of courtship in nature, without extruding their anal gland and often without preliminary strutting and fanning of the wings. Thus, the anal and alar glands apparently do not take part in the final act of copulation. Indeed, it is possible to bring about copulation by placing the tip of the male abdomen into contact with that of the female. Only in nature, under free-flying conditions, does the process of courtship take place.

LEGS

The mesothoracic (middle) and metathoracic (hind) pairs of legs of the monarch butterfly are similar in structure, as in all species of butterflies. They consist of two small basal joints, the *coxa* and *trochanter,* a large, inflated segment, the *femure,* and a large slender joint, the *tibia*. Attached to the tibia is the *tarsus* (foot), which in the middle and hind pairs of legs consists of five joints of variable lengths. Attached to the end joint is a pair of

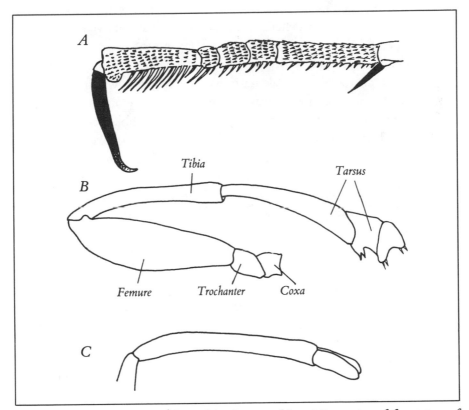

The tarsus (foot) of the middle and hind pairs of legs (A) consists of five joints of variable lengths, with a large, black, curved claw attached to the last joint. In contrast, the front pair of legs are small and are tucked neatly under the head. These aborted legs are covered with long hairs, giving them the appearance of tiny brushes. The hairs must be removed in order to see the various joints. The front foot of the female (B) consists of one elongated joint and two small clublike joints armed with paired spines. The front foot of the male (C) consists of one elongated joint and two oval terminal ones placed in juxtaposition. The function of these modified front legs is unknown.

long, curved, sharply pointed claws. In the monarch butterfly, as in all species of the so-called brush-footed butterflies (family Nymphalidae, in which the monarch butterfly was at one time placed), the prothoracic (front) pair of legs is much reduced in size and tucked inconspicuously beneath the head. Since these legs are so inconspicuous, the monarch butterfly appears to possess only two pairs of legs.

If you wish to examine the tiny front legs, carefully remove them, preferably from a specimen that has recently died and is still in a soft condition. Then remove the dense clusters of hairs that cover them. To remove the hairs, I use an artist's paintbrush with the bristles cut short. Hold a leg with a pair of fine forceps, and pass the brush over the leg with a gentle scrubbing action. Once the hairs and scales have been removed, the leg can be examined by means of a strong magnifying glass.

An interesting feature of these aborted legs is the structure of the foot. If you compare the foot of a female with that of a male you will find a striking difference. The female's foot consists of three joints; the one attached to the tibia is elongated, and the apical two joints form a clublike structure armed with pairs of small spines. The foot of the male, in contrast, consists of one elongated joint and two terminal joints placed in juxtaposition.

Those who have studied insect behavior and its relation to body structures realize that rarely, if ever, does one find anomalies without a definite purpose. The front legs are not reduced in size simply because they are of no use. If such were the case, the legs would have entirely disappeared, or become mere remnants of the original legs. One must also answer the questions, Why is the foot of a female's front leg so very different from that of the male? and, Why are the front legs so densely covered with long hairs?

I do not know the answers to these questions. I have spent many hours on numerous occasions under various circumstances observing these small legs. For instance, if you hold a live monarch butterfly in your hand, particularly the female, you will see the front legs vibrate intermittently. In the act of copulation the tiny legs of both the male and the female will vibrate. Thus, it would appear that they perform some function when the insect is under stress, but the mystery of the purpose of the aborted front legs remains for further study.

PROBOSCIS

A scene familiar to many of us, especially as children, is a field or garden of flowers with colorful butterflies flitting from one blossom to another in search of sugary nectar. Each butterfly's sucking tube, coiled under its head when not in use, is extended. You may have wondered how this slender, apparently simple tube, resembling a soda straw, operates in sucking up the nectar.

If you examine the proboscis under the microscope, you will see that it is a complicated structure, not a simple tube. To examine it carefully, it is necessary to remove it, preferably from a recently deceased specimen, and place it on a glass slide in a drop of water. Using a sharp blade, cut the tube into sections along its length, as well as across its width. Then examine the sections under a microscope or with a strong magnifying glass. Some of the structures I describe can be seen only under quite high magnification, $200\times$ to $400\times$.

The proboscis is composed of two parts *(maxillae)* that are concave on the inner surface and convex on the outer surface, similar to a hose pipe that has been cut in half lengthwise. These two halves are held together by means of hundreds of minute hooks and interlocking spines that act in the same manner as a zipper. Along the outer, or convex, surface is an elastic rod of cuticle that is cross-striated to make it more flexible. Its function is to cause the proboscis to become coiled like a watch spring when not in use. The inner surfaces of the maxillae consist of a row of hundreds of minute, somewhat branched, chitinous rings, each one separated from its neighbors by a flexible membrane. Each of these rings consists of a row of quadrangular plates bearing spines that are directed inwards toward the proboscis channel; these plates resemble tiny thumbtacks. A nerve, along with a *tracheole* (small breathing tube) to supply oxygen, extends the length of the proboscis. All along the proboscis are numerous small, transverse muscles. Scattered over the surface of the proboscis, especially near the tip, are numerous small circular plates, each one bearing a projection, or papilla, that responds to touch. Thus, if you touch the proboscis of a monarch while it is feeding, these tactile sense organs immediately send a response to the nerve, resulting in the coiling of the proboscis. These sense organs also inform the monarch butterfly of the nature of the blossom, guiding the tip of the proboscis to the nectar cup. Other sensory cells at the tip of the proboscis respond to the presence of the nectar, resulting in the contraction of the muscular pharynx that acts like a pump to suck up the nectar.

The coiling and uncoiling of the proboscis is accomplished as follows. When the butterfly is preparing to feed, a nerve impulse excites the transverse muscles; these muscles, by their tension, flatten out the proboscis, causing it to extend. When feeding has been completed, the muscles relax, and the proboscis is coiled by the striated rod of cuticle, which holds the proboscis in a coiled position until the muscles are once again stimulated to contract.

Situated at each side of the proboscis is a pair of feelerlike appendages termed the *labial palps*. The palps are covered with numerous spinelike hairs. It is necessary to remove these hairs in order to see that the palps are composed of three distinct parts. The palps vibrate while the monarch butterfly is feeding, which indicates that they perform a tactile function.

ANTENNAE

The antennae, or feelers, are composed of numerous small, cylindrical joints of uniform size except at the apex, where the joints become larger and form a clublike structure. Between each joint is a flexible membrane that allows for a degree of curvature. The segments and the intervening membrane can be seen with a magnifying glass. Remove an antenna from a monarch butterfly, preferably one recently deceased, and place it in a drop of water on a glass slide. Holding the base with a fine pair of forceps, gently stroke the antenna from base to apex with a razor blade. This will separate the individual joints. In carrying out this procedure you will note that there are few scales on the antenna; those present are very small and can be seen only under the microscope at 100× magnification.

The antennae lack any discernible modifications such as hair clusters or scent pockets and hence do not seem to play an important role in detecting odors such as those emanating from flowers. Under caged conditions, live monarch butterflies from which I removed the antennae were still able to locate food. However, I have observed that while a monarch is feeding the antennae are lowered towards the blossoms, which would indicate some sort of sensory response.

It would appear that the antennae inform the monarch butterfly while it is in flight of its orientation with respect to gravity, much as the semicircular canals of humans operate. When one witnesses the complex flight of the monarch, one can appreciate the function of the antennae in flight orientation.

EYES

If you observe two butterflies chasing each other, performing numerous aerobatics, you cannot help but be impressed with the visual responses of these winged creatures. I have often been asked the question, Do butterflies see images as humans do? To answer this question, one must examine the eyes of both the adult and the larva in order to see the various structural elements that are involved. Having done so, one can then speculate as to how such eyes function.

When you examine the head of a monarch butterfly, you are immediately aware of the presence of a pair of large, black, bulging, ball-like eyes. To the unaided human eye, they do not seem to possess any complex structures. However, if you view the eye through a strong lens or a microscope, you see that the surface is covered with what appear to be a great many small, six-sided plates joined closely together so as to give the impression of a honeycomb. To determine what these tiny six-sided plates are, it is necessary to dissect the eye and examine it with a high-power microscope. One can then see that the eye is composed of small, rodlike elements, each lying beneath one of the six-sided plates. Each of these rods is an individual eye, referred to as an *ommatidium* (Greek, little eye), and is made up of the

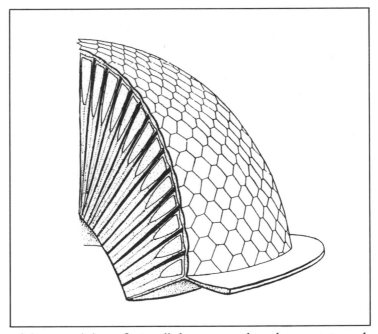

The eye of the adult monarch butterfly is called a compound eye because it is made up of hundreds of simple eyes. Each simple eye, termed an ommatidium, has a six-sided lens composed of transparent cuticle. The lenses fit together to form a honeycomb pattern.

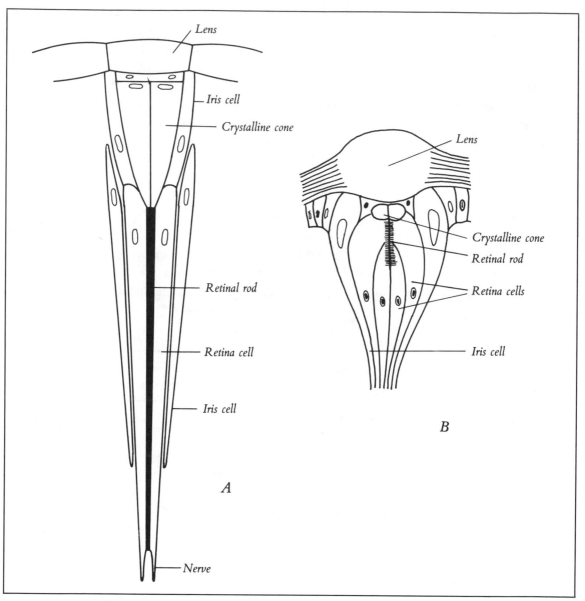

Lens

Iris cell

Crystalline cone

Retinal rod

Retina cell

Iris cell

A

Nerve

Lens

Crystalline cone
Retinal rod

Retina cells

Iris cell

B

If one simple eye is removed from the compound eye and examined under a microscope, you can see the many parts (A). Light entering through the lens is focused through the crystalline cone to a light-sensitive body termed the retinal rod (rhabdom). The photochemical reaction resulting from the light rays stimulates the retinal cells. Then the message passes via the nerve to the brain. In order to prevent stray light from affecting neighboring eyes, the structures are surrounded by pigmented iris cells. The larva (B) has two groups of simple eyes, one on each side of the head. Their structure is similar to that of the ommatidium, or simple eye, of the adult.

following parts. The six-sided plate is the *lens,* which is composed of clear cuticle. Beneath the lens is another transparent structure termed the *crystalline cone.* As light enters the eye and passes through the lens and the crystalline cone, it is scattered in all directions. In order to direct the light in one direction to the *retinal rod,* or *rhabdom* (Greek, a rod), which is the active body in recording vision, the crystalline cone is surrounded by pigment cells, similar to those of the iris of a human eye, and so they are called *iris cells.* The retinal rod is surrounded by *retinal cells* that conduct the impulses from the retinal rod to the nervous system. Surrounding the retinal cells are pigmented cells, or iris cells, similar to those surrounding the crystalline cone.

Are the eyes of the larva the same as those of the adult? If you examine the head of the larva closely you will see, situated on each side of the head, an irregular row of tiny, clear, beadlike eyes. Each one is a single, or simple, eye. The basic structure of one of these simple eyes is similar to that of the individual eye of the compound eye of the adult. Beneath the bulbous lens is a small crystalline cone that directs light to the retinal rod. Retinal cells relay the nerve impulse to the central nervous system. The iris cells prevent the scattering of light.

We can never know what a butterfly sees when it looks at an object, any more than we can tell what an individual human sees, since it is not possible to examine the interpretation of the brain when stimulated by light passing into the eye. However, if you remove the outer cuticle of the butterfly's eye, with all its multitude of lenses, and pass a light through it, you obtain a picture of many individual parts of the object, like a mosaic.

When light rays fall on the retinal cone, a chemical termed "visual purple" is produced. This substance stimulates the retina, which passes the stimulation on to the brain where it is interpreted. The chemical reaction is somewhat similar to the one that occurs in making a photographic negative.

Although it is impossible to see through the eye of a monarch butterfly and to know the resulting brain response, we can test the sight of butterflies as they respond to various colors and objects. There have been many such experiments carried out for a number of different species of insects, but none specifically for the monarch butterfly. It has been shown from such experiments that not all butterflies respond to light in the same way. Some species can detect and respond to ultraviolet light, which is not visible to humans, while others do not. Some species react more to the red-orange part of the color spectrum, while others react more to the green-blue part. Relatively few experiments have been carried out with respect to butterflies' responses to size and shape of objects, but it would appear that they do react. Thus, a female in the act of ovipositing can distinguish a particular food plant by its size and structure. Perhaps the most remarkable eye response is seen during flight, particularly when a male is pursuing a female in prenuptial flights in which the angle and direction of flight vary rapidly. In social flight, one butterfly will follow another as it flies in circles while moving in a given direction. The avoidance reaction at the approach of a moving object is well known to all who have attempted to capture a monarch butterfly that is resting on a flower.

In contrast to the adult, a larva is not capable of rapid response. Its eyes can perceive objects and can discriminate between a large and a small object, as evidenced when it is preparing to enter the pupa stage and is searching for a suitable supporting object. To examine its surroundings, the larva will raise the front portion of its body and move from side to side to allow light to fall on the simple eyes on each side of the head. If you cover all of the eyes but one on each side of the head, the response is the same as if all the eyes were exposed.

Unlike the visual response to light in an adult, a larva can respond to light that passes through the thin skin of its body. If all the eyes are covered with an opaque substance, the larva can still distinguish light from darkness. This effect of light passing through the larval skin, which can respond to changes in the amount or duration of light, is related to the migratory response, which I discuss at length in part 5.

The eye of the monarch butterfly is a marvelous structure that has evolved over millions of years. The eyes of other insects are equally as remarkable and, in some species, much more so. Indeed, one could write a book dealing with but one topic, the eyes of insects.

EGG LAYING (OVAPOSITION)

When the reproductive organs are completely developed and mating has taken place, the female deposits her eggs on the leaves of the milkweed plant. Females exercise considerable selectivity as to the particular milkweed plant on which to deposit an egg. As if aware that the very small larva hatching from the egg requires a tender leaf for its first meal, the female deposits her eggs on the small leaves of the milkweed plant rather than on the older, tougher ones — small seedling plants are most often chosen. These small plants, usually 7 to 48 centimeters in height, possess leaves that are soft to the touch and yellow-green in color, with a thin epidermis and a thin layer of pubescence on the undersurface. In contrast are the blue-green leaves, with their thick epidermis and heavy pubescence, of the more mature plants. During the month of August, in fields where the majority of the milkweed plants have reached maturity and there are few, if any, small seedling plants present, eggs will be deposited on the larger leaves of plants of various stages of maturity.

To investigate the egg-laying behavior, I made some observations in the field. The area chosen for the purpose contained plants in various stages of development: tall milkweed plants possessing flowers and small seed pods; second growth plants less than 60 centimeters in height; and a great many seedling plants 8 to 20 centimeters in height. The following results were obtained: 400 plants possessing flowers and seed pods yielded only one larva; 200 plants without flowers or seed pods yielded two eggs and one larva; and 400 small plants (less than 20 centimeters in height) yielded seventy-four eggs and twelve larvae.

The ovipositing female not only chooses small tender leaves but also avoids unhealthy plants, such as those that have a virus disease that turns the leaves yellow and those infested with aphids that cluster together in dense masses on the underside of the leaf.

In choosing a particular plant, the female first employs a purely visual response. Flying slowly, in gliding flight, she weaves back and forth across the field within a few centimeters of the top of the vegetation. Occasionally she will pause to examine a plant that is not a species of milkweed, but after touching it with her tarsi, she continues her search. Now and then she discovers a small milkweed seedling hidden by tall grass. Having located it by sight, she will crawl slowly through the tangle of tall grasses to reach it and deposit an egg. Then she will crawl back through the tall grasses, an action that accounts for much of the wing destruction seen in older females. Sighting a free-standing milkweed plant, a female will approach it slowly, flying into the breeze, which assists in retarding her forward motion. Her two pairs of long legs are extended in preparation for testing the plant as to its suitability for depositing an egg. This is done by placing the tarsi on the surface of the leaf, thus bringing numerous scent-receptor cells, located in the tissue, into contact with the leaf.

If you wish to test the presence of these sensory cells, you can carry out the following simple experiment. Soak a piece of cloth in a honey and water solution. Hold the folded wings of the monarch butterfly firmly but gently, and bring the butterfly close to, but not touching, the honey-soaked cloth. You will observe that the butterfly displays no positive response. Touch its antennae to the cloth, and again there is no response. Now, extend one of the legs and place the tarsus on the saturated honey cloth. The butterfly immediately extends its proboscis in preparation for feeding. For best results, this experiment should be carried out when the butterfly is hungry.

If a leaf is accepted, the female bends her abdomen under it so that the tip comes into contact with the underside of the leaf membrane close to the central rib. A yellow, waxy egg is extruded, the blunt base foremost, together with a mucilagelike secretion that firmly cements the egg to the leaf. Depending on the position of the female's thorax on the upper surface of the leaf, her abdomen may reach a distance of 2 to 19 millimeters from the margin. I measured the lengths of the abdomens of fifty females and found that the average length was 17 millimeters. If half the length of the abdomen is curved beneath the leaf, then the egg would be deposited at a distance of 8 to 9 millimeters from the leaf margin. On numerous occasions, however, more than three-quarters of the length of the abdomen was curved beneath the leaf, thus allowing the egg to be placed closer to the central area of the leaf, near the midrib. I examined 240 milkweed leaves on which eggs had been deposited and found that the majority of eggs were located between 5 to 18 millimeters from the leaf margin. Rarely does the ovipositing female deposit eggs on the upper surface of the leaf or on the undersurface if another egg is present. Under caged conditions, however, eggs may be deposited on any part of the milkweed plant, regardless of the presence of other eggs.

Occasionally a female may deposit an egg on the leaf of a plant that is not a species of milkweed. When I found such eggs, I wondered how this could happen. Realizing that the female exercised considerable choice during the egg-laying and that the tarsi performed the essential function of testing whether or not the plant was suitable, I carried out the following simple test.

Holding a female butterfly's wings together, I placed her tarsi on a milkweed leaf. She responded by bending her abdomen in readiness to deposit an egg. Then I placed the tip of my finger at the tip of her abdomen, and she deposited an egg on it. The scent receptors on the tarsi informed the ovipositing female that she was standing on a milkweed leaf. This response passed via the nervous system and caused an egg to travel from the oviduct to the genital opening. Since there are no scent receptors on the tip of the abdomen to inform the female whether or not she is touching a milkweed leaf, the egg is extruded and cemented to the object that comes into contact with the tip of the abdomen, in this case, my finger. Eggs found on plants growing next to a milkweed plant probably result from a similar action.

I found it possible to have an ovipositing female deposit eggs on any medium. Eggs deposited on filing cards were useful for many experiments and tests, such as times and frequency of oviposition, cross-mating with respect to color and size variations, and the effect of environment factors on rates of development. Such cards could be placed in different environmental conditions and the data recorded on the same card.

Having deposited an egg on a leaf, a female, in leisurely flight, searches for another suitable plant. Within a short time she alights on a second plant, deposits an egg, and then leisurely continues her survey of milkweed plants. The intervals between each egg-laying vary; shorter intervals occur at the beginning of egg-laying and longer ones toward the end. To find out what these intervals might be and, at the same time, obtain information on the number of eggs laid in nature (not in the laboratory under artificial conditions), I followed ovipositing females as they flew from one milkweed plant to another. I found that the interval between each egg deposition varied from twenty seconds to ninety seconds, with an average of fifty-nine seconds. During an observation of one female, carried out over a period of forty-five minutes, 42 eggs were deposited. After depositing eggs, the female came to rest on the leaf of a goldenrod plant for a period of ten minutes, during which she remained with wings partly spread. At my approach she flew to a group of small milkweed plants and, in a period of three minutes, deposited 2 more eggs. Once again she came to rest on the goldenrod plant for a period of twenty minutes. Then she took to wing on speed flight to an adjacent field.

I have often been asked, How many eggs does a female monarch lay? This is a difficult, perhaps impossible, question to answer with any degree of accuracy. It is not possible to seek the answer in the laboratory, because a caged female does not live as long as her counterpart in nature, hence the period of egg-laying is greatly reduced under laboratory conditions. Also, there is undoubtedly a stimulating effect of free flight, together with the physiological attribute of nectar, giving rise to a greater production of eggs by stimulating the cells of the ovaries. However, on the basis of field data, one can speculate. From many years of rearing and tagging monarch butterflies, I know that a female can live up to thirty days during the breeding period. If an ovipositing female is capable of laying 42 eggs in one day, then during her life she could produce 1,260 eggs. Even if we assume that her active egg-laying period is limited to only half of her life, or fifteen days, this would still give a figure of 630 eggs.

ADULT LIFE SPAN

How long does an adult monarch butterfly live? To answer this question, it is necessary to consider two different physiological states: nonmigrants and migrants.

Nonmigrants are those one finds in the fields during the summer months;

they mate, and the females deposit eggs on milkweed plants. In some places, such as southern California, Florida, southern Mexico, and some of the islands of the Pacific Ocean, breeding populations occur throughout the year. These are referred to as "resident populations." The adult female life span is between thirty and forty days, because food is available and the temperature remains above freezing. I do not have data on the longevity of breeding males.

During the fall migration, when the monarch butterflies are leaving the breeding areas for overwintering sites, the migrants enter what I have termed "reproductive dormancy." During this period their reproductive organs do not develop. Such individuals probably live for eight to ten months, based on the data from my laboratory specimens, though some of my associates have been able to keep such migrants for periods up to twelve months. This longer life span allows migrants to journey from breeding grounds to overwintering sites and return. Once the reproductive organs have developed and mating has taken place, however, the life span for migrants is the same as that for the nonmigrants. For more information on migration, see part 5.

NUMBER OF GENERATIONS

When the female monarch butterflies leave the overwintering sites in Mexico and California, their reproductive organs have developed and mating has taken place, either at the site or along the return route to the breeding grounds. As the migrants proceed northward, females deposit eggs on milkweed plants along the migratory route. Thus, in the more southern parts of the route, larvae and eventually adults appear early in the breeding season, March and early April. The adults from this first generation also migrate northward, the females depositing eggs along the route. This second generation will also proceed northward, eventually reaching the more northern limits of the breeding range. By the end of August and early September, there are three or four generations. In addition, some females that are not in reproductive dormancy will deposit eggs along the southward migratory routes in the fall, giving rise to yet another generation. Thus, from the time the overwintering monarchs leave the various sites, there is a rapid population buildup involving three or more generations.

By estimating that each female may lay up to 700 eggs, one can calculate how many butterflies would result from a single female returning to the breeding grounds, assuming four generations and survival of all members of each generation. The first female would give rise to 700 adults in the first generation. Of these, 350 would be females. They would produce a second generation of 245,000 adults; of this number, 122,500 would be females. They would produce 85,750,000 adults; the 42,875,000 females would give rise to a population of 30,012,500,000 adults in the fourth generation. This possible rate of increase is referred to as "biotic potential" and reflects the maximum rate at which an insect can increase its population if there are no deaths. However, the actual rate of increase is influenced by numerous hazards encountered by the migrants on their journey from breeding areas to overwintering sites and back, by a great number of diseases to which monarch butterflies in various stages of development are prone, by various parasites and predators, and by unfavorable weather conditions. A virus disease can so reduce a population that, in some parts of North America, monarch butterflies may become rare in certain years.

Numerous records sent to me from my associates living in various parts of the United States and eastern Canada indicate that the annual dates for the arrival of the spring migrants are approximately as follows:

Southern areas (lat. 32°–37°N): March–April
Central portions (lat. 37°–42°N): April–May
Northern portions (lat. 42°–48°N): May–June

As the Eastern Population of spring migrants moves northeastward from the overwintering sites to the breeding grounds, the females deposit their eggs en route, giving rise to a population of adults in the southwestern parts of the continent. These first-generation adults then move northeastward, and the females deposit eggs en route, giving rise to a second generation of adults. Since both generations move northeastward, there is a complete absence of monarch butterflies in the southwestern parts of the continent during the summer months; the region is later repopulated during the fall migration. The individuals occurring in any given locality are, of course, not the offspring of a single migrant returning from an overwintering site. The population spectrum is far more complex.

If you observe the return of the monarch butterflies to northern breeding grounds, such as the New England states, you will notice that the early arrivals, in late May or early June, have faded, tattered wings. These are the migrants that overwintered in Mexico. Later arrivals are only slightly faded and not so badly tattered; these are the first generation offspring of the earlier migrants, arriving from the southwest. Still later, fresher individuals arrive, mixed with more faded and tattered specimens and slightly faded ones. Finally, newly emerged, brightly colored monarchs will be seen, representing the generation produced on local breeding grounds. Similar observations may be made with respect to migrants and later generations of the Western Population returning to their breeding grounds from the overwintering site in California.

FLUCTUATIONS IN NUMBERS

It is well known to entomologists involved in studies of insect behavioral patterns that many insect species fluctuate in numbers from one year to the next. For example, mass outbreaks of forest tent caterpillars and of gypsy moths follow periods of scarcity. Such fluctuations in numbers also apply to the monarch butterfly.

I can recall one summer when I was able to collect only four adult monarchs. That particular year of extreme scarcity was followed by a few years in which the number gradually increased. Then great numbers could be found for three years in a row. This was followed by another decline. In order to obtain data on the relative abundance of monarchs across North America, I sent forms to members of the Insect Migration Association, who resided in most of the states of the United States and the provinces of Canada. The members were asked to estimate abundance in their particular areas. The results were plotted on outline maps of North America for each year from 1965 to 1968, which covered a period of change from scarcity to abundance. In addition to the data contained in the reports I kept an account of the number of monarchs found in my area with particular reference to those located on overnight roosting trees. I also recorded data on the presence of disease in laboratory specimens that were collected in the field. The results, as presented here, apply mostly to North America east of the Rocky Mountains. Although I did not receive records of comparative abundance from associates in the mountain states, where the Western Population occurs, I did obtain considerable data on the numbers in the overwintering site in California.

During the period when the population had been greatly reduced, I experienced considerable difficulty in maintaining my laboratory specimens. On one occasion I had a laboratory population of over five thousand specimens, which were being raised to obtain data on sex proportions and rates of development when reared on various species of milkweed. All specimens reached the last larval instar, many hanging from the frame of the cages in preparation for entering the pupal stage. Within a short period of three days, all but five died of a disease that turned a larva into a soft black sack that ruptured when touched, releasing a black, ill-smelling fluid. My students and my attendant cleaned all of the cages, glassware, and growth chambers with a strong solution of formaldehyde, but to no avail. Other specimens introduced into the cages and glassware succumbed to the same virulent disease.

Over the next two years, specimens collected and placed in the same cages and glassware showed fewer deaths recorded, although the disease persisted. Then one year, only 5 percent of the specimens died. I made a water solution of the black, inky fluid from the dead insects and sprayed it on milkweed leaves, which were then given to 100 test specimens. Of these only 2.2 percent died of the disease. I discovered that the disease, referred to as an "epizootic," was caused by a polyhedrosis virus.

I concluded that the virus epizootic caused the decimation of the monarch butterfly population throughout most of North America during this particular period. Then, a strain of monarch butterflies appeared in the midwestern states that was resistant to the virus. Eventually this resistant strain was responsible for the buildup of the population.

At first, on examining my records of many years, I concluded that the population fluctuations were somewhat cyclical, occurring every six or seven years. However, more recently I decided that such is not the case. There is no true cycle, but rather the fluctuation in population is irregular, and periods of scarcity and abundance occur in any year, depending on environmental factors that permit the production of a lethal virus. The factors governing the formation of the various strains of viruses and their lethal effects are as yet unknown. Monarch butterflies in all stages of development contain within their bodies a multitude of viral and bacterial particles, as do all insects and, indeed, humans. Why such parasitic organisms, or virus particles, can sometimes become lethal is a matter for speculation.

In certain years, monarch butterflies are abundant, which is most obvious during the fall migration. In contrast are years when they are scarce; then I receive many letters expressing fears that monarchs are becoming extinct because of the use of insecticides. In 1963 and 1964, monarchs were scarce, so during the years 1965–1968 members of the Insect Migration Association made observations in their areas on whether monarchs were scarce (○) abundant (●), or increasing in number (▲). When plotted on a map (see the following two pages), these observations show an increase in number starting in the Midwest (Iowa and eastern Nebraska) and spreading across the continent, reaching a peak in 1968.

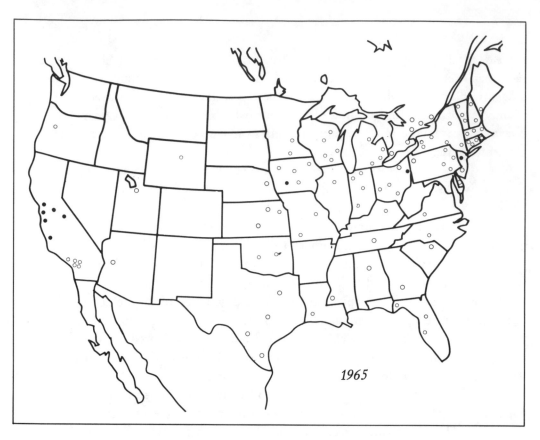

1965

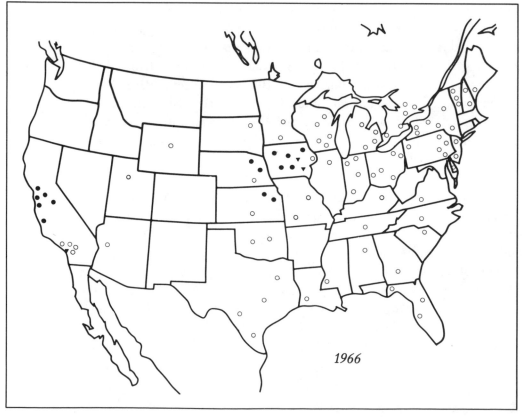

1966

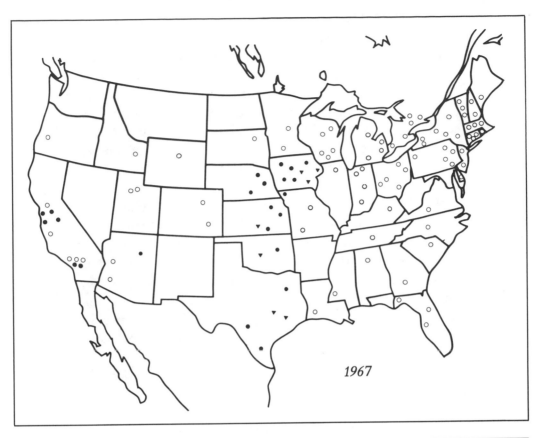

1967

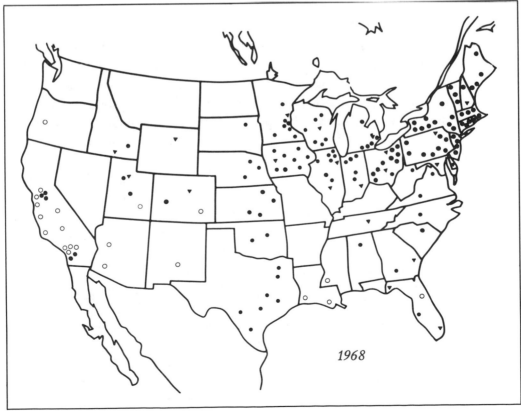

1968

The overwintering monarchs in California did not follow the same change in population as that of the eastern ones. The California population decreased in 1968 at a time when the Eastern Population was abundant and increased when there was a marked decline in the Eastern Population. I have concluded that the virus disease spread westward from the Eastern Population and that the delay in its effect was due to the mountains separating the two populations. Relatively few of the Eastern Population crossed the barrier to mingle with the western members.

Weather conditions can also greatly reduce populations in some areas, as exemplified during the summer of 1983. Norah and I saw only five monarch butterflies in our area that summer compared to the hundreds we were used to seeing during the previous years. I believe this was caused by two weather conditions: low to freezing temperatures in early summer throughout most of northeastern North America and torrential storms along the southwest migratory routes. Unlike the effects of a virus epidemic, when five or six years are needed for a population to recover, population declines caused by weather conditions are usually shorter in duration, taking from two to three years for complete recovery.

NONMIGRATORY RESIDENT POPULATIONS

In 1935, when I first started an intensive study of the migrations of the monarch butterfly by placing instructional alar tags on the wings of the migrants as they passed through my area of Ontario, Canada, I believed that all monarchs were migrants. It was not until 1951, during a field trip to peninsular Florida, that I came to realize that not all monarch butterflies migrated. A few remained in parts of Florida throughout the year. In the years following, I found similar situations in southern California and Mexico. I came to the conclusion that there exist two physiological states among monarch butterflies, one migratory and one nonmigratory.

Utilizing control cabinets in my laboratory at the university, I found that if I kept the temperature uniformly high at 24°C and the light periods at seventeen hours, it was possible to maintain a breeding population throughout the year. I later found that the same results could be achieved by simply keeping the butterflies in cages in the laboratory; the room temperature was fairly constant at 21°C, and laboratory lights were on during the day and at intervals during the night as the guards made their rounds. The specimens involved were collected during the summer months when their reproductive organs were functional.

If I used migrants collected in the fall, when their reproductive organs were nonfunctional, it was possible to keep them alive for periods in excess of ten months. In contrast, the members of the breeding population died within a month after mating and egg-laying had taken place. Thus, longevity depended upon whether or not the reproductive organs were functional.

In geographic areas where the temperature remains warm throughout the year and where species of milkweed are present, one can expect to find resident monarch butterfly populations. Such areas include Florida, southern California, Mexico, and islands of the South Pacific and Atlantic oceans. An interesting anomaly exists in certain areas, for example in southern Florida,

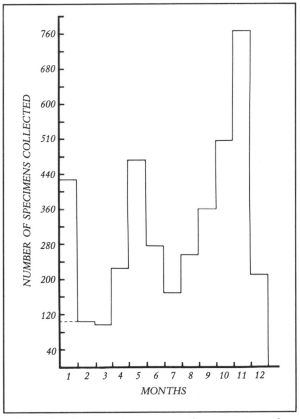

A research program on the relationship between migratory and nonmigratory butterflies was carried out over an eight-year period in three localities of peninsular Florida. It showed that two population peaks existed—one in the fall and one in the spring. The reduced number between the two peaks represents the resident or nonmigratory population.

where both resident and migratory populations exist together for part of the year. My associates and I made a study of the Florida populations over a period of eight years. During this time observations were made, and an intensive tagging program was carried out throughout the year. As a result of this effort, I was able to show that there were two population peaks each year, one during April, May, and June and the other during August to November. The spring peak was due to an influx of migrants moving northward from Guatemala via Yucatan; the fall peak was due to aberrant

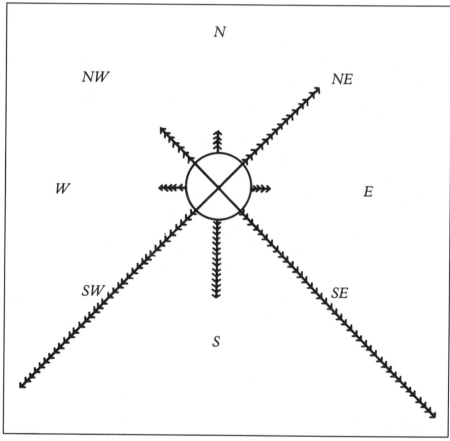

An alar-tagging program was carried out in southern California at Whittier over a period of five years. When the results were plotted on a Williams graph (in which each arrow represents a tagged and recaptured specimen and the lines indicate the direction of flight), it was apparent that the nonmigratory, or resident, population moved over short distances in directions similar to those of the migrants — south in the fall and north in the spring.

fall migrants moving southward. The reduced population during January to March and July and August represented the nonmigratory resident population.

The question occurred to me: Do these resident populations exhibit any tendency to migrate or move in a particular direction? To answer this question I carried out a study over a five-year period of the movement of the monarch butterflies in southern California. The study was based on reared specimens, all of which were reproductively active. By plotting the data on flight direction, I found that there was a definite tendency for the butterflies to move in a certain direction at different times of the year: there was a strong southerly movement between September and December and a northerly one between March and July, movements similar to those found for true migrants. There was very little movement during July to September, which corresponds to the breeding period of the migrants. However, the flight direction of the migrants is to the southwest in the fall, while the resident population in southern California moved to both the southwest and the southeast. Since publishing this study, I found two large overwintering loci, one southeast and the other southwest of the area (Whittier, California) where the study was carried out. It would appear that resident populations of monarch butterflies that are not in a state of reproductive dormancy do exhibit a migratory tendency, although it is not carried out over long distances or to an overwintering site with a return movement.

During the period I have been studying the migrations of the monarch, a number of species of other butterflies native to North America have also been alar tagged. None of them show any unidirectional movement over long distances that would indicate a migratory habit.

INTERNAL ANATOMY

When I was teaching entomology at the university, I spent a considerable amount of time on the anatomy, both external and internal, of the various orders of insects. The students showed considerable surprise at the complexity of these tiny creatures, particularly those less than a millimeter in size. Indeed, I am always impressed with the complex structure that adapts insects for their various ways of life, not to mention the amazing transformations that take place as the insects pass from the various juvenile states to the final adult. I marvel at the magnificent color patterns of moths and butterflies that develop from an immature form that resembles a worm. Many other species of insects, such as beetles, flies, and bees, also pass through miraculous transformations.

At the end of the term when I reviewed the course, I would hold up a fly swatter and, looking at an imaginary insect crawling across the lecture desk in front of me, I would state, "I trust that when you see an insect crawling across your floor or desk you will take time to consider what an amazing little creature it is before you destroy it." With this parting remark, I would bring the swatter down upon the surface of the table with a resounding smack, emphasizing my point and, at the same time, awakening the more nonentomologically minded and more lethargic members of the class.

The external anatomy of the monarch butterfly is most complex. Numerous small segments, or plates, serve as a "skeleton" to which muscles are attached, allowing for the various mechanisms involved in walking, flying, breathing, feeding, and so on. Each of these segments has a scientific name. Because of this complexity, I have omitted such a discussion from this book and refer those who wish to explore this complex anatomy to my book, *The Monarch Butterfly,* listed in the references.

To successfully remove the internal organs of both male and female butterflies, it is necessary to use freshly killed specimens. In those preserved in alcohol or formaldehyde the fatty tissue tends to stick to the organs, making it difficult to separate the various parts. Also, formaldehyde causes the organs to become stiff and brittle, resulting in the organs breaking as one attempts to remove them.

In constructing the accompanying drawings, I used eight separate sketches, each one drawn with the help of an instrument termed a camera lucida. When placed over the eyepiece of a microscope, this instrument reflects the object being examined onto a sheet of paper next to the microscope. The outline of the object can then be accurately traced on the paper. The organs being examined were in a shallow vessel of water with a layer of wax on the bottom. This made it possible to fully extend the various organs and hold them in place with fine pins.

Remove the wings, and place the body in a dish, the bottom of which is covered with a layer of wax a centimeter or more thick. Make an incision with a razor blade along the back of the body from behind the head to the tip of the abdomen. Spread the two halves apart and secure them to the wax by inserting pins through the flaps and into the wax. Fill the dish with water to cover the dissected specimen. Then, using a needle, gently free the organs from the large, yellow mass of stored fat. The internal anatomy will now be exposed. For a clearer view of the anatomy, the various organs can be removed and placed in the water, where they can be freed from the fatty tissue.

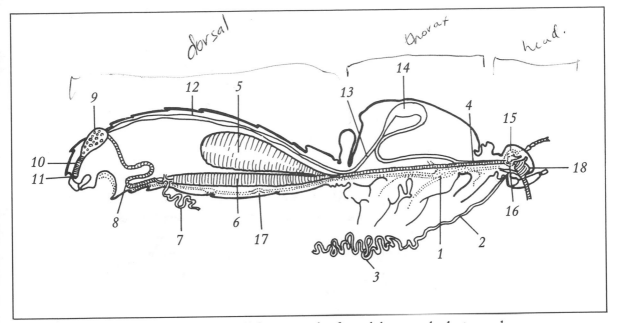

If you were to remove the body wall from one side of an adult monarch, the internal organs would be arranged as shown in this stylized drawing. The nervous system extends from the head to the end of the body and consists of the brain (15) and a nerve center (16) beneath the brain from which nerves pass to the various parts of the head. In the thoracic region is a large nerve center, the thoracic ganglion (1), that sends out nerves to the various parts of the thorax, legs, and wings. A nerve cord then passes along the ventral side of the body. Various nerve centers, the abdominal ganglia (17), are located in the abdomen. Nerves pass from these centers to the various parts of the abdomen. In the digestive system, the pharynx (18) pumps nectar through the sucking tube and into the esophagus (4), which leads to the stomach (6) and an associated pouch, the food reservoir (5), in which the nectar is stored. The salivary gland (3) empties its contents, by way of a connecting tubule (2), into the anterior end of the esophagus to mix with the nectar from the pharynx. The small intestine (8) leads to the colon (9), then to the rectum (10), and finally the anus (11), from which undigested material is expelled. The excretory system, termed the malpighian tubules (7), functions like the human kidneys. This cluster of tubules, of which one is indicated here, passes its contents into the small intestine. The circulatory system is situated in the upper, or dorsal, part of the body and consists of an elongated tube, the heart (12), which has several openings termed ostia through which the body fluid passes. Body fluid is pumped toward the front end of the body through a tube, the aorta (13), which bends upward in the thoracic region to an inflated portion termed the aortal chamber (14). The fluid moves on through the aortic artery to the head region and then spills out into the body cavity. There are no other arteries or veins. This type of circulatory system is referred to as an "open" system.

The above is a simplified method of dissection, and you may fail to see the finer structures that I describe next. I suggest that, before reading the following descriptions, you examine my drawings to familiarize yourself with the scientific terminology that applies to the various parts.

FEMALE REPRODUCTIVE SYSTEM

When we observe a female monarch alight on the leaf of a milkweed plant to deposit an egg, we little realize the complexity of the butterfly's anatomy and of the physiological processes involved. It is only by careful dissection that the various anatomical structures can be seen. But even this fails to disclose the millions of active cells that are involved in the processes; these can be examined only with the help of a compound microscope or the electron microscope. Such examinations reveal only the structure of the cells involved. We still have not seen the tremendously complex cellular activities that finally produce a fertilized egg.

The reproductive organs of the female may be divided into two groups: one is concerned with receiving and storing male sex cells (copulatory organs) and the other produces the female sex cells, together with those involved in fertilization (ovulatory organs).

THE COPULATORY ORGANS

A heavily chitinized tube, termed the *ductus copulatrix,* receives the long, needlelike penis of the male. The duct leads to a large saclike structure called the *bursa copulatrix,* usually referred to as the *bursa.* A heavily chitinized valve is located where the ductus copulatrix meets the bursa; when closed, the valve prevents the escape of male sex cells.

The bursa is a comparatively large organ (approximately 4 mm long and 3 mm wide) that is capable of considerable expansion when filled with the male *spermatophore,* a membranous sac containing the male sex cells. The bursa is somewhat pear-shaped, being broad in the central region, rounded at the anterior end, and constricted at the posterior end. To one side of the entrance of the ductus copulatrix is a slender tube, termed the *ductus seminalis,* that is somewhat swollen along part of its length. This swollen section is called the *bulla seminalis* (Latin: *bulla,* bubble). When you view the bursa under the low power of the microscope or with a strong hand lens, you will detect two dark bands, one located on each side. On closer inspection, these dark bands present an irregular rhomboidal configuration, or pattern. Using a sharp scalpel or razor blade, you can cut open the bursa to reveal the inner wall. There you will notice that the dark bands are actually

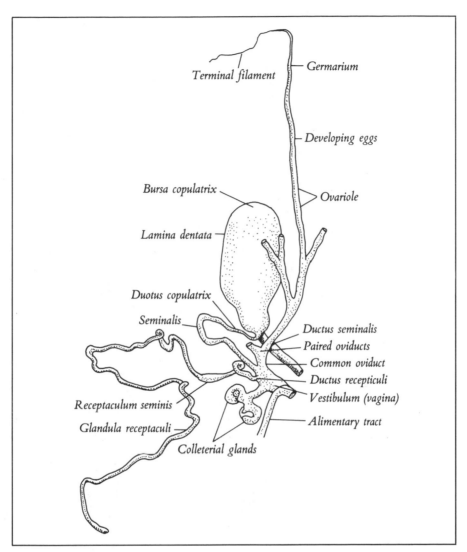

The female reproductive system is complex. Each part performs a specific function: one part produces the ova, or eggs; another part produces the nutritive material for the developing embryo; and yet another makes the gemlike egg shell. The sperm cells received from the male during copulation are held in the saclike bursa copulatrix and are released to fertilize the ova that pass down the oviduct.

the bases of numerous spines, or teeth, that are heavily chitinized and variable in size. The smaller teeth are arranged at the outside margins and the larger teeth in the central portion; the teeth point in opposite directions from the midline. Well-developed longitudinal muscles are associated with the bursa. A shallow channel may be seen in the wall of the bursa, which is located adjacent to the valvular mechanism of the ductus copulatrix. The channel leads to the ductus seminalis.

OVULATORY ORGANS AND ASSOCIATED STRUCTURES

Owing to the presence of large amounts of fatty tissue, it is difficult to remove intact the reproductive organs and related structures, particularly if the organs are not well developed. Therefore, only females that are mature will give satisfactory results. Females that are ovipositing will have eggs in all stages of development.

There are two *ovaries,* each composed of four smaller units termed *ovarioles,* of which one is illustrated in my drawing. The ovariole is a long slender tube consisting of a fine, hairlike *terminal filament,* which broadens out into a granular area, the *germarium,* where the ova develop. The ovariole shown in my drawing appears to be distinctly separated from the others. However, in the body cavity the ovarioles are close together and, since each

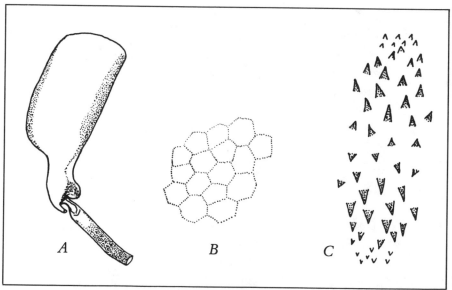

If you remove the bursa copulatrix of the female and examine it with a strong hand lens, you will detect two dark bands, one on each side (A). On close inspection, these dark bands present an irregular rhomboidal pattern (B). If you cut open the bursa and examine the interior walls, you will see a number of spines, or teeth, the bases of which give the rhomboidal pattern seen on the outer surface (C). Note that each set of teeth points in opposite directions. Muscular action of the bursa causes the teeth to rip open the spermatophore and liberate the sperm cells when they are needed to fertilize the ova.

one is longer than the length of the abdomen, they are folded to form a compact mass. During dissection, this mass must be carefully teased out in a water bath in order to isolate each individual ovariole.

Ducts from two ovarioles join to form a larger duct, which in turn joins its counterpart from two other ovarioles, thus forming one large duct from all four ovarioles. This duct then joins with that of the other four ovarioles. The two ducts are termed the *paired oviducts,* which enter the *common oviduct.* The common oviduct leads into a swollen area termed the *vestibulum* (Latin: *vestibulum,* porch). Also leading into the vestibulum is an elongated, somewhat twisted structure, the *ductus receptaculi.* Close to the junction of the ductus receptaculi to the vestibulum is a marked swollen area, the *receptaculum seminis,* which is the receptacle that receives the male sex cells. The remainder of the ductus receptaculi, which is of uniform diameter and with a slightly granular appearance, is termed the *glandula receptaculi.* It appears to be glandular in nature producing certain biochemical substances. Finally, there is a rather compact mass of tissue, somewhat resembling a small mushroom, termed the *colleterial gland* (Greek: *kolla,* glue), which secretes the substance of the egg shell and also the glue that cements the egg to the leaf of the milkweed plant.

Briefly, these anatomical structures function as follows: A spermatophore is deposited by the male in the bursa copulatrix. Ova from the germarium develop as they pass down the oviduct, finally arriving in the vestibulum. By means of the teeth contained in the bursa, the spermatophore is ripped open, liberating the sperm cells, which pass down the ductus seminalis and collect in the receptaculum seminis. When the ova are ready for fertilization, the sperm cells are released into the vagina. Then, secretions from glands, especially the colleterial glands, supply the necessary nutrients and the egg shell, as well as the substance that glues the egg to the leaf.

Unfertilized eggs can be seen in the oviducts and in the vestibulum. When a certain complement of fertilized eggs have been deposited by the female, a rest period occurs to allow more eggs to be fertilized and to pass down the oviducts. This accounts for the rest periods during the egg-laying process. It also accounts for the rapid rate of egg-laying during morning periods of eggs that have accumulated during the night.

MALE REPRODUCTIVE SYSTEM

The elongated male organs are, in life, twisted and folded within the body. To examine them, I stretched them out. This shows the comparative lengths of the various structures and the variation in circumference along their lengths. If, in attempting to remove the male organs, you break some of them, you can still identify the broken section by comparing it with my drawing.

The *testis* is the most conspicuous element of the male reproductive system. It is comparatively large and in life is purple in color. Holding the purple testis in place and supplying it with oxygen are a great many small, pale tubes called *tracheae,* which I discuss in the section dealing with the respiratory system. Two tubes, each called a *vas deferens* (Latin: *vas,* vessel; *deferre,* to carry away), originate from the posterior margin of the testis. These tubes are tightly twisted around each other near their point of origin. At first glance they appear to be one large tube instead of paired tubes. The swollen part of a *vas deferens* is termed the *funnel* and is approximately one-quarter the length of the organ; the rest of the vas deferens is slender and threadlike. The *vasa deferentia* enter the paired *vesicula seminalis* (Latin: *vesicula,* small bladder), which are joined together at their posterior ends. In their natural position in the body they are so closely pressed against one another that they appear to be a single organ. Each vesicula seminalis is comparatively large, white (in contrast to the surrounding yellow fatty tissue), and slightly U-shaped, broad at one end and tapering at the other. Appearing as a continuation of the tapered end is a long, twisted, threadlike *accessory gland.* A single tubelike structure, the *tubular gland,* originates at the point of attachment of the paired vesiculae seminalis. Near the *penis (aedeagus)* the gland becomes wider, forming the *ductus ejaculatorius;* at the entrance to the ductus, the tubular gland enlarges to form the *bulbus ejaculatorius.* The ductus ejaculatorius, which is a relatively narrow duct, is surrounded by circular muscles; the bulbus ejaculatorius has very thick, muscular walls and is attached firmly to one side of the heavily chitinized penis.

When mating takes place, the male inserts the penis into the chitinous ductus copulatrix of the female, which opens into the bursa copulatrix. At the same time the male maintains a firm grip on the tip of the female's abdomen by means of strong chitinous claspers. Thus firmly united, the mated pair may fly from one resting place to another, the male carrying the inert female below him. It is during this rather lengthy period that the sperm packet, the spermatophore, is formed from secretions of the tubular and accessory glands, and the sperm cells are added to the spermatophore from the testis via the vas deferens and the vesicula seminalis.

If you examine the inside of the bursa of the female about fifteen minutes after copulation begins, you will see that it contains a small gelatinous structure formed from secretions from one of the male glands. Thirty minutes after copulation the gelatinous structure will be found to contain no sperm cells. Forty minutes to one hour after copulation, the gelatinous structure will contain sperm cells. Thus, it takes forty minutes to an hour or more from the initiation of copulation for the spermatophore to be formed and the sperm cells to be added to it.

The female's acceptance or rejection of the male does not depend on the presence or absence of sperm cells in the receptaculum seminis. It is not unusual to find two or three spermatophores in the bursa of a female even though her ovaries are not fully developed and there are no eggs in the oviduct. In many cases, however, an examination of the spermatophores

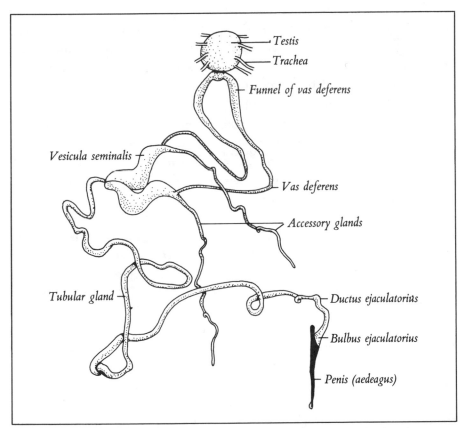

Testis
Trachea
Funnel of vas deferens
Vesicula seminalis
Vas deferens
Accessory glands
Tubular gland
Ductus ejaculatorius
Bulbus ejaculatorius
Penis (aedeagus)

The male reproductive system is somewhat simpler than that of the female. Sperm cells are produced in the testis, pass through a pair of slender tubes, and are stored in a pair of elongated sacs, vesiculae seminalis. Nutritive material and sperm cells are stored in a sac termed the spermatophore, which is introduced into the bursa copulatrix of the female during copulation.

taken from a bursa shows secretions from the glands but no sperm cells. Copulation may take place even though both male and female possess undeveloped reproductive organs, although this is rare. In most cases the presence of spermatophores in the female bursa is coincident with the presence of fully developed ovaries and of eggs in the oviducts.

DIGESTIVE SYSTEM

One of the most remarkable transformations in the life of the monarch, as well as other species of butterflies, takes place in the digestive system. In the immature stage, the monarch larva feeds on the leaves of a plant, chewing its food with chitinous jaws; the mature butterfly feeds on the nectar of flowers, which it draws into its body by a long sucking tube, the proboscis. In addition to such obvious anatomical changes, there is also a change in the entire digestive process from one that converts milkweed leaves into other chemical substances of the body to one that converts sugary nectar.

When you examined the reproductive structures, you probably noticed the long, tubular digestive tract, which can be readily removed, placed in a water bath, and the various parts identified as follows.

The proboscis, or sucking tube, is coiled beneath the head like a watch spring when not in use. The proboscis enters the *pharynx* (Greek: *pharynx,* gullet) which acts as a miniature pump. It possesses two muscle layers, an outer one of longitudinal fibers and an inner one of transverse fibers. The combined actions of the muscle layers expand and contract the pharynx, thus drawing the nectar up the proboscis. A triangular flap, termed the *epipharynx* (Greek: *epi,* above or upon), is located over the opening to the esophagus and acts as a valve. It is opened while the butterfly is feeding and closed when feeding has been completed.

The *salivary glands* consist of two coiled tubes that unite in a common duct opening into the pharynx close to the entrance of the proboscis. It is assumed that these glands, which in the larval stage produce the liquid that forms silk, have some digestive functions as yet not clearly understood.

The *esophagus* is a straight, very slender, thin-walled tube that leads from the pharynx, passes through the region of the thorax and the anterior portion of the abdomen and opens into the *food reservoir.* This is a conspicuous, somewhat pear-shaped organ; its walls are composed of longitudinal and transverse muscle fibers. Like the pharynx, the reservoir acts as a pump, and it also stores nectar.

The *stomach* is a straight, sausage-shaped organ lying along the ventral wall of the abdomen. The stomach walls are relatively thick and are composed of both muscular and glandular layers of tissue. Certain digestive processes take place in the stomach as the result of secretions from the cells of the glandular layer.

Six small, somewhat twisted, wormlike structures unite to form a common duct that opens into the posterior end of the stomach. These structures are known as *Malpighian tubules,* named after the Italian anatomist Malpighi, who first described them. They function as kidneys in removing waste material from the body fluid.

The *small intestine* is a narrow, somewhat S-shaped tube arising from the posterior end of the stomach. The walls of this organ are composed of digestive cells that produce the enzymes that convert the sugar and other substances contained in nectar into various biological entities used in the maintenance of the body and in body functions.

The small intestine passes into the *colon,* which is somewhat pear-shaped in the female and more cylindrical in the male. It is covered with numerous small glands that probably are responsible for removing waste material from the body fluid that surrounds it. The colon narrows posteriorly before entering the short cylindrical *rectum* in which waste material is stored until it is excreted through the anus.

CIRCULATORY SYSTEM

The circulatory system in the monarch butterfly is termed an "open system," because there are no walled arteries and veins leading the blood from a heart to all parts of the body and back to the heart again. The "blood," better termed "body fluid," simply moves freely throughout the body cavity.

The main pumping mechanism, which may be considered the *heart,* consists of an elongated tube, the *dorsal vessel.* It is located in a space termed the *sinus* in the dorsal area of the body and extends the length of the body. In the abdomen, the dorsal vessel is slightly constricted at the juncture of each abdominal segment; in each of the expanded portions between the constrictions there is a pair of openings, termed *ostia* (Latin: *ostium,* door). In the thorax the dorsal vessel loops upwards, and at the top of the loop it expands to form the *aortal chamber.* The dorsal vessel is closed at its posterior end and open at the anterior.

The manner in which the blood circulates in this simple circulatory system is as follows. The body fluid, or blood, enters the paired ostia in the dorsal vessel, which, acting as a heart, pumps the blood forward. The blood is held in the dorsal vessel as the ostia, by means of expanded lips, close the openings. The blood is also pumped forward by the aortal chamber, which has a rear valve that prevents the blood from flowing backwards. In the region of the head the blood is discharged into the body cavity through two or more branches termed *cephalic arteries*. Pulsations of the thorax and abdomen drive the blood backwards through the body cavity and sinuses and into the sinuses of the abdomen, where it is taken up again by the dorsal vessel through the ostia. In the appendages and wings, the blood flows along definite channels that are analogous to blood vessels.

The body fluid of the monarch butterfly is light green in color due to the presence of chlorophyll and is 85 to 90 percent water. It is slightly acid and contains various dissolved substances, including organic ions (sodium, potassium, and chloride), proteins, fats, sugars, and organic acids. These substances, resulting from the digestive processes, are carried by the body fluid to all cells of the body. The body fluid does not transport oxygen, since there are no oxygen-carrying erythrocytes. Oxygen is carried to the cells by the *tracheal system,* discussed in the next section. Body fluid carries only a small amount of carbon dioxide in the form of bicarbonate. A few specialized blood cells are present, including *haemocytes,* which act like human white blood cells. They ingest particles of debris and bacteria, especially at the site of a wound, where a plug composed of haemocytes and debris is formed.

The body fluid, directed by muscular action of the abdomen and thorax, functions as a kind of hydraulic system that can extrude or expand various parts of the body. An illustration of this is the expansion of the wings when the butterfly emerges from the pupa.

RESPIRATORY SYSTEM

All living creatures have a means of taking oxygen into and removing carbon dioxide from their cells. The monarch butterfly possesses such a system, the equivalent of a "lung," for carrying air to the cells where the oxygen is removed for cellular functions.

If you examine the sides of the abdomen of the adult monarch, using a fairly strong magnifying glass, you will observe small, oval structures, one on each side of the five abdominal segments. Each oval structure is termed a *spiracle* (Latin: *spiraculum,* a hole) and opens into a tube called a *trachea* (pl. *tracheae;* Latin: *trachea,* windpipe). In addition to the five pairs of spiracles on the abdominal segments, there is one pair on the thorax that is difficult to see since the thorax is covered with scales and hairs. The tracheae are the main air trunks; they divide within the body into numerous small, thin-walled tubes called *tracheoles,* or little tracheae.

By rhythmic pulsations of the abdomen—which can be observed in a live butterfly—and muscular action of the thorax during flight or walking, air is drawn into the tracheae through the spiracles and travels through the hundreds of tracheoles to the vital organs of the body, where oxygen is brought to the cells.

A number of small, bladderlike swellings of the tracheae form air sacs. In freshly killed specimens, the sacs are white and, because of the air contained in them, glisten by reflected light. Such air sacs not only increase the air supply but also add buoyancy to the body during flight.

Thus, the respiratory mechanism of the monarch butterfly is markedly different from that found in man. Such a respiratory system is particularly advantageous to the monarch in that if one tracheal tube is nonfunctional, there are thirteen others to continue to supply oxygen. In man, there is but one trachea. It is therefore not surprising that the monarch can fly rapidly and over long distances, possessing as it does a most efficient respiratory system and an abundant supply of stored energy-producing fat.

NERVOUS SYSTEM

Does the monarch butterfly possess a brain? This question has been submitted to me on numerous occasions. Not only does the monarch possess a nerve center in its head, which might be referred to as a "brain," but it also possesses eight other nerve centers. Like the brain, these centers can receive stimuli to a limited extent and will respond to control muscular actions in various parts of the body. Those unfamiliar with the nervous system of insects express surprise when a monarch butterfly will attempt to fly and to walk when its head has been removed. This peculiar response, which is common to all insects, is due to the presence of these individual nerve centers that act like small local brains.

The brain, or nerve center, the seat of all controlled responses, lies immediately above the esophagus in the head region. Two nerves from the brain send impulses to the eyes and the antennae; these nerves are termed the *optic* and *antennal nerves.* Immediately beneath the esophagus is a sort of secondary brain, which because of its location is termed the *subesophageal ganglion* (Greek: *ganglion,* a little tumor). It is joined to the brain by two nerves that surround the esophagus like a collar and are termed collectively the *circumesophageal connectives.* Nerves sending impulses to the various parts of the mouth arise from the subesophageal ganglion.

Two fairly large nerve centers, the *thoracic ganglia,* are found in the thorax. From these centers nerves pass to the legs and wings. The central nerve cord is ventral in position (unlike that in man, which is dorsal). On each of the second to the sixth abdominal segments are nerve centers, or ganglia, from which nerves extend to the various muscles of the abdomen and to the intestinal tract.

The complete nervous system, with its multitude of nerve tracts sending and receiving impulses to and from various parts of the body, is highly complex. For example, the brain is not one unifunctional mass; it is divided into three major regions, each one of which presents its own distinctive complexities. In addition to a central nerve system, there is a sympathetic system, as in man, which supplies nerves to various parts of the body and which acts independently of the central nerve system to a certain degree. Because this sympathetic system sends nerves to parts of the digestive tract and the reproductive system, it has been termed the *visceral nervous system.* Finally, there is a network of nerve cells that receive impulses from outside the body. These include receptor organs, cells connected to hairs and sensory organs, and cells covering the surface of muscles and the walls of the digestive system.

Thus, in attempting to decide whether a butterfly possesses a brain, we are led into an elaborate system of nerves, nerve networks, and nerve cells that receive impulses from both outside and inside the body and transmit them to the various nerve centers. In addition to such nerve responses involved in mating, escaping danger, and seeking food, the nervous system controls the production of hormones, cellular division, and the arrangement of tissues and organs. Like a complex computer, it brings about the transformation of a wormlike larva into a completely different organism, a butterfly.

PART 5

Fall Migration

In late summer and fall, the monarch butterflies move southward to their overwintering sites. They can be seen flying over fields, pausing now and then to feed on the nectar of autumn flowers or, what is most dramatic, clinging in groups of many hundreds to the branches of trees chosen to be overnight roosting locations. They fly across highways in a steady stream, and thousands are smashed by passing cars. In years of abundance they are among the most striking and ubiquitous members of the insect world in North America.

The journey from northern breeding grounds in New England and the regions of the Great Lakes to the overwintering site in Mexico or from the valleys of the Rocky Mountains as far north as Idaho and Montana to the site in California is hundreds of miles. Many dangers await the travelers along these migratory routes. The most severe are violent rain and wind storms. It is a common sight to see thousands of dead and dying monarch butterflies strewn for miles along the shores of large lakes, such as the northern shores of Lake Ontario and Lake Erie, following severe storms. Tropical hurricanes along coastal areas cast migrants against tall grasses, bushes, and trees, damaging their wings. And many butterflies drown in turbulent ocean waves. Millions of migrating monarch butterflies are destroyed; only a relative few reach their destination in the overwintering sites.

Even after the monarchs arrive at their winter retreats, the danger of storms is still a major factor in their survival. In some respects, the danger is greater, particularly in Mexico, where cold temperatures, strong winds, and snow kill thousands. For those that survive there remains the long return trip north, with the hazard of freezing temperatures common in the spring and early summer in the northern breeding areas. However, the few that survive the round trip build up the population to the countless millions that, come fall, will once again follow the migratory routes of their ancestors.

When I completed my undergraduate years at the University of Toronto, I entered graduate school to study various aspects of the ecology and morphology of the Orthoptera (grasshoppers and crickets). My studies of the monarch butterfly continued more as a hobby than as a research project. My work on the Orthoptera was carried out under the B. A. Bensley Fellowship at the Royal Ontario Museum. Each year the director of the museum was required to submit an annual report about the various activities of the museum, and I suggested that my studies of the monarch might be included. The director, however, was of the opinion that the government would not look kindly on an activity that involved "putting paper tags on the wings of butterflies." Later, when I became the director, I was able to continue the study of the monarch butterfly in my spare time, since the research activities of the museum concerned collections that were used in taxonomy and in the preparation of exhibits.

During World War II, when I was attached to the Royal Canadian Air Force as a meteorological officer, I was stationed at various airports across western Canada. I carried out a number of observations of the presence or absence of monarch butterflies and species of milkweed. After four years of such observations, I concluded that, although there were at least two species of milkweed present, there were no monarch butterflies in western Canada, except the occasional one found near Winnipeg, Manitoba. This observation proved to be of importance for my later studies of migratory routes.

When I returned from military service after World War II, Norah and I were able to establish a group of interested individuals, living in various parts of the United States, who were willing to assist us in our work, as taggers and/or donors of funds to be held in trust by the University of Toronto. Our studies eventually were financed by the Committee on Research and Exploration of the National Geographic Society and by the National Research Council of Canada. As a result of this financial support and the voluntary assistance of thousands of interested individuals, our investigations into various aspects of the ecology, morphology, and behavior of the monarch butterfly gathered momentum, and we were able to organize numerous field expeditions to many parts of the United States, Canada, and Mexico (including Yucatan), the islands of the Caribbean, and the Antilles. As in all major endeavors, there were many trials and tribulations, but for the most part it was a most enjoyable experience, and it had a most fascinating and rewarding conclusion.

When I started an in-depth study of the monarch butterfly in 1935, very little was known about its migrations. Various suggestions had been made, but these were based on little definitive data. One notion was that they overwintered along the coast of the Gulf of Mexico. Another was that they overwintered on the Florida peninsula. Some biologists were of the opinion that they moved southward, never to return, in the manner of a migrating lemming population; the northern populations continued because some of the adults or pupae overwintered under logs in the breeding areas. This suggestion was proposed because there are species of butterflies that do overwinter as adults or in the pupa stage.

All that was known from field observations was that during late summer and fall thousands of monarch butterflies moved southward to an unknown overwintering site. My suggestion that they migrated in a manner common to many species of birds was considered quite impossible. But that they might move to an overwintering site could not be denied, since it had long been known that thousands of monarchs gathered on the trees in the Monterey Peninsula of California. I came to the conclusion (later proved erroneous when I discovered the Mexican site) that, by some unknown circuitous route, the migrants traveled to the southern parts of the continent, then west to California, where the large clusters of overwintering monarch butterflies had been reported. I wrote a short article, published in a scientific journal in 1955, presenting this possible solution to the migratory puzzle, but I received no reactions from my colleagues.

Such was the state of my knowledge of the migrations in 1950 when Norah and I began the alar-tagging program that included numerous field expeditions to many parts of the continent.

DEFINITION OF TERMS

Before proceeding with the details of the migrations of the monarch butterfly, it is necessary to consider what is meant by "migration" as it applies to the monarch butterfly, or indeed to any animal that possesses a similar habit. We have become accustomed to using the word *migration* in relation to birds that move annually from breeding grounds to overwintering grounds and back. However, there are many types of movements found among most species of animals that could be called migration, for example, the congregation of snakes in a particular location during hibernation; the movement of frogs to a pond in spring; and the movement of salmon from the ocean to freshwater streams. Occasionally, for reasons that are not clear, certain species of animals appear suddenly in great numbers far beyond their normal geographic range and in places where conditions are not suitable for their survival.

In the above examples I have used the word *movement* as a generalized term for any act of passing from one place to another. This may be divided into three major categories: *involuntary dispersal, nomadism,* and *migration.* The category of involuntary dispersal would apply to any organism carried to a different locality outside of its normal range by forces beyond its control. Examples include a bird carried by strong winds; an insect carried on a drifting log; and a monarch butterfly carried on a ship. The category of nomadism would apply to those animals that move in various directions.

Within the category of migration are three major subcategories: *emigration, immigration,* and *remigration.* If an individual animal or a population moves away from a particular area, this would be emigration. Movement into a particular area is immigration. Movement from one area to another and back again is remigration.

Remigration is divided into two more subdivisions: *daily remigration* and *annual remigration.* If an animal or a population leaves overnight roosting site A, moves to feeding area B in the morning, and returns to site A in the afternoon, this would be a daily remigration. If an animal or a population migrates from breeding grounds in the fall to an overwintering site, returning the following spring to the breeding grounds, this is an annual remigration.

The monarch butterfly is classified in this system as an "annual remigrant." However, some individuals within the monarch population do not take part in an annual remigration, for example, the early generations that mate, deposit eggs, and then die. Such individuals are considered to have taken part in an immigration. While on the breeding grounds, males and females move in random fashion from one field of milkweed plants to another and hence are categorized as nomadic.

Some monarch butterfly populations do not take part in an annual remigration but remain on the breeding grounds throughout the year. These are termed "resident populations" and occur in areas where the temperature remains above freezing and where species of milkweed grow throughout the year, as in southern California, Mexico, and Florida.

Thus, several movement patterns are found among monarch butterflies: annual remigration, immigration, and nomadism. This part of the book, however, is concerned with the annual remigration of monarch populations.

WHY DO MONARCH BUTTERFLIES REMIGRATE?

I have often been asked why monarch butterflies move southward in the autumn. A simple explanation is, to avoid the lack of food during the winter months. However, the monarchs leave the breeding areas when food for both larvae and adults is abundant. Another reason often given is that they move south in order to avoid the cold of the winter. But how do the butterflies "know"—to use an anthropomorphic term—that the winters are cold if they have not experienced a winter?

Similar explanations have been offered for many migrating species of animals that move from colder to warmer climates. But, while moving away from an area that will eventually become uninhabitable is indeed the end result of migration, it cannot be the causative factor involved. For a possible explanation, one must look to the far more involved subject of inheritance and attempt to understand how such an inherited behavioral pattern came about.

While analyzing the habits of the monarch for a plausible answer to this phenomenon, I came to realize that migration is related to three principal factors: (1) monarch larvae feed exclusively on species of milkweed; (2) the migratory pattern is from northeast to southwest; and (3) there is a long history, extending over eons of time, of the distribution of the milkweed species of the genus *Asclepias*.

Before presenting my conclusions, I would mention that I have given considerable thought to the suggestion that the recent ice age that ended about ten thousand years ago in North America may have given rise to the migratory patterns of the monarch butterflies. I have concluded, however, that the ice age was not the factor responsible for the migratory movements, since it had little or no effect on the east-west distribution of the milkweed.

The northeasterly-southwesterly migrations are correlated with the changing distribution of the species *Asclepias* resulting from changes in the

North American land mass over millions of years. During that time the ancestors of the present monarch butterfly species undoubtedly existed, for insects have a palaeontological record dating back to the Carboniferous period, which commenced 350 million years ago and lasted for 75 million years.

After a most exact and exhaustive study of the species and subspecies of the genus *Asclepias* occurring in North America, Dr. Woodson, in his monograph *The North American Species of Asclepias,* came to the following conclusion:

> The great diversification of *Asclepias* in the Floridian center may be due in part to the fluctuating "Orange Island" archipelago in early Tertiary, and partly to the southward migration to the coastal plain, as it became available, of certain Appalachian elements in late Tertiary and Pleistocene; it is difficult to distinguish them except by special methods. Of one thing we can be fairly certain that the Antilles contributed nothing.
>
> With the draining of the Cretaceous seas from the Rocky Mountain geosyncline, the western United States and Mexico gradually received asclepiad immigrants from the east, from the Ozarks and from Florida. The crest of this westward migration may have been approached in Pliocene. It is obvious that migration from the Ozarks could have taken place far earlier than from Florida. Lastly, the great diversification of the rich asclepiad flora of Mexico may be ascribed to adaptive radiation in response to the repeated Cenozoic orogenies culminating in Pleistocene. The Californian center, with its few species, so slightly related to the Appalachian and Ozarkian and so closely to the Mexican, may be considered the terminus of the westward movement.

Many researchers tend to overlook the millions of years of evolutionary history when they study various aspects of animal behavior and base their conclusions only on factors now operating in the environment. From Woodson's study of the distribution of species of milkweed in North America together with the fact of the east-west migration of the monarch butterfly, I have concluded that the migration pattern as we now observe it originated in the distant past when the milkweed species spread westward. Eventually, through some evolutionary process, the east-west movement was incorporated into the monarch's genetic code to produce a cyclical migration related to some as yet unknown response to seasonal changes on the planet.

Since there are more species of milkweed in central and southern Mexico than in any other area of North America, it has been suggested that perhaps this was the birthplace of the genus *Asclepias* and that the various species spread eastward. Thus, monarch butterflies in the fall migration would be returning to their palaeontological home. Concomitant with this suggestion is the fact that there are more species of butterflies of the genus *Danaus* in South America and Central America than in North America, hence the monarch may have originated in South America and moved into North America as conditions permitted. However, there are very few species of milkweed in South America and Central America.

In concluding this brief discussion of the possible origins of the monarch migratory habit, it is interesting to note that the species *Danaus erippus* of South America also migrates. Data on the migratory routes of this species is scanty, however, and based on observations only.

When I consider the phenomenon of migration, I wonder what factors act on the larvae of the monarch to produce a population of migrants and, at the same time, stop the development of the reproductive organs. Norah and I have been involved each year in alar tagging thousands of migrant monarch butterflies, which we remove from their overnight roosting clusters during the fall migration. We have been aware of the presence of many species of migrating birds in the same places at the same time. Flocks of redwing blackbirds gather for a short visit on the monarch butterfly trees, and then, with much twittering and cries of och-a-ree, continue on their southward journey. Flocks of small, chirping warblers search for the occasional insect clinging to the bark or feeding on the leaves. Swallows line up in long rows on the electric and telephone wires. Overhead, flocks of Canada geese pass in V formations. There is an air of expediency, of restlessness and excitement, as these migrating birds gather, then fly away in flocks. What kind of neurophysiological alarm clock informs these migrants that now is the time to leave the breeding grounds? Norah and I have often pondered this question and have suggested to ourselves many hypotheses. One is rather intriguing, if perhaps farfetched.

As our small planet earth travels in its elliptical orbit around the sun, it is possible that twice each year it passes through an area rich in some sort of radiation that impinges upon animal life. The radiation cycle might affect in some manner the cells of the body, causing reproductive organs to abort in the fall and develop in the spring and to initiate the migratory response. Perhaps our astronomy researchers may add a missing part to the migration puzzle. Perhaps animal life on our earth is being controlled by what is happening in outer space more than we now consider feasible. It's a thought, if not a possibility.

ALAR-TAGGING METHOD

In order to follow the movements of a particular member of a moving population of animals, it is necessary to have some distinctive device that will identify one individual wherever it may journey. When dealing with a large animal such as a deer or bear, one can attach a large object, but in the case of a small insect one is limited by the size and weight of the object being attached. What method can one use to mark an animal as small and seemingly as delicate as a butterfly, as well as to inform the person capturing such a marked specimen where to send it? In the case of migrating birds, a band is attached to a bird's leg. Instructions as to where the specimen is to be sent are printed on the band. However, one cannot attach such an object to the leg of a butterfly.

The first recorded attempt to mark insects to trace their movements was that of an Indian silk-producer who put marks on the wings of male silkworm moths. Each district where the moths occurred was represented by a distinctive mark. As a result of this method, male moths were traced for distances of 160 kilometers. Subsequently, a number of marking methods have been used, including making distinctive incisions in the insect's wing; putting different combinations of colored spots on the wings; spraying the wings with different types of dyes; stamping a letter and number on the upper surface of the wing; and spraying with a radioactive material.

In the early years of my studies, in 1935 and 1936, I attempted to use a combination of dyes and oil paint. Using a small spray gun, I could mark hundreds of butterflies as they clung to the branches of an overnight roosting location. None of these butterflies were ever returned. I also tried placing combinations of spots of various colors on the upper surfaces of the front wings, each combination identifying a particular specimen. This brought no results. Using an ink stamp, I applied numbers, or a combination of numbers, on the wings, again with no results.

It became apparent after so many unsuccessful attempts that it was not sufficient to simply mark a specimen. It had to bear some sort of tag that would inform the person collecting the specimen to whom it should be sent. The word *tag* rather than *label* is used because tag refers to something attached to something else, whereas label refers to the nature of the object to which it is attached. The word *alar* is an adjective referring to a wing and is well known among scientists working in many different languages.

Through the University of Toronto Press, I arranged to have printed sheets of tags bearing the notation "Return to Museum, Toronto, Canada."

Each sheet contained fifty tags that had to be cut out. A watery glue was applied to the back of the tag, which was then applied to the upper surface of the right front wing. This method proved to be very cumbersome. The glue got on other tags as well as my fingers, and it was necessary to wait until the glue had set before liberating the tagged specimen. Of butterflies so tagged, none were returned.

To avoid the use of liquid glue, I obtained the same type of sheets but with an adhesive already applied. The glue was similar to that found on postage stamps. I moistened the label and stuck it to the upper surface of the right front wing. Specimens so tagged were then placed in a large flight cage in order to test the adhesive property of the tags. Within a short period of time, all of the tags fell from the wings. I realized that it was necessary to remove the scales from the surface of the wing so that the tag could be applied directly to the wing membrane. This method was more successful, but still a number of tags did not adhere to the wing. The wing veins, which lie above the plane of the wing, caused the edges of the tag to stick up, and the passage of air over the wing surface pried them loose.

By accident, one of the labels I was preparing to attach to a wing of one of the migrants was creased, and it occurred to me that the tag could be folded and placed over the leading edge of the wing. I removed the wing scales from the upper and lower surfaces of the wing in the area of the discal cell, thus avoiding the raised veins, placed the tag over the leading edge, and glued it in place. As a result of using this method, a number of specimens were returned to me. The flight distances were very short—none exceeding 1 kilometer.

In order to test the adhesive property of the water-soluble glue, I placed tagged monarchs in large flight cages and then sprayed the cages and the butterflies with water. As I anticipated, the labels came off. To overcome this difficulty, I devised a method whereby a tag could be glued to itself, thus giving the glue a greater adhesive property. I placed a piece of light cardboard, such as a filing card, on the underside of the wing and, using a paper punch, I made a round hold through the wing membrane (the cardboard was used to prevent tearing the wing). The moistened gummed tag was then placed over the leading edge of the wing in the vicinity of the discal cell, as close to the body of the butterfly as possible, and glued to itself through the hole. When I used this method, many hundreds of specimens were returned from distances up to 1,288 kilometers.

Some of my associates in the tagging program reported that under wet conditions, even when the tags were glued through the hole, they fell from the wings. It was not until the winter of 1954 that I learned how true these reports were. At this time, Norah and I were attending meetings of the

American Association for the Advancement of Science at the University of California at Berkeley. We took advantage of the opportunity to visit the overwintering clusters of monarchs in the Monterey Peninsula. With the assistance of two students from the university, we tagged over a thousand monarch butterflies that were roosting in large clusters on the branches of Monterey pines in Washington Park. During the evening it started to rain, and throughout the night there was a continuous light drizzle and heavy fog. The following morning we visited our tagging area. The monarch butterflies were still in large clusters on the branches of the pines, but our tags, like scattered confetti, littered the ground. Obviously, a water-soluble adhesive was useless. Rather than leave the area with no tagged specimens, we tagged over a hundred using a waterproof glue that we purchased from the local hardware store. However, none of these specimens were ever returned to me.

On returning home, I began to investigate adhesives that might be used in place of the water-soluble one. I contacted a number of business establishments as well as my chemistry colleagues for an answer to this problem. It was suggested that a label similar to those commonly used to designate the price of glass merchandise might work, since this type of label would adhere to a smooth surface and did not require moistening. As a result of correspondence with the firm that manufactured these labels, a tag was produced that would cling to the smooth surface of the wing membrane, after the scales had been removed, by applying a slight pressure with the thumb and index finger and that, when bent in half, would fit into the area of the discal cell.

Placing the tag on the wing does, of course, add a slight amount of extra weight to it, but if this weight is kept close to the body of the butterfly the weight to be lifted by the wing is greatly reduced. This is illustrated in the accompanying diagram where T^1 is the tag placed at the apex of the wing W, and T^2 is the tag placed near the base of the wing close to the body. The distance the weight must be lifted in position T^1 is much greater than in T^2, and hence the weight at the position T^1 is much greater than at T^2. This can be compared to lifting a weight on the end of a long pole and lifting the same weight when it is located at the base of the pole near one's hand.

How much does a tag weigh? About .01 gram. The average weight of one butterfly is .41 gram, based on the average weight of five males and five females. Hence, the weight of a tag is approximately one-fortieth the weight of the butterfly.

As a result of this simple technique, a great many migrants could be tagged in a relatively short period of time. Once the butterfly is in one's hand, it takes, on the average, eight seconds to apply the tag. In addition, the tag eliminates the need for liquid glue. By bending the tag over the edge of the wing, the adhesive surfaces are brought along the line of the crease, thus further assisting in holding the tag to the wing. Having the tags arranged on a sheet or in a roll makes it easier to type numbers on each tag and, at the same time, is an automatic record of the tags used on a particular day.

In the early stages of tagging, the numbers were written on the tags by hand. Although different kinds of ink were tested, only numbers written with a hard graphite pencil lasted under adverse weather conditions. Later, numbers typed with a carbon ribbon were found to be durable. Eventually, arrangements were made to add a piece of equipment to the printing press so that the numbers were automatically printed serially on the tags using a carbon-type ink.

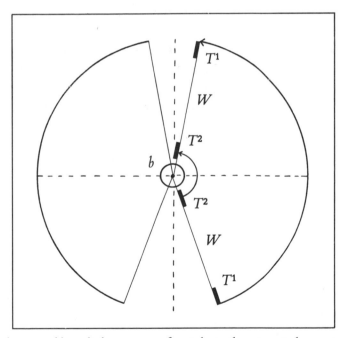

Although the small alar tag adds a slight amount of weight to the wing, it does not interfere appreciably with the butterfly's power of flight. If we placed the tag (T¹) at the tip of the wing (W), it would add weight to the degree of lift for the distance the wing would travel. However, if we place the tag (T²) close to the insect's body (b), we decrease the distance through which the wing travels, and there is less degree of lift.

During the past few years I have used thin water-resistant labels with a strong adhesive backing. The labels come in various colors so that butterflies tagged at the overwintering sites can be differentiated from those tagged during the fall and spring migrations. Since we wanted many thousands of tags consecutively numbered and since the space on each tag is limited to not more than six digits, we finally incorporated a letter along with the number, thus giving an unlimited numbering system as well as eliminating duplication of numbers from year to year.

The method of applying the alar tag is as follows: Remove the wing scales from the left or right front wing in the area of the discal cell by gently rubbing the area between the thumb and index finger, thus exposing the wing membrane. Take a tag from the sheet or roll, bend it in half so that the adhesive surface of each half faces inward, and place the tag over the discal area. A gentle pressure secures the tag to the wing membrane. The specimen is then released.

Tagging has made it possible to plot, with considerable accuracy, the migratory routes during the fall and spring migrations. Tagged specimens have been returned after having flown distances of over 3,000 kilometers (2,050 miles). Occasionally a specimen we collected had a broken wing, a fracture of the costal vein. The tag placed over the fractured vein allowed the butterfly to continue its flight. Many such damaged specimens have been recaptured at distances of over 1,288 kilometers.

My associates and I have used this alar-tagging method for a number of species of butterflies with considerable success. In the case of small species, a much smaller tag is employed; the size of the tag to be used is dictated by the amount of space available in the discal cell. If the tag is too large, the free edge on the underside of the wing will be slightly elevated over the vein, thus catching on the front margin of the hind wing and making flight impossible. It is also possible to use this tagging method to follow the movements of migrating dragonflies. I found that one must apply the tag to the front edge of the hind wing because flight was impaired when the tag was put on the front wing. I have not, however, pursued a tagging program for migrating dragonflies.

Many of the specimens that were alar tagged were captured in fields where they were feeding, but the most successful way to alar tag thousands of migrants was to locate the overnight roosting trees. Norah and I were able to tag as many as twelve hundred specimens in a single morning at such roosting sites.

In order to follow the movements of any animal that travels hundreds of miles it is necessary to tag thousands of specimens, so that a few of them may be recaptured and the data sent to the researcher. Since it is not possible for one individual to tag thousands of migrants in many different localities along the migratory routes, we decided to enlist the support of others who might be interested in the study of the monarch butterfly migration. In 1952 Norah wrote an article dealing with our research project, and it was published in *Natural History,* a magazine produced by the American Museum of Natural History. A request for assistance was appended to the article, and a few individuals responded, some of whom still continue to work with us. From this nucleus of "research associates" grew the Insect Migration Association (IMA), which over the years has numbered over four thousand persons living in almost every state of the United States, including Hawaii (but not Alaska, where the monarch butterfly does not occur), three provinces of Canada, Mexico, Australia, and New Zealand.

As tagged specimens began to appear in various towns and cities, our migration study was reported in newspapers and magazines across the continent, and over the period of the investigations I received clippings of three thousand eight hundred articles. The publicity proved important, since it aroused the interest of the general public and made them aware of the possibility of finding such a tagged specimen.

Those who captured a tagged migrant either reported the number on the tag and released the butterfly to continue its flight or sent the tagged specimen to our laboratory at the University of Toronto, along with the date and place of recapture. Norah handled all such correspondence and would inform the person who had tagged the specimen about its recapture, together with the name and address of the person who had found the specimen and the place and date of the recapture. The person who found the specimen was informed about where it had been tagged and given a brief description of the investigation.

When a recaptured specimen was reported, the places of tagging and of recapture were indicated on a large topographic map hung on the wall. A black thread was used to join the two places. The line of flight was thus indicated and referred to as a *release-recapture line* (RRL). From such lines it was possible to trace the direction of migration from various localities in Canada and the United States to the overwintering sites in Mexico and California, as well as the aberrant migration through Florida to Yucatan and the islands of the South Atlantic.

TWO POPULATIONS

When I first started investigations on the migratory routes and final destinations of monarch butterflies in North America, the overwintering site in

California was well known and widely advertised as a natural science phenomenon. But no one knew where the butterflies came from or where they went after leaving California. It was suggested that all of the migrant monarchs from the United States and Canada overwintered in California.

Norah and I made field trips to various parts of the coast of the Gulf of Mexico, particularly the north coast of Florida, where we observed thousands of migrants flying westward. When we visited the overwintering site in California, it became obvious to us that the relatively small numbers of monarchs in California could not possibly account for the great masses of migrants leaving the eastern parts of the continent.

As a result of the alar-tagging program, it was evident that there were two populations, one that overwintered in California, which I have termed the "Western Population," and another far more extensive population that had its breeding areas east of the Rocky Mountains, which I have termed the "Eastern Population." I was eventually able to show that the Eastern Population overwintered in the Neovolcanic Mountains of Mexico. These two populations were once thought to be morphologically distinct on the basis of comparative studies of wing lengths. However, after measuring wing lengths of more than a thousand monarch butterflies taken from both populations, I was able to prove the fallacy of this conclusion. Eventually, I was also able to demonstrate that the two populations were not geographically isolated. Migrants from east and west of the Rocky Mountains moved through the river valleys, particularly in Montana and Idaho, along the tributaries of the Snake River. It is quite likely that other passages through the mountains also allow for an exchange of genetic material, thus maintaining a uniform population in North America.

OVERNIGHT ROOSTING CLUSTERS

One of the characteristic features of the southward flight is the establishment of overnight roosting sites. These sites consist of one or more trees

Two populations of monarch butterflies occur in North America. The Eastern Population (●) breeds in areas east of the Rocky Mountains and overwinters in Mexico or, in the case of the aberrant migrants, in the mountains of Guatemala. The Western Population (■) breeds in the valleys of the Rocky Mountains and overwinters along the coast of California. Members of the two populations are similar in color and size, since there is a degree of intermingling that prevents genetic isolation, which would give rise to two distinct races of monarchs.

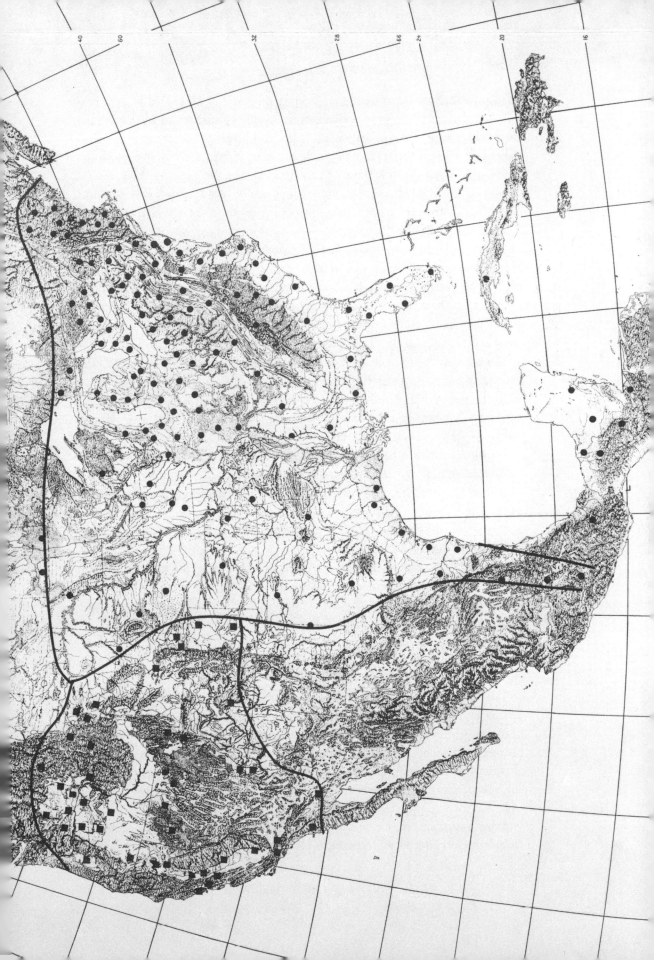

that are usually located near a large body of water and especially on peninsulas that extend in a southerly direction. Many thousands of migrants may be found clinging to the branches, twigs, and leaves of roosting trees. With wings closed, the butterflies resemble clusters of dead, brown leaves. In the morning, when the first rays of sun reach them, they spread their wings, exposing the abdomen and thorax. These are covered with a dense mat of fine black hairs that absorb the penetrating rays. An observer is presented with a most unforgettable sight—a tree ablaze with the orange color of thousands of butterfly wings. As the butterflies warm up, their wings begin to vibrate rapidly—a sort of shivering motion that, it has been suggested, assists the warming process by muscular activity. Finally, when their body temperature has risen to the point at which flight is possible, the butterflies drift away from the roosting trees, singly or a few at a time, to continue their solitary, leisurely flight southward.

When the sun is shining and the air temperature is above 13°C, the migrants continue their flight, pausing en route to feast on nectar from various species of autumn flowers. As evening approaches and the sun's rays diminish in intensity, the air becomes cooler, and the migrants seek suitable trees on which to spend the night.

It is imperative that the migrants find suitable resting trees while the temperature is above 10°C, because temperatures below this figure cause a state of semiparalysis, making flight impossible. By clinging to the foliage with their needlelike claws, the butterflies remain firmly attached to the support during the night, safe from insectivorous ground-dwelling animal life.

To test what would happen if a semiparalyzed migrant were placed on the ground, ten specimens were so arranged beneath the roosting trees. The following morning, five of the butterflies had been removed by some predator, and the abdomens of the remaining five had been consumed, or partly so. The test was repeated on another occasion, and only one specimen was consumed, while the others remained unharmed. Such animals as shrews, mice, and voles are the most likely predators.

The characteristics of clustering behavior vary with temperature. At temperatures well above 13°C the migrants tend to spread out over the branches of the roosting trees or to form relatively small clusters. When the temperatures drop below 13°C, and especially if there is a strong wind, the clusters become much larger and more concentrated. Generally, the lower the temperature, the denser the clusters.

It has been suggested that the mass clustering during periods of cold weather assists in preserving the body temperature of individuals. However, thermometers placed in the center of the clusters indicated no appreciable difference in the temperature there and that of the surrounding air. However, dense clusters may provide protection from the cooling and drying effects of wind. Large clusters may also provide protection against the whipping action of branches. If there are only a few individuals on the end of a small branch, the whipping action may dislodge them, while the weight of large clusters causes the branch to sway in the wind rather than to whip about. I have also observed that large clusters tend to shed the rain, thus preventing the migrants' wings from becoming soaked, which would prevent or impede flight.

Certain trees in a given area are chosen year after year as overnight roosting sites. It has been suggested by some scientists that migrants from one year leave some sort of odor on the trees that attracts migrants the following year. However, when a roosting tree is removed as a result of rural development, construction of roads, or agricultural expansion, the migrants choose another tree or group of trees nearby. I have also observed that the migrants frequently choose to roost on deciduous trees, and since the leaves fall to the ground in late autumn, any odor left on leaves would be gone. To determine whether or not odors are left by successive generations requires scientifically controlled experimentation.

To arrive at a possible explanation for the choice of roosting trees, the following observations and experiments were carried out. A site was chosen for observation that was located .6 kilometers from the north shore of Lake Ontario, where countless thousands of migrants fly each fall. Monarchs flying along the shore in a southwesterly direction moved inland in the evening, coming to rest on the leaves of a large silver maple. Observations on flight and wind direction are summarized in the accompanying figure. Path "b" represents the route of migrants that were moving southwestward following the lake shore; path "a" is the route of those that passed this particular site and then returned to it; and path "c" is the route of those that were moving from the northeast. The two diagrams are based on two separate sets of observations, with clustering taking place on two separate locations on the tree. From these data I concluded that the migrating monarch butterflies are attracted by sight to a particular group of trees. Upon reaching one of the trees, particularly one with large clusters of leaves, they roosted on the leeward side, where they were protected from the wind.

How are clusters formed after the migrants have selected certain branches of the roosting tree? To answer this question, the following observations were recorded. When a monarch seeking an overnight roosting site approaches a given tree, it flies around the tree to the leeward side. It chooses a leaf and comes to rest, clinging to the leaf by means of its curved claws.

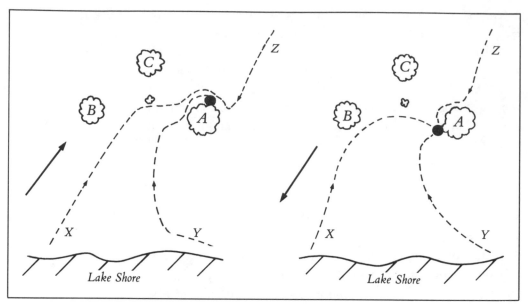

This diagram is based on many observations of monarchs as they chose an overnight roosting site. In the observation area were three trees: a small willow (C), a slightly larger cedar (B), and a large silver maple (A). Some of the migrants flew southwestward (Z); some flew westward (Y); some followed the lake shore; and others passed the area and then returned (X). Migrants chose the largest tree (A) and, depending on wind direction (indicated by arrows), came to rest on the leeward side (●). Thus, the three principal factors in the choice of a roosting site are: elevation, size of the tree or group of trees, and wind direction.

When its wings are brought together and only the undersurfaces are exposed, the monarch closely resembles a dead leaf. When a second migrant approaches, the first one snaps its wings open, revealing the bright orange coloration of the upper surfaces. At first I concluded that this was a signal to attract others to the particular branch in order to form a cluster, but later I discovered that such was not the case. Exposing the bright orange wing surfaces was a warning by the first butterfly to the approaching migrant not to land on it.

If opening wings in this manner is not done in order to attract others to a particular branch, how do the migrants signal to each other to form overnight clusters? In an attempt to obtain an answer to this question, a field experiment was carried out.

I considered the possibility that monarch butterflies emit a scent—

referred to as a "pheromone"—that attracts the butterflies to each other. I extracted this substance using the alcohol-chloroform method. The solution was diluted, one part of solution to fifty parts of distilled water. A similar solution was made, as a control, without the addition of the macerated monarch butterfly bodies.

In an area that I had studied for a number of years, I selected a group of trees along the line of flight. The extract made from the bodies of the monarch butterflies was sprayed on the branches of one of the trees. On the branches of another tree in the row, but 40 meters distant, the control spray was applied. As the migrant monarch butterflies entered the area, Norah and I recorded their line of flight and noted whether or not the butterflies were attracted to the sprayed trees. This experiment was carried out on four separate occasions with completely negative results. The migrants continued on their flight to other roosting trees without pausing at the sprayed trees.

There remained the possibility that the monarch migrants were attracted by sight alone to branches on which one or more monarchs had already come to rest. To test this possibility, seventy-five dead monarch butterflies were mounted in trees with wings arranged like those of the living specimens—some folded, some partly opened, and others widely spread to show the bright orange color of the upper surfaces. These specimens were pinned to the leaves to form small clusters. Twelve butterflies with their wings spread as if they were flying were suspended on fine nylon fibers and attached to the ends of the branches of the tree so that, with the action of a slight breeze, they appeared to be in flight and attempting to come to rest. Such tests were carried out on a number of possible roosting trees in an area where there were trees used for overnight roosting. The results were negative. The migrants were not attracted to the dead specimens.

I next considered the possibility that monarch butterflies emitted some sort of signal, such as a pheromone or a sound, only while they were alive. Sound signals have been shown to occur among various species of moths. To test the possibility of such signals by living migrants, I carried out the following experiment.

Twenty specimens, ten males and ten females, were placed in bags constructed of fine nylon netting. Since there was the possibility that the free-flying migrants might see the butterflies in the bags, they were carefully secreted behind clusters of leaves on the branches of the trees. The results were truly remarkable; within twenty minutes, free-flying migrants approached the trees in which the nylon bags of live monarchs were secreted and came to rest upon neighboring branches. A few flew through the cluster of leaves to come to rest on the nylon bags. I concluded that, in some manner as yet unknown, live monarch butterflies do communicate with each other.

Although the southward movement may commence as early as July 17 in the northeastern sections of the breeding range, large overnight roosting clusters are not formed until mid to late August, reaching a peak in numbers by mid or late September. After a number of years of collecting monarch butterflies for alar tagging at different roosting sites, we found that the appearance of the largest numbers of migrants coincided with a rapid drop in nocturnal air temperature. With the passage of a cold air mass that results in clear skies and maximum radiation at night, the number of migrants always increased remarkably. I concluded, therefore, that low temperatures might be responsible for initiating the formation of roosting clusters.

Through August and September we made frequent observations on the presence (or absence) of migrants on a particular roosting site located on the north shore of Lake Ontario. The information obtained from these observations is summarized in the accompanying chart. The number of migrants observed on the roosting site is given on the right side of the chart and the dates on the left side. Minimum temperatures, taken from the monthly summaries published by the Meteorological Branch of the Canadian Department of Transport, are given at the top of the chart, with a reading from left to right indicating the degree of falling temperatures. Observations were made before August 12, when there were no roosting migrants. On August 13 only one specimen was found on the tree (the previous year five had been found on the same tree on August 15). After September 28 there were so few migrants on the tree that the observations were discontinued. This sudden drop in numbers might have been due to freezing temperatures that would have destroyed pupae and larvae.

There appears to be a correlation between the passage of cold fronts, which produce minimum temperatures below 13°C, and the presence of migrants on the roosting trees. On only one occasion prior to September 12 did the minimum temperature drop below 13°C; this occurred on July 6 with a minimum temperature of 12°C. On that occasion no weather was associated with the passage of the front, and maximum wind speed did not exceed 19 kilometers per hour. The chart indicates that migrants had a slight urge to form clusters from August 12 to September 4, with a maximum of twelve specimens on the trees on September 3, but there was very little weather associated with the fronts, and wind velocity did not exceed

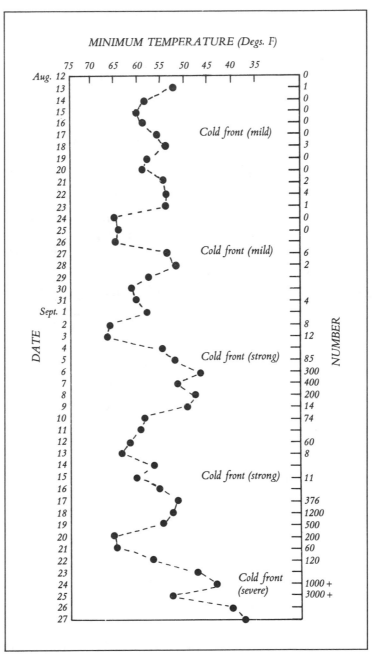

This graph shows the relationship between the passage of cold frontal systems and the numbers of fall migrant monarch butterflies found on overnight roosting trees during August and September at one observation area. With the passage of strong cold frontal systems, the number of roosting migrants increased dramatically, with estimated counts of over a thousand. [Note: (Fahrenheit − 32) ÷ 9 = Centigrade ÷ 5]

27 kilometers per hour. The cold front that passed on September 4 had a great deal of rain, and winds of 32 kilometers per hour with gusts to 56 kilometers per hour were associated with it. Following the passage of this front, the number of monarch butterflies on the roosting trees rose rapidly.

That atmospheric pressure is an important factor in the activity of the migrants was strikingly demonstrated by the following observation. On September 12, 1957, more than a thousand butterflies clustered on the roosting trees. Norah and I collected a number of them for alar tagging, using a large net fastened to a 6-meter rod. As the net was placed over a cluster, those outside of the net were disturbed and took to wing. Usually, disturbed specimens immediately fly southward on their migratory route, but to our surprise, on this particular morning, the migrants refused to leave the roosting trees even though the temperature had risen to 17°C. They flew but a short distance, circled around the tree, and came to rest again, forming small clusters. At this time the sky was slightly overcast with cirrostratus clouds, the wind was approximately 11 kilometers per hour, and there was no indication of an approaching storm. By 11:00 A.M., the sky had become overcast with heavy altocumulus clouds, and by 1:00 P.M., strong winds and thunderstorms swept the area. Meteorological reports indicated rapidly falling barometric pressure, which was the only meteorological factor that might have affected the activity of the migrants. This leads to the conclusion that the monarch butterflies respond to changes in atmospheric pressure—such a response has been well documented with research on the activity of muscoid flies.

The sudden appearance of many migrants on the overnight roosting trees may be explained as follows. As the cold air mass advances, the butterflies move southward in the warmer air mass ahead of it. Eventually, the cold air overtakes the migrating butterflies, causing them to remain in a particular area until the return of another warm air mass. Since the body temperature of a monarch butterfly is the same as that of the surrounding air, cold temperatures will slow up development of larvae and pupae and will also delay the flight of migrants. If air temperatures are below 13°C, adults will be unable to fly and will remain in the same area until the advent of higher temperatures. When a warm air mass replaces the cold, migrants will move southward within the warm air mass. These temperature changes that occur throughout the migratory period give rise to the numerous reports that I have received from various parts of the continent concerning variations in monarch butterfly populations, particularly with respect to the numbers occurring on the roosting trees.

DIRECTION OF MIGRATION

WESTERN POPULATION

The breeding areas of the Western Population are located in the river valleys of the Rocky Mountains. During the fall migration, these migrants move southwestward to the coast of California. A number of loci exist within the California site, extending from Bodega Bay in the north to Ventura in the south. As indicated in color plate 12, migrants alar tagged in the mountain valleys have been recaptured in the California site. Specimens alar tagged and released at Gibsons Landing in British Columbia have been recaptured in California, indicating a southward movement along the Pacific coast.

EASTERN POPULATION

Since the breeding area of the Eastern Population is much more extensive than that of the Western Population, encompassing the area east of the Rocky Mountains, the population density is much greater. Thousands of monarch butterflies cover the branches of trees on the overnight roosting sites. On leaving the roosting sites, the air may be filled with migrants, giving rise to reports of mass migrations. Actually, the migrants proceed southwestward singly, not in flocks. During the peak of migration, those passing over roadways are hit by passing cars, their dead bodies littering the sides of the roadways. On one occasion, in a locality north of Toronto, Canada, a count was made of monarch butterflies hit by passing cars. In a distance of only .3 kilometers a total of 111 dead or mangled living specimens were collected. Countless thousands of monarchs are destroyed on the highways and roads of North America every year.

As a result of alar tagging over 400,000 migrants over the period of my investigation, my associates and I have worked out the migratory routes with considerable accuracy. Migrants from the more eastern portions of North America, particularly from breeding areas in the vicinity of the Great Lakes, move southwestward. Upon reaching the coast of the Gulf of Mexico they follow the coastline westward, passing through Florida, Mississippi, Louisiana, and Texas. They finally orient their course to the southwest, eventually arriving at the overwintering site in Mexico. Migrants from breeding grounds in the Great Plains regions move more directly southward. Except for a few migrants (discussed later), the Eastern Population eventually reaches the mountains of Mexico.

The time taken for the migrants to fly from their breeding grounds to

Mexico varies. Those from the northern sections of North America take from eight to ten weeks to reach the Mexican site, while those from the more southern sections arrive in four to six weeks.

ABERRANT MIGRATION
OF THE EASTERN POPULATION

The majority of migrant monarchs move in a southwestward direction, eventually reaching the mountains of Mexico. However, alar-tagged recaptures indicate that a considerable number move eastward toward the Atlantic Coast of the United States; migrants have been reported from the Florida Peninsula, Bermuda, the Atlantic Ocean (lat. 19°-0'N, long. 63°-32'W; lat. 35°-19'N, long. 63°-42'W; lat. 32°-31'N, long. 59°-48'W); the Bahama Islands; the Greater Antilles (Cuba, Jamaica, Hispaniola, Puerto Rico); the Lesser Antilles (Guadeloupe, Martinique); and the Gulf of Mexico (lat. 29°-11'N, long. 88°-4'W). Large overnight clusters have been reported in Yucatan. During an expedition there, I witnessed numerous migrants flying in from the Atlantic Ocean to the mainland following strong northerly winds.

The reports of migrants from the Lesser Antilles presents confusion in identification, since there is a subspecies, *Danaus plexippus megalippe,* that closely resembles the subspecies in North America with which this book is concerned. In order to answer some of the questions concerning the relationship between these two subspecies, a series of cross experiments were carried out. These are discussed in part 7.

It has been shown that migrants of various species of insects tend to maintain a direct course. If the migrants encounter strong winds, they may be blown off course, but on entering areas of relatively calm conditions, they immediately return to the original direction of migration. Migrant monarch butterflies are sometimes blown off course during periods of strong northwesterly winds. Those from breeding areas east of longitude 90°W are

As shown by numerous release-recapture lines (point of release ▼; point of recapture ■), the fall migrants travel in a southwest direction (C) east of the Great Lakes and south-southwest in areas west of the Great Lakes (D). Those that reach the Gulf of Mexico (E) follow the coastline in a continuous stream — a spectacular sight during late October. They continue in a southwest direction (at G), eventually reaching the overwintering site in the Neovolcanic Plateau of Mexico (▲). Occasionally a migrant may fly over the Gulf of Mexico directly to the Mexican site (A).

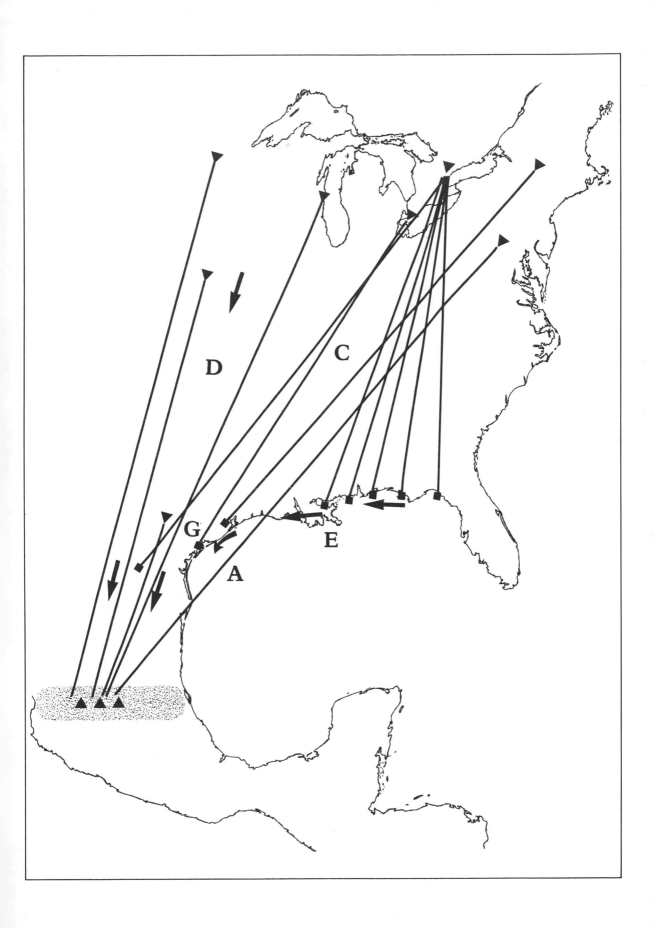

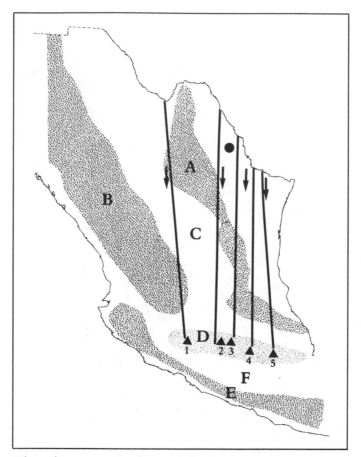

The release-recapture lines to the overwintering sites in Mexico indicate that migrants from the Great Plains region west of the Great Lakes reach the westernmost loci (1), those flying directly from the Great Lakes region reach the more central loci (2 and 3), and those from the Great Lakes region that fly south to the Gulf of Mexico and those from areas east of the Great Lakes reach the more eastern loci (4 and 5). Destinations are the Sierra Madre Occidental Mountains (A and B), Sierra Madre del Sur (E), Central Mesa (C), Neovolcanic Plateau, or Cross Range (D), and Balsus-Mexican Basin (F).

blown towards the Atlantic coast or over the Atlantic Ocean. That migrants can be blown far out over the ocean is attested to in a letter from Vincent Varey, of Stockport, England:

> I was a deck boy on the MV *Laguna* on a voyage from Liverpool to New York during September 1944. It was a convoy seven days out of Liverpool when order was given to scatter and make

for New York without escort. This was due to the imminence of a hurricane in the path of the convoy. We encountered the edge of the hurricane and soon afterwards steamed into fair weather and blue skies. We were then 5 days or 1000 miles from New York when we ran through a massive swarm of monarch butterflies. I remember standing on deck watching this mass of colourful creatures fluttering around the ship's rigging. On arrival in New York I learned that the hurricane had turned westward, crossing Long Island, N.Y.

Since there are no release-recapture data available, except for the Florida Peninsula, one can only speculate as to the direction of migration and final destination of the aberrant migrants. Migrants moving down the Florida Peninsula fly, by way of the Florida Keys, across the ocean to western Cuba, from which island I have received numerous specimens and reports of overnight roosting clusters. From Cuba they pass down the Yucatan Peninsula, where migrants are common in the fall. Norah and I spent a considerable amount of time in Yucatan with our field assistant, Señora de

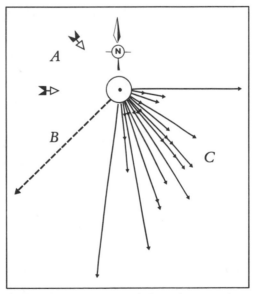

A considerable number of Eastern Population migrants traveled southeastward instead of the usual southwestward direction (B). This was due to strong west and northwest winds (A), which blew the migrants off course (C). On reaching the Atlantic Coast, these migrants followed the shoreline south. I refer to such migrants as "aberrant."

Montes, a local ornithologist, observing migrants flying in from the ocean, assisted by a strong onshore wind. Our field assistant also made numerous observations of overnight roosting clusters. Specimens were observed and collected along the east shore of Yucatan and in Guatemala. From these observations, together with specimens collected, it would appear that the aberrant migrants may overwinter in the mountains of Guatemala. At the time of writing this portion of the book, Norah and I arranged for a field assistant to investigate certain areas in the mountains of Guatemala, where we suspect the overwintering clusters are located.

Migrants blown far offshore have been observed in considerable numbers in Bermuda and by ships in the vicinity. It would appear that they travel southwestward, assisted by strong ocean winds, to the Bahama Islands. A number of observations have been made of their presence, one island reporting overnight roosting clusters. From the Bahamas the migrants travel to Cuba and Jamaica, where many specimens have been collected and observations of overnight roosting clusters have been reported. From Cuba and Jamaica they travel to Yucatan, Mexico.

I have received a number of specimens of *D. plexippus,* as well as *D. megalippe,* and hybrids from Haiti, Dominican Republic, and Puerto Rico. Whether or not the *D. plexippus* migrants eventually reach the mainland of South America is speculative.

Reports of *D. plexippus* occurring in the Lesser Antilles I believe to be due to erroneous identifications. Norah and I spent a number of years investigating the monarch butterflies in the islands of the Lesser Antilles and found only *D. megalippe.* However, it is possible that on occasion *D. plexippus* from North America may be carried to the Lesser Antilles by ships or by strong hurricane winds.

The possibility of migrant monarch butterflies that are blown far offshore over the Atlantic eventually reaching the Bahama Islands is slight. This would entail a very long ocean flight. Monarch butterflies will not fly at night, which raises the question of the possibility of such a long flight taking place. It has been suggested, based on recorded observations of monarchs resting on the ocean surface during daytime, that they might also do so during the hours of darkness. To test this possibility, I carried out the following experiment.

A large plastic dome (circumference 18 cm; height 150 cm at the center) was constructed and attached to a frame so that it could be placed over a free water surface. Since there were no places to land within the dome, the butterflies were forced to fly or to come to rest on the surface of the water. When a specimen remained on the water surface and was apparently unable

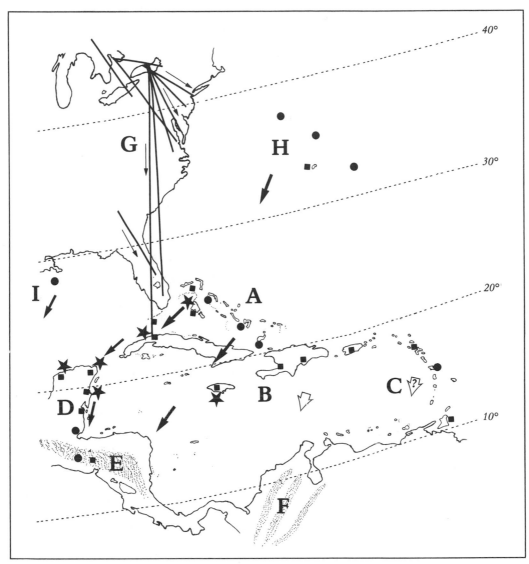

Migrant monarch butterflies that are blown off course to the Atlantic Coast follow the shoreline south (G) through peninsular Florida to Cuba via the Florida Keys, to Yucatan (D), and then to Guatemala (E). Migrants that are blown out over the Atlantic, reported from Bermuda and the surrounding ocean (H), travel southwestward to the Bahama Islands (A) and then via Cuba and Jamaica to Guatemala. Migrants reported from the Greater Antilles (Haiti-Dominica and Puerto Rico) (B) might reach Colombia (F). Those reported from the Lesser Antilles (C) might be erroneous identifications or perhaps were carried by ships or blown by hurricane-force winds. (Specimens observed, •; migrants collected, ■; overnight roosting reports, ★.)

to take off, it was removed and examined. The time of landing on the surface and time of removal were noted. Remaining on the surface of the water for periods in excess of twenty minutes caused the wings to become saturated, allowing only short flights when the butterflies were thrown into the air. If a butterfly's wings had been flat upon the water's surface, the butterfly experienced difficulty when attempting to become airborne and eventually became completely submerged.

To test the degree of water saturation of the wing, a drop of water was placed on the upper wing surface after free water had been blotted up with filter paper. If the wing was saturated, the droplet spread rapidly over the wing surface; if the wing had become partly saturated, the drop assumed a flattened ellipsoid; if the wing was perfectly dry, the drop assumed a spheroidal configuration, similar to the shape of a water drop placed on a hot plate, because of the water repellent nature of the dry wing.

In flying over the ocean, monarch butterflies would encounter not only strong winds that might force them onto the surface but also large-wave action. If a migrant were forced beneath the surface as the result of wave action, would it be able to continue flight? To answer this question, Norah and I carried out the following simple experiment. Five specimens were held beneath the surface of the water in the lily pool in our front lawn. When liberated, the monarchs floated to the surface and flew off without difficulty. This was repeated a number of times, and only one specimen, after floating to the surface, was unable to take off. On examining the butterfly we found that the right front wing was fractured. We then repeated the experiment using monarch butterflies with fractured front wings. In all cases, though the butterflies floated to the surface, they were unable to take off. I conclude from this experiment that, as long as the butterflies have not suffered wing damage, they can land on the surface of the ocean for brief periods and, if submerged by wave action, can return to the surface and take to wing.

If, on their flight from the vicinity of Bermuda southward to the more northerly islands of the Bahamas, a distance of approximately 620 kilometers, the migrants were assisted by a strong ocean wind of 48 kilometers per hour, making a combined speed of 96 kilometers per hour, the distance could be covered in approximately sixteen hours, or one daylight period. If we also take into account that ocean winds often exceed 80 kilometers per hour, the time taken could be considerably reduced. Hence, offshore migrants could reach the Bahamas and some of the more easterly islands of the Greater Antilles without having to rest on the surface of the ocean during the night.

During the fall migration in North America in periods of peak population, a few monarchs are captured in England. Some ornithologists, aware of the long-distance flights of birds, have concluded that the butterflies flew across the North Atlantic assisted by strong westerly winds, arriving in England usually in the vicinity of London, a straight-line flight of over 5,632 kilometers. There are, however, a few objections to such a conclusion.

I have shown that the fall migration is southwestward, a movement inherent in the species complex and perhaps associated with the earth's magnetic lines of force. To fly to England the migrants would have to move in a northeastward direction.

I have also demonstrated that monarch butterflies do not fly during hours of darkness. Therefore, one must assume that to make such a long-distance flight they rest on the surface of the ocean at night. However, monarch butterflies can rest on the surface of water for only a short time before their wings become waterlogged, making flight impossible. Hence, the journey would have to be accomplished in one daylight period.

It has been suggested that strong westerly winds at low levels would assist in accomplishing such a long distance flight. However, as the result of the passage of pressure areas over the ocean, wind direction would be variable. Perhaps strong vertical wind currents would carry the butterflies to the zone of prevailing westerly winds, at a height of 6 kilometers. However, at such a height freezing temperatures occur.

One of the most important objections to the suggestion that monarchs might reach high altitudes was presented by Dr. Glick, a research entomologist. Glick attached an insect-trapping device to the wing of an aircraft and made over seventeen hundred flights at different altitudes. No butterflies of any species were captured at heights above 366 meters (1,200 feet) from ground level. What, then, is the explanation for the occurrence of monarch butterflies in England? The answer is quite simple: They are carried across the ocean on ships. I offer the following in support of this conclusion.

Asclepias syriaca, the common milkweed growing in eastern North America, occurs on sandy, gravelly soil, such as one finds in railway yards and shipyards. When mature larvae leave milkweed plants growing in these places to choose a suitable support for attachment of the pupae, they may select material that is in transit to England. On one occasion I found a monarch pupa attached to a large wooden crate on which was printed in large letters "London, U.K." Since the pupa can take as long as nineteen days to reach full development, there is adequate time for the journey before the emergence of the mature butterfly. The greater the abundance of monarch butterflies in North America in a particular year, the greater the chance of pupae being fastened to shipments and carried across the ocean. It has been shown that monarch butterflies occurring on the islands of the Pacific Ocean were transported by vessels from the west coast of North America, and the same explanation may account for the occurrences of monarch butterflies in England.

EFFECTS OF LOW TEMPERATURES ON MIGRATION

Low temperatures during the last weeks of the fall migration are responsible for the destruction of many larvae and pupae. On October 18, 1956, following the passage of a cold frontal system that resulted in subfreezing temperatures, 148 out of a total of 264 pupae in our outdoor rearing cages were dead. Of those surviving, 60 produced normal butterflies; the remainder emerged but were unable to fly. Out of a total of 48 larvae, only 1 survived. In addition, the cold temperatures destroyed the milkweed plants.

To test the effect of low temperatures on pupae and adults under controlled conditions, 10 pupae were placed in a control cabinet at a temperature of 3°C. Two weeks later, 1 pupa was removed. It developed into a perfectly formed adult. After seventeen days, 2 pupae were removed from the cabinet; 1 developed normally and 1 died. After forty-four days, the remaining 7 were removed. Of these, 5 failed to mature; the remaining 2 developed to the point when the adult butterfly could be seen through the transparent pupal skin, but they failed to emerge.

To test the effect of low temperatures on mature butterflies, 10 butterflies were placed separately in plastic envelopes and exposed to a temperature of −4°C for a period of twelve hours. When removed from the chamber and liberated from the plastic envelopes, they were able to fly without any apparent ill effect. The experiment was repeated subjecting the butterflies to a temperature of −5.5°C for a period of twenty-four hours. All recovered without ill effects. Specimens were then subjected to a temperature of −6.7°C for a period of twenty-four hours. Of these, 2 died and the remainder were unable to fly; although still alive, they had difficulty walking.

To test the effect of environmental low temperatures, 10 specimens were placed outdoors in one of the large flight cages for a period of two days when ambient temperatures ranged from 1°C to −12°C. The specimens were then taken indoors. Six failed to recover, and the remainder exhibited the same paralysis described above.

Although these tests are by no means conclusive, they indicate that pupae are more susceptible to low temperatures than are adults and that adults can withstand below-freezing temperatures for short periods of time. This is most important to their survival during the overwintering period. However, prolonged periods of low temperatures, in the absence of incident radiation, are either fatal or produce paralysis. This also occurs at the overwintering sites.

Low temperatures in late summer and fall are responsible for the termination of the fall migration. Breeding stops and the larvae, pupae, and, to a more limited extent, adults are destroyed. Certain members of the fall migrants remain sexually mature, so breeding does continue as the population moves southward into warmer areas, where the food plants have not been destroyed by freezing temperatures.

BREEDING ACTIVITY
DURING THE FALL MIGRATION

At various times throughout the summer months (June-August) I have collected female monarch butterflies and dissected them in order to estimate the number of eggs that might be laid by one female. In the process of doing so I noted that during the peak breeding period (June and July) all females contained active ovaries with numerous eggs in the oviducts. I also noted that throughout the breeding period there were no clusters of butterflies on the overnight roosting trees. During the last two weeks of August, some females possessed inactive ovaries with no eggs in the oviducts and a few migrants were found on the roosting trees. During September and early October, large clusters of migrants formed on the overnight roosting trees; an examination of these individuals showed inactive ovaries and testes, a condition that I have referred to as "reproductive dormancy." However, collecting in the fields produced an occasional male and female with active reproductive organs. Thus, as the fall migrants move southward, there are two sexually different groups—one with active reproductive organs and the other in reproductive dormancy.

This difference in sexual activity during the fall migration accounts for the occurrence of larvae and breeding pairs in areas where they are absent during the summer months. Fall breeding results in an increase in the size of the migrating population and an extended migratory movement over a longer period of time. The absence of monarch butterflies in the southern parts of the North American continent during the summer period will be discussed when I deal with the spring migration in part 6.

CHARACTERISTICS OF FLIGHT
DURING THE FALL MIGRATION

As described in part 4, there are five monarch flight patterns: gliding, cruising, speeding, prenuptial, and social. With the exception of prenuptial flight, all of these flight patterns are present during the fall migration. With rare exceptions, the southward movement is slow and rather casual, with periods of gliding, cruising, and, most characteristic of all, social flight, involving two or more individuals circling about each other while at the same time drifting slowly toward the south.

When an overnight roosting cluster breaks up in the early morning hours, there is rarely a sudden mass exodus as there is with a flock of migrating birds; rather, there is a slow breaking up of the clusters, a few individuals at a time. Only when the roosting tree is shaken violently by the wind or when the cluster is alarmed is there a mass movement. When such an exodus occurs along the migratory route, and particularly along the shores of large bodies of water, one will witness thousands of monarch butterflies flying in a continuous stream, giving the impression of a migrating flock.

DIRECTION OF FLIGHT

I have observed on numerous occasions that when migrants were released on my screened porch, they would move in the direction of the sun. In the morning they would cluster on the east side, moving to the south by noon and to the southwest in the afternoon. This, I have concluded, is an escape response. Caged butterflies will fly to the area of maximum illumination in order to escape; if you liberate a monarch butterfly in a room, it will fly to the window and flutter against the pane.

To investigate flight direction during the day, from sunrise to sunset, migrant monarch butterflies were collected from overnight roosting trees, alar tagged, and liberated by tossing them into the air. This was done at hourly intervals and under various wind conditions. Flight direction was determined by compass and recorded. Butterflies released in the morning, from 8:00 A.M. to noon, flew toward the southeast under light wind conditions and to the south with strong northerly winds. Those liberated in the afternoon, from noon to 8:00 P.M., flew to the southwest. On one occasion six of those released during the morning were found the following morning on the overnight roosting trees located 1.6 kilometers southeast of my home. From these release experiments I concluded that during the morning period the monarchs moved toward the sun in search of flowering plants in order to feed. In the afternoon, they flew in their inherent fall migratory direction, toward the southwest.

What is the mechanism involved in flight orientation? Is it a visual response? Do the antennae play an important part? To test the latter suggestion, I carried out the following experiment. Thirty monarch butterflies were liberated in groups of ten: the first ten specimens had antennae intact; the second ten had one antenna removed; and the last group of ten had both antennae removed. The tests were carried out at 11:00 A.M. on a day when the sky was clear and the winds calm. Specimens with both antennae flew to the east or southeast; those with only one antenna flew to the east and southeast; those that had no antennae flew in various directions—two went south, four west, and four flew to the northeast.

The test was repeated under the same conditions. Those with one or both antennae intact flew to the east or southeast, while those that lacked antennae flew in various directions. Three flew south; two flew east; three flew northwest; and two flew in erratic circles, eventually landing, with difficulty, on trees 35 meters from the point of liberation.

Recently, researchers have located magnetite in the bodies of monarch butterflies, a substance that has also been reported in the bodies of pigeons and dolphins. Perhaps monarch butterflies follow the earth's magnetic lines of force. This would explain the dispersal, rather than migratory, habits of the population inhabiting the islands of the South Pacific (discussed in part 7). Perhaps researchers will one day locate magnetite in the antennae of the monarch butterfly.

HEIGHT OF FLIGHT

Although monarchs have been observed at heights exceeding a thousand feet above ground level, this is usually the result of strong updrafts, particularly in those areas where thermal air pockets exist or in hilly and mountainous areas. Migrants typically remain close to the ground throughout their migration. They do so in order to find nectar-producing flowers and to avoid adverse winds by taking advantage of the frictional effect of the ground and vegetation.

I have received a number of reports of migrant monarch butterflies being seen and/or captured at heights of from 1,500 to 1,900 meters, and such reports have been given in the literature as though the measurements were above ground level. It is not unusual for migrant monarchs to fly over mountains that exceed 3,600 meters in height. However, the butterflies remain close to the ground.

When a migrant monarch encounters obstacles such as wooded areas, tall buildings, hills, and mountains that lie across the line of migration, it will usually fly over them in order to maintain its flight direction. However, with only a slight change of direction, migrants will also follow passages, such as city streets, broad roadways, clearings in wooded areas, and river valleys through hilly or mountainous regions, always flying close to the ground. My office window faced a broad street with a northeast-southwest orientation. During the fall migration, I could see the migrant monarchs flying leisurely over the city lawns and visiting the flower beds in adjacent gardens while maintaining their southward movement. In an adjacent street with an east-west orientation, migrants were rarely seen flying close to the ground; rather, they flew over the tops of buildings and maintained their southwestward direction.

SPECIMEN TRANSFERENCE

Would monarch butterflies continue to travel southward or southwestward during the fall migration if they were transferred from one part of North America to another? To obtain data that might answer this question, thousands of migrant monarchs were alar tagged in one area and transferred to another. The specimens were placed individually in small glassine, or plastic, envelopes (6.3 × 10 cm). A small piece of moist cotton was placed in each envelope in order to maintain a high humidity, for monarchs dry out rapidly in the absence of sufficient moisture. The envelopes were sealed after introducing a small amount of air. The flap of the envelope was folded twice and then secured with adhesive tape. The envelopes were packed loosely, but compactly, to prevent bouncing about during transit, in strong cardboard cartons. The cartons were sent airmail to their destinations where the butterflies were immediately released by my associates.

The following transfers were carried out during the fall migration; the butterflies were either collected from overnight roosting locations or captured by net in the field.

1. East to west transfers. From Toronto and Port Hope, Ontario, to Gibsons Landing, British Columbia; Reno, Nevada; Lethbridge, Alberta; Denver, Colorado; Pearsall, Texas; Salt Lake City, Utah; Quemadeo, Texas; Tonapah, Arizona; and Rapid City, South Dakota.
2. West to east transfers. From Muir Beach, California, to Towner,

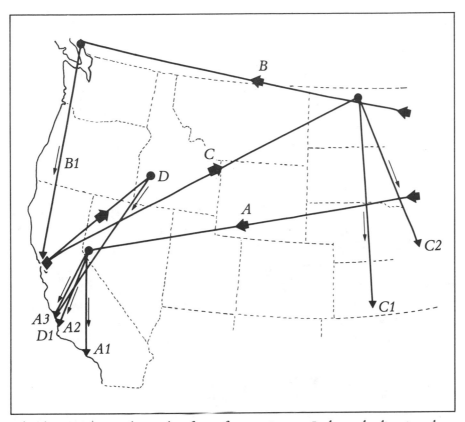

This diagram depicts the results of transfer experiments. It shows the direction along which monarchs were transferred (➤), the area of capture (◆), the point where the monarchs were released (●), the flight of the monarchs from the release point (→), and the point of recapture (▼). Monarchs transferred from Port Hope, Ontario, to Reno, Nevada (A), a distance from east to west of 3,220 km in the direction 260° WSW, were recaptured at Morro Bay, Ventura, and San Luis Obispo, California. The same southwestward movement occurred when specimens were transferred from Hayward, California, to Boise, Idaho (D), a distance of 773 km in the direction 40° NNE, and were recaptured at Morro Bay, California. When monarchs were transferred from Muir Beach, California, to Towner, North Dakota (C), a distance of 2,060 km in the direction 60° NE, they were recaptured at Pratt, Kansas, and Omaha, Nebraska. They followed the same general southward movement as the populations in the Plains regions. Fall migrants tend to follow coastlines. When specimens were transferred from Toronto, Ontario, to Gibsons Landing, British Columbia (B), a distance from east to west of 3,280 km in the direction 280° WNW, they followed the coastline to be recaptured in southern Washington and northern California.

North Dakota; Boise, Idaho; Reno, Nevada. From Hayward, California, to Boise, Idaho. From Santa Cruz, California, to Reno, Nevada.

3. North to south transfers. From Sault Ste Marie, Ontario, to Clearwater, Florida. From Toronto, Ontario, to Pensacola and Lakeland, Florida. From Berkeley Heights, New Jersey, to Port Charlotte, Florida. From Castro Valley, California, to Mercedes, Mexico. From Whittier, California, to Eagle Pass, Texas. From Wichita, Kansas, to Laredo, Texas.

I plotted a few of the long-distance recaptures of the transferred specimens, as shown in the accompanying chart. When specimens were transferred from one part of North America to another, they tended to follow the same migratory direction as those butterflies inhabiting that particular area. Thus, specimens transferred to the mountain areas flew southwest, the same as the resident population. Specimens transferred to the plains regions flew south along with the resident population. Unfortunately, I was unable to arrange for transfers from the plains and mountain regions to the east. I am confident, however, that if such transfers had been carried out, the butterflies would have followed a southwestward flight direction.

It would appear that some force, perhaps magnetic, directs the migration in a southwestward direction in the eastern and mountain areas and in a more direct southward direction in the plains regions. If transfers were made during the spring migration it is probable that the same migratory routes would be followed, but in the opposite direction.

A question remains to be answered: What physiological change takes place in monarch butterflies during the overwintering period that directs spring flight in the direction opposite to that of the fall migration? At the present time there is no clear answer to this question.

PART 6

Overwintering Sites and Spring Migration

THE MEXICO SITE

Those who have had a dream and have lived to see that dream come true will have some conception of my feelings when I first entered the Mexican forest and there, before my eyes, was the realization of a dream that had haunted me since I was a lad of sixteen. It was then that I first pondered the question, Where do the monarch butterflies go when they leave their northern breeding grounds in the fall? I had found the answer. The following passage from an article disclosing the discovery, published in *National Geographic,* August 1976, describes the moment.

> I gazed in amazement at the sight. Butterflies—millions upon millions of monarch butterflies! They clung in tightly packed masses to every branch and trunk of the tall, gray-green *oyamel* trees. They swirled through the air like autumn leaves and carpeted the ground in their flaming myriads on this Mexican mountainside.
>
> Breathless from the altitude, my legs trembling from the climb, I muttered aloud, "Unbelievable! What a glorious, incredible sight!"

This was the climax of years of effort involving many people and a great deal of detective work. As a result of tagging thousands upon thousands of fall migrating monarchs, I had finally succeeded in tracing the travelers from my own backyard in Toronto, Ontario, Canada to a small village, San Luis Potosi, in Mexico.

But did the recapture report of one alar-tagged monarch mean that all the butterflies from east of the Rocky Mountains spent the winter in Mexico? I spent the winter months sending letters to various personnel in Mexican universities requesting information about a possible overwintering area where masses of monarch butterflies might be found. No one knew of any such place. So, I decided that there was only one way to solve the mystery and that was a field expedition to Mexico and Texas. I included Texas because there had been many reports of monarch butterflies clustering on trees along the Rio Grande.

During the winter of 1969–70, Norah and I established headquarters in the Biology Department of the University of Texas in Kingsville. Since there was a possibility that monarch butterflies might remain in Texas along the Rio Grande River, we drove thousands of miles searching for them, from Corpus Christi in the south to Big Bend National Park in the north. During our travels we interviewed biology teachers in many schools and colleges, but although all those interviewed were aware of the presence of the monarch butterflies, no one knew of an area where they congregated in great numbers. A few scattered clusters occurred, particularly in an area near Eagle Pass, but these could not account for the thousands of migrants that had to pass through this part of Texas. We eventually concluded that the eastern monarch butterflies passed through Texas on their journey to an as yet unknown part of Mexico.

We left the University of Texas and crossed into Mexico to continue our search for the elusive monarchs. We had no idea where to look. Day after day we journeyed across Mexico's desert regions, through the sparse growth of xerophytic plants and tall, columnar cacti, our eyes searching air and ground for a monarch butterfly. We interviewed science teachers in primary and secondary schools; we spoke to classes of Mexican school students; we discussed the presence of monarch butterflies with farmers, who were well aware of these *mariposas* and knew their life cycle from larva to pupa to adult. We questioned professional entomologists in departments of agriculture and biology professors in the universities. Most knew about the monarch butterflies, but no one had heard of an area where there were great numbers of them. As we journeyed through lush tropical valleys and arid deserts, we saw only two monarch butterflies. Finally, we headed back to our headquarters at the University of Texas, our mission a failure. Where could the monarch butterflies be?

Our next method of attack was to write articles in both English and Spanish for popular magazines and newspapers in Mexico. In these articles we asked for information concerning the presence of large masses of orange butterflies and requested assistance in locating them. As a result, I received a letter from Kenneth Bruger offering his assistance in the search. Mr. Bruger, an engineer who worked in a garment factory in Mexico City, enjoyed roaming through the countryside, accompanied by his small dog. Although Ken had never collected butterflies and did not know one species from another, his enthusiasm for the search won us over. Provided with pictures of monarch butterflies and notes on where migrations had been observed, Ken began his travels. Fortunately, I was able to cover many of his expenses, thanks to generous grants from the National Geographic Society of the United States. A year passed and no overwintering site was located. Then, a most happy event occurred; Ken met and married Cathy, who is a native of the area in which we were interested. Now, traveling on a motorcycle, Ken and Cathy visited towns and villages, enquiring of the inhabitants where a mass gathering of monarch butterflies might be found. Ken sent me numerous reports of his journeys and the locations where he found monarch adults and larvae. The four of us—Norah, Ken, Cathy, and me—worked as a team of detectives, ferreting out clues to the whereabouts of our elusive migrant monarch butterflies. Then, after months of travel, the locus near Angangueo was discovered.

After leaving the small Mexican village of Tuxpan, where the four of us were staying at a local motel, we journeyed by jeep up a dusty, winding mountain road, passing through colorful hamlets, to a mountain plateau. Here there were no roads. We drove on across the plateau heading toward the mountain rim. The ground at this altitude was white with frost; a small, crystal-clear mountain stream wended its way across the plateau, slipping around volcanic boulders and making gurgling sounds as it went. Except for clusters of grasses, the only vegetation consisted of widely scattered bushes, with leaves that were leathery and glossy, reminding me of holly. In the distance near the rim of the plateau I could see a wall of evergreen trees. We traveled across the plateau as far as the jeep could take us, bumping along rutted terrain and up dusty, steep inclines. Then we parked our bone-shaking vehicle and continued the rest of the way up the mountain on foot.

Norah and I live in Toronto, Canada, which is a few hundred meters above sea level; now we were climbing a mountain that was 3,200 meters (10,000 feet) above sea level. We felt the strain of the elevation on our lungs; our hearts beat rapidly. We gasped for breath, and our feet felt as if they were encased in lead. The mountain rim seemed to be retreating. We realized that we should have spent a few days at a lower level to allow our bodies to adjust to the increase in altitude. Step by torturous step, and with frequent pauses, we eventually reached the summit. From the mountain rim we could look down to the mountain valley, thousands of feet below. As we gazed along the mountainside, which was covered with a dense growth of spruce trees, Norah and I felt that we had reached the end of a long journey. Somewhere below us the migrant butterflies had gathered to spend the winter months.

In the absence of a path, we descended the steep mountainside by slipping and sliding over rough stones and huge boulders. Halfway down we found a narrow path that had been cut into the mountain by the cattle that roamed freely on the mountainside. The path wound through volcanic boulders that, when dislodged, rolled down the side of the mountain, loosening other rocks as they hurried to reach the valley below. We realized that one false step, stumbling over a rock or a protruding root of a spruce tree, and we would tumble down the slope like the boulders we had dislodged. I now appreciate the skill and daring of those obsessed with the desire to climb mountains.

Before leaving Toronto, I had concluded that being butterflies, monarchs would travel to tropical valleys where it was warm and where sweet, sugary nectar oozed from thousands of brilliantly colored flowers. I imagined the air filled with monarch butterflies, flowers ladened with them as they fed on the nectar, colorful tropical birds joining them in flight, and the sounds of tropical animals in the background. Now I stood on the top of a mountain in Mexico, 3,000 meters above sea level. It was damp and cold—not tropical. Snow occasionally sifted through the branches of the northern-type spruce trees; there were no tropical palmlike trees covered with blossoms. And all was quiet; there were no sounds of tropical animals. No colorful, noisy birds flew about—only silent, drab little birds flitted through the spruce branches.

"Why," I asked myself, "would monarch butterflies travel thousands of miles to spend the winter months on the trees of this cold volcanic mountain when only a few miles further on lay warm tropical valleys?"

We stumbled along the narrow mountain path. Then, as if a curtain had been drawn revealing a theatrical scene, there before me were hundreds of lofty spruce trees, some covered from top to bottom with monarch butterflies. I gasped in awe. What a sight! I had at last found the overwintering site of my beautiful monarch butterflies.

The dense growth of spruce trees was festooned with giant clusters of

monarchs that resembled so many dead leaves, for at the time not one butterfly was stirring. They blocked out the light, except for a small gap that
permitted the rays of the sun to penetrate to the forest floor, which looked
like a gigantic Persian carpet because it, too, was covered with orange
monarch butterflies. The stillness of the air, the damp, somber darkness of
the forest, the blue-gray beams of light like ethereal pathways to the blue of
the heavens above all gave the impression of a cathedral where one should
converse in whispered tones for fear of breaking the enchantment. As we
gazed in silence at the scene before us, the sun, which had been hidden
behind a gray cloud, emerged and beamed a warm ray of golden light upon
one of the great clusters of dormant butterflies. As if on cue from a director,
the tree was transformed into a blaze of color as the butterflies spread their
bright orange wings to the warm sunlight. What a magnificent sight!

To reach the trees on which the butterflies were clustered, we had to
slither down the mountainside to an exposed area where trees had been cut
down. Partway down the sand and gravel slope, we arranged ourselves for
the task ahead of alar tagging as many of the monarch butterflies as possible
in the hope that some of them would eventually be recaptured as they
journeyed to their northern breeding grounds. Working on the side of a
mountain was by no means an easy task, since gravity kept dislodging us
from our precarious foothold. We draped ourselves over fallen logs and dug
our heels into the gravelly sand. We kept to the margin of the butterfly
forest and tagged migrants we found on bushes and on the ground—
together with those that left the clusters and, having flown for a short
distance, came to rest on us! We avoided venturing into the area where the
butterflies covered the forest floor, because we did not want to step on
them.

While I was sitting on the ground tagging one butterfly after another, a
cow poked its head through the lower branches of a nearby bush. She eyed
me with bovine curiosity, then proceeded to eat some of the monarch butterflies that were on the ground. I was at first alarmed at this peculiar action
on the part of a vegetarian cow; then I wondered if this grazing would have
an impact on the numbers of monarchs in this particular spot. Later, I read
in a natural history magazine that Mexican farmers deliberately led their cattle to such areas to feed on the butterflies. This statement I found to be
without foundation, as were many of the other statements in the article.
Farmers living in these mountain valleys simply let their cattle roam
through the forest to forage on the meager amounts of grasses and low
plants. They have neither the interest nor the inclination to lead cattle
anywhere. It is merely by chance that cattle come upon the butterflies and
sample a few.

Norah and I regularly scanned the butterflies clustered on the spruce trees using our binoculars in hopes of locating specimens bearing white alar labels attached to their wings during the fall migration. As we sat enjoying the quiet of the forest and the beauty of the trees covered with butterflies, a branch that measured about 4 centimeters in diameter at its base broke with the weight of a great cluster of monarchs and fell at my side, casting hundreds of fluttering butterflies on the ground. I leaned over to examine this fluttering mass, and my eyes rested on a white label attached to the wing of one of the fallen members. With a trembling hand—my excitement was very great indeed—I picked up the specimen. At first I was speechless, but after regaining my composure, I shouted to Norah, who sat some distance away busily tagging. I could not have been more excited if I had uncovered a buried treasure of fabulous value. Here I had undeniable proof that monarch butterflies overwintering on this mountain had come from distant breeding grounds.

On returning to our motel, we waited anxiously while Mitzi, the motel owner, placed a phone call from this remote village to Toronto, by way of Mexico City. This took a great deal of time and much discussion in Spanish to accomplish. Finally, after what seemed an eternity, the call was put through to my assistant at Scarborough campus of the University of Toronto. After examining my files, she was able to give me the name of the person who had tagged this particular specimen and the location where it was tagged: Chaska, Minnesota, on September 5, 1975. I had picked it out of the mass of fallen butterflies on a mountain in Mexico on January 18, 1976, almost five months later. It had flown a distance of 2,020 kilometers (1,225 miles) from where it had been captured, tagged, and released.

When the first locus was discovered, I concluded that all of the migrating monarch butterflies from east of the Rocky Mountains spent the winter in this particular area, since the clusters covered hundreds of trees. I wondered what would happen to the monarchs if the trees were removed. Then, during the summer months, as the result of lumbering operations, the trees were indeed cut down at this particular locus. The following winter my field assistant found that the overwintering monarch butterflies had simply chosen a new locus a few kilometers distant. Thus, for lumbering operations to completely destroy the monarch butterfly population, it would be necessary to remove all of the trees on all of the mountains of the Neovolcanic Plateau. This is highly unlikely, but if lumbering were carried out during the winter months at a time when the migrants were roosting, then the destruction would be considerable. As our studies in Mexico continued, I was delighted to learn that there were a number of separate butterfly groves on various mountains, further protecting against the possible annihilation of the species.

The first locus was located on a steep, nearly inaccessible mountainside. The new locus was much more accessible, and we were able to reach it by jeep over a bumpy, rock-strewn road. Although the place was also on the side of the mountain, the walk to the place where the migrants were clustered on trees was not too strenuous. However, this time, Norah and I made use of small cylinders of oxygen in order to ease the burden on our lungs.

As a result of alar tagging over 100,000 migrants in nine places on four separate mountains, I came to the following conclusions: Overwintering migrants located in the more western loci migrated in a northward direction (the release-recapture lines, when extended, led to breeding grounds in the Great Plains regions). Migrants from the more central loci migrated northeastward (their release-recapture lines, when extended, led to breeding grounds in areas east of the Mississippi drainage and the Great Lakes). Migrants from the more eastern loci traveled to the east-northeast and northeast. (Their release-recapture lines, when extended, indicated flights to breeding areas in the Atlantic regions.)

These alar-tagging records raise certain questions. Do the migrating monarch butterflies from a particular breeding area overwinter only in loci on particular mountains? Or, do they arrive at loci merely by chance, influenced by their particular flight pattern and by wind direction? When they leave Mexico, do the monarchs simply fan out over the eastern parts of the continent, moving in a general north to northeast direction? Or, do they return to the same breeding areas from which they departed during the fall migration?

One of the tagged fall migrants that had overwintered in the Mexican site and that had been recaptured during the spring migration gave us a clue. This particular specimen was tagged at Decorah, Iowa, during the fall migration and was recaptured at Richmond, Texas, during the spring migration. By extrapolating the release-recapture line of flight from Mexico to Richmond, it would appear that its final destination was the broad area of the Great Lakes around lakes Superior, Michigan, and Huron. This area encompasses the northwest section of Iowa where the specimen was tagged, indicating a return to the original breeding area.

Of course it is not reasonable to come to a conclusion based on one specimen that was released at one point and recaptured on its way back to approximately the same general area. However, for the present, I believe that migrant monarch butterflies do travel to specific loci on certain moun-

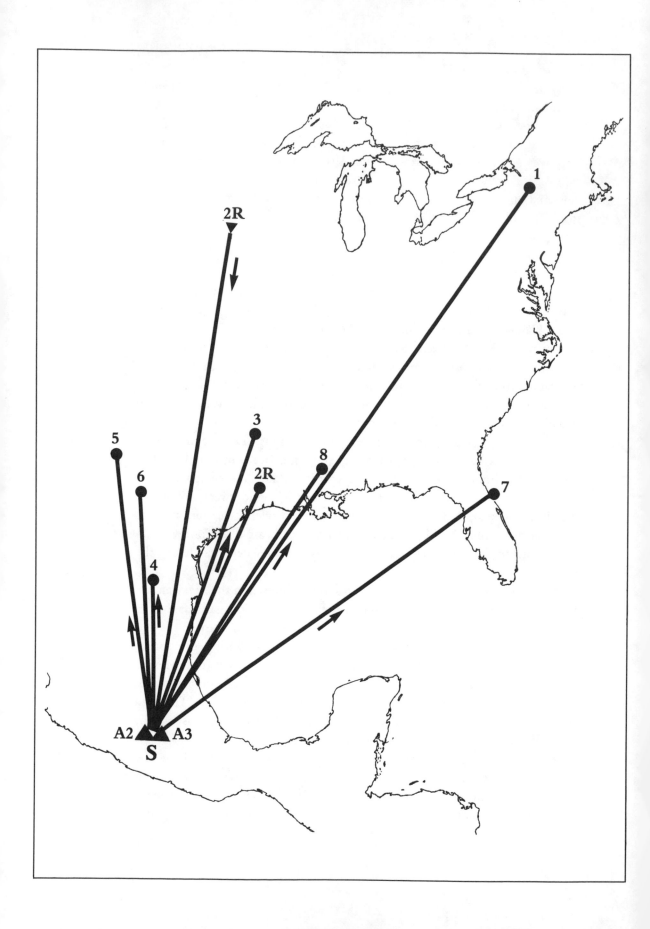

tains and that during the spring migration they return to their original breeding area—but not to the specific point from which they began their journey, such as my garden. Only further tagging of fall migrants will give conclusive data showing whether or not migrating monarchs return to their original breeding areas. I have also concluded that offspring from eggs deposited en route by the spring migrants follow the same migratory route and arrive in the same general areas as their migrating parent.

While I sat on the mountainside observing the actions of the overwintering butterflies and admiring the beauty of the forest festooned with colorful butterflies, I pondered the many questions related to this amazing phenomenon. The thought occurred to me that perhaps by clustering together on this chilly mountain the butterflies could raise their body temperature above that of the surrounding air (as discussed in part 5). On numerous occasions during fall migration I had noticed that when the weather was cold and migrants were dislodged from their clusters, they would crawl slowly over the ground vibrating their wings in a shivering motion. Perhaps the action of the wing muscles tends to increase body temperature, just as muscle activity increases body temperature in humans. Here in Mexico I observed this shivering motion by individuals that had fallen from the clusters and were crawling about on the ground or climbing up the stems of bushes and trunks of trees. Those that remained in the clusters did not exhibit this shivering motion. In most cases, they did not show any movement at all except when alarmed by a passing cloud. Then they would open their wings as if preparing for flight, and at times they would leave the cluster for short flights, depending on the temperature and the time of day.

To test the possibility of a temperature difference between the cluster and the surrounding air, maximum-minimum thermometers were placed in

Monarch butterflies alar-tagged at the overwintering site in the Neovolcanic Mountains of Mexico (S) exhibit the following spring migratory pattern: those from the more westerly loci (A2) move northward (4, 5, 6) to the Great Plains region; those from the central loci move north-northeast (2, 3) to the Great Lakes region; and those from the more easterly loci travel northeast (8, 1, 7) to the Atlantic region. An occasional migrant crosses the Gulf of Mexico (7) to Florida and then to the Atlantic coastal region. Specimen 2R was alar tagged at Decorah, Iowa (▼2R), flew to the overwintering site, and was recaptured at Richmond, Texas (●2R). From this study it would appear that the monarchs return to the regions where they spent their larval stages.

clusters that were well hidden among the branches so as to eliminate as much as possible any effect of direct incident radiation. Thermometers placed at the bases of the trees recorded the air temperature. Taking into account those situations where there was an indication of exposure to direct sunlight, I was unable to find any significant difference between the temperature in the clusters and that of the surrounding air during the twenty-four-hour period.

Not all of the butterflies spent the winter months in a somewhat comatose state. During the three-month period, we saw a few individuals leave the clusters, circle above the trees, and fly to a spring or wet ground to drink or to the few clusters of flowering plants adjacent to the area. Such departures, for the most part, occurred early in the clustering period or close to the time when the butterflies were to begin their long trip north.

From a casual observation, one might have concluded that the clusters massed on the branches of the trees were composed of butterflies arranged one on top of the other. A close examination, however, revealed that, in most cases, the monarchs were in close proximity to, but not usually on top of, one another. Only when individuals left a cluster and then attempted to rejoin it did pile-ups occur. For the most part, the migrants arranged themselves in an orderly manner, resembling a stack of playing cards placed on end. Each member of the cluster occupied a very small space, its wings held above its body, which was pressed closely against that of its neighbor. This was most evident when the clusters formed on the trunks of the trees. When an individual that had left a cluster attempted to regain its position, the members of the cluster opened and closed their wings in a snapping motion, as if to warn the new arrival: "Don't land on top of me!" (This is the same reaction I observed in overnight roosting clusters during the fall migrations.) It is also a sort of jockeying reaction that finally allows the new arrival to fit itself into the cluster.

The migrants begin to arrive in the Mexican mountains in November and continue to the end of December. Large numbers appear as early as the first week of November, the number decreasing throughout the month, and by the middle of December most of the migrants have completed the journey. They begin to leave the mountains in mid-February, a few small clusters remaining as late as mid-March in some loci. The differences in the times of arrival and departure may be explained as follows. The departure from breeding areas extends over a period of six to eight weeks, from mid-August to the end of October, with a few stragglers leaving as late as November—the latter most likely never reach the overwintering site, and may account for reports of monarch butterflies appearing in clusters on the islands off the coast of Georgia, along the Gulf coast, and in Florida. Those that leave the breeding grounds late may eventually reach areas in Texas as late as December and January. These individuals, having passed through the winter reproductive dormancy period, begin mating. The females deposit eggs that result in the larvae and pupae that have been reported in these places. For the most part, however, migrants that leave the breeding areas late arrive at the overwintering site later than those migrants that leave the breeding area earlier.

Various environmental factors affect departure from northern breeding grounds. Where temperatures are high, development will be more rapid than in areas of lower temperatures, and butterflies can leave the breeding grounds earlier. Heavy rains also impede development. And migrants from breeding areas in the more northern sections of the continent have further to travel than their more southern relatives and hence arrive later.

Over a period of many years, Norah and I have watched the fall migrations along the coast of the Gulf of Mexico. At first, there are only a few migrants, but the numbers gradually increase with the greatest concentrations occurring in mid-October, followed by a rapid decline. This pattern applies also to the arrival of the migrants at the various loci in the Mexican overwintering site.

The onset of reproductive dormancy in migrants of the fall migration and its cessation at the overwintering site is correlated with the summer and winter solstice. Approximately two months after the summer solstice, about August 21, the majority of migrating monarchs have entered a state of reproductive dormancy. This is not, of course, a fixed time. The dormancy state starts for many migrants as early as the first week of August, depending on the occurrence of cold temperatures. The cessation of reproductive dormancy occurs about two months after the winter solstice—as early as the first week of February for a few and as late as mid-March for others—low temperatures again playing an important part in hastening or delaying this physiological change.

Monarch migrants choose a particular place on a particular mountain because of two factors: topography and wind direction. The first arrivals approaching mountains of the Neovolcanic Plateau are attracted to the highest points of land lying across their migratory route; these places are covered in part by a dense growth of evergreen trees. A cursory flying about takes place as the migrants test out the wind direction, eventually choosing a locus on the leeward side that will give them protection from the mountain winds. Hence, clusters form on various sides of the mountain at each locus. These first arrivals, having located a protected area, form clusters on the branches of the trees. Those arriving later join the clusters.

As the clusters form, another factor appears to draw later arrivals, regardless of wind direction. Observations both at the overwintering sites and during the fall migration seem to indicate that some sort of signal, the nature of which is still unknown, draws the monarch butterflies together to form the larger clusters. Apparently neither sight nor odor (pheromone) is the factor involved.

I had considered the possibility that the migrants were particular about the kind of tree on which they formed their clusters. However, clusters were found on five different species of pine, one species of spruce (*Abies religiosa,* recorded as *Oyamel mexicano* in one publication; *oyamel* is a native term and not a scientific generic name), and one species of cypress *(Taxodium macronotum).*

When a change in wind direction occurs, the clusters, having been established on the leeward side of the mountain, are now exposed to the wind. Mountain winds can reach almost gale proportions with the passage of a frontal depression. The upper portions of the trees are whipped about, and clusters formed near the tops of the trees are shaken loose from the branches. The butterflies, unable to fly at low temperatures, fall to the ground. The passage of cold fronts is often accompanied by heavy rain or wet snow, resulting in the destruction of the butterflies that are on the ground. I have seen the ground beneath the trees covered with a wet blanket of snow and thousands of dead butterflies lying on it. Such incidents usually take place in late December and early January, when polar weather outbreaks are most common.

The first large clusters form on trees near the tops of the mountains in early winter (December-January). During late January and February, the migrants tend to move down the mountainsides toward the valleys, forming smaller and more scattered clusters on the trees. Hundreds now leave the clusters to gather on the margins of small puddles or on marshy ground to drink, their colorful wings reflected in the calm surface of the water. Having obtained their fill of water (which undoubtedly is correlated with physiological changes taking place—the development of the reproductive organs and the utilization of stored fat), they return to the roosting trees to form small, scattered clusters or they begin their journey to their breeding grounds.

Over the past forty-odd years, I have noted that birds do not usually attack monarch butterflies that are flying or at rest (at which times they resemble so many dead leaves and hence do not evoke in the birds a feeding response). However, if the resting monarchs exhibit a quivering-wing motion, birds will on occasion attack them and devour the bodies after removing the wings. In the overwintering loci, where temperatures are often low, this quivering action is common, and birds passing through the area will attack the butterflies. This explains the presence of bodiless wings scattered over the forest floor in some places, especially during cold weather.

On one of my expeditions, a field assistant shot two small birds that were flitting about the clusters of monarch butterflies. I examined the intestinal contents of the birds and found the remains of monarchs in one of them. An ornithologist identified the bird as a species of flycatcher, *Myiarchus tyrannulus.* Since I found very few birds among the overwintering clusters, I concluded that the flycatcher was a migratory species, thus accounting for the presence of detached monarch wings being more abundant in the early part of the winter when such birds would be most abundant.

As the days went by and we continued our alar tagging and observations, we became aware of a gradual increase in the numbers of monarch butterflies that were leaving the roosting clusters and flying above the tops of the trees. When a passing cloud cast a shadow over the clusters, the roosting members would release their hold on the tree and, like a golden waterfall, flow down the branch before taking to wing. We referred to this action as "cascading."

As I watched the thousands of butterflies cruising about the treetops, silhouetted against the blue of the sky, I noticed that many of them were flying in circles, similar to the flight pattern I described earlier as prenuptial or social flight (part 4). By mid-February, mating had begun to take place. At first, only the occasional pair was seen copulating on the ground. By the end of February, there were many small clusters forming. In some cases the clusters were composed of one female and three or four males; in other cases, the clusters consisted only of males. I had noted this behavior many years previously when I received a shipment of live monarch butterflies in February from the overwintering site in California. These specimens were sent to me by a colleague so that I might investigate the functions of the alar gland. I put the butterflies in a large flight cage. Three days later I noticed the same frantic mating behavior in the cage that I now witnessed in Mexico.

When the migrant monarch butterflies leave their breeding grounds during the fall migration, the reproductive organs of the majority are undeveloped or in a state of dormancy. Within two months after the winter solstice, hormones liberated from the central nervous system stimulate the development of the reproductive organs and initiate the act of copulation. Watching the frenetic mating activity of the butterflies, I was led to the conclusion that perhaps following the dormancy period there was an excessive amount of hormone liberated compared to the amount released during the summer months on the breeding grounds. This might account for the frenzied behavior.

Norah and I stood on the crest of the mountain and watched the migrants flying in great numbers toward the northeast, heading back to their respective breeding areas in distant parts of North America. It was indeed an awe-inspiring sight, and we asked ourselves, Is it possible that one of the butterflies we are now observing will find its way to our garden in Toronto, Canada? What compelled these butterflies to travel hundreds of miles to this mountain? And what finally released them from this particular Mexican site to return northward, back to the breeding grounds?

THE CALIFORNIA SITE

The gathering of monarch butterflies on the pine and eucalyptus trees of California was a well-known phenomenon when I first started to study the migrations of the Eastern Population, and it eventually led to my discovery of the Mexican site. Many articles about this had been published, along with photographs showing the large clusters of monarch butterflies in California, and the spectacular sight attracted thousands of tourists from many parts of the United States and Canada. It became a source of income for hotels, motels, and merchants, particularly in Pacific Grove.

So important are the migrant monarch butterflies to the local economy that a day is set aside each fall to celebrate the arrival of these long-distance travelers. Motels are named "Butterfly Trees Lodge" and "Monarch Lodge." Replicas of monarch butterflies made of various substances are sold as brooches, pins, and decals, and mounted specimens are sold in local stores. School children put on a special display. Dressed in a variety of colorful costumes, some representing monarch butterflies, they parade through the streets of Pacific Grove. Refreshment booths are set up and special exhibits are displayed by school classes — all in honor of the butterflies that choose to spend the winter in Pacific Grove. Neither residents nor visitors are allowed to collect specimens or to disturb the clusters on the trees. Anyone found doing so is liable to a large fine. When Norah and I arrived at Pacific Grove, we had to call at the local police station to obtain a permit allowing us to carry out our investigations, and motel owners would not permit us to interfere with clusters located on their properties.

Norah and I arrived in the Monterey area in late December 1955 after a very bumpy, noisy flight in a plane that had little air pressure control—which resulted in damage to Norah's inner ear. It was a painful experience for Norah, and the effects lasted for many years thereafter. We immediately began alar tagging the migrants, but as I mentioned in part 5, we used alar tags that had a water-soluble glue backing. With the advent of rain and fog, all of the tags came loose from the butterflies' wings and fell to the ground beneath the roosting trees. The expedition was a complete failure.

In the years following our first visit to California I was able to locate nine separate overwintering loci extending from Muir Beach in the north to Ventura in the south. The number of butterflies at each of these loci varied from small clusters of less than fifty to masses of many thousands. The largest clusters occurred in the more northern loci, particularly in the areas of Santa Cruz and Pacific Grove. Recently, however, an associate who had worked with me in the northern loci reported that the clusters in areas near Ventura are far larger than those in the north; this was corroborated by another associate, who recorded very large clusters in the vicinity of Carlsbad. These two important records indicate that there are two large migrations, one in the north and one in the south, with smaller migrations between. This is correlated with the breeding areas in the valleys of the mountains, as shown in the map on plate 12. Most of the large clusters form on pine trees—those on the eucalyptus trees are more diffuse. The sicklelike claws of the butterfly are better adapted to clinging to pine needles than to the broad blades and rounded petioles of the eucalyptus leaves. However, as in the case of the Mexican sites, the position of the trees is an important factor in influencing their being chosen by the migrant butterflies.

The choice of an overwintering site depends on the height of the land and the presence of roosting trees; the position of clustering depends on wind direction, the migrants choosing the side away from the prevailing winds. In the Mexican site, the highest land is the Neovolcanic Plateau; in California, however, the situation is quite different. The migrants leave the breeding areas in the mountain valleys and fly southwestward until they are stopped by the Pacific Ocean. They then cluster on the largest trees present in a particular place. If the wind changes direction, as happens with the passage of a frontal depression, the clusters are exposed to the full force of the wind. Migrants that are dislodged and fall to the ground may become waterlogged and at times are exposed to freezing temperatures. Hundreds may die. On December 9, 1957, a total of 1,980 dead monarchs were collected from beneath roosting trees in Natural Bridges State Park, located near Santa Cruz, their deaths the result of a cold front that passed through. I have no reports of similar storm effects occurring in any of the nine loci south of the San Francisco Bay area. This, I believe, is due to the fact that temperatures there, even after the passage of a cold frontal depression, remain sufficiently high to permit flight, and the dislodged migrants can return to their roosting trees.

In some of the Mexican sites, the ground beneath the roosting trees is littered with monarch butterfly wings, the result of bird predation. In the northern loci of California, similar predation takes place, but I have no reports of predation south of the San Francisco Bay area. The reason for this absence of predation is probably the warm temperatures. Migrants, when exposed to low temperatures, will vibrate their wings, and it is this wing action that attracts the attention of insectivorous birds. (I will discuss the importance of this shivering motion when I deal with Batesian Mimicry in part 7.)

There seem to be two types of loci in California—one static, the other temporary. Loci where migrants do not remain throughout the winter months I refer to as "transient hibernal roosting loci"; these occur frequently in the northern areas such as San Jose. Loci where migrants remain in fairly constant numbers throughout the winter months, such as those in the Monterey area, I refer to as "static hibernal roosting loci." Considerable variation exists in the numbers of monarch butterflies present in each loci from the time of arrival during the fall migration to departure during the spring migration. In some loci, such as the Bay Area, the numbers reach a maximum in November, drop rapidly in December, and gradually diminish up to departure in late February or March. Elsewhere, the migrants remain through November and then completely disappear in January, as happens in the Natural Bridges locus.

Within a given area there is a certain amount of intermingling among the various clusters located on different roosting trees—tagged butterflies from one group of roosting trees have been recaptured in other, distant groups. In the more northern loci, free flight away from roosting trees is minimal; relatively few monarchs have been found feeding on the nectar of local flowers. Migrants in loci further south are more inclined to leave the clusters to feed on local flowers. This difference in the habits of northern and southern migrants may account for the difference in their average dry weight (the weight being lower in the southern migrants as compared to the northern), which in turn is related to the utilization of stored fat.

I once believed that when migrants left the northern loci they traveled to the more southern ones. To test this suggestion, 99,000 specimens were alar tagged over a period of five years. Of these tagged migrants not one was recaptured at any of the more southern loci. And, not one of these specimens was recaptured over long distances. From the short release-recapture data, it appears that the flight away from loci is to the northeast, the same direction as that taken by spring migrants at the end of the over-wintering period. Where do these migrants go after leaving a particular locus during the overwintering period? So far, I do not know. I suspect that they leave the ocean area and fly northeastward to the Sierra Madre Mountains, there to cluster and remain for the rest of the overwintering period. Then they journey to the valleys where milkweed can be found.

By mid-February, the overwintering migrants become more active. Many leave the clusters to fly above the roosting trees or to visit nearby beds of flowers. An occasional pair are seen copulating, and this activity increases in intensity towards the end of the month, with the same frenzy as that observed in Mexico. Flight direction away from the various loci is north-eastward (the same as that found at the Mexican site), the migrants eventually populating the mountain valleys.

SPRING MIGRATION

The direction of flight away from the overwintering sites is northeastward. Mating takes place at the overwintering sites and along part of the migratory routes, and males, for the most part, do not return to the more northern breeding areas.

While Norah and I were staying at the University of Texas at Kingsville, we conducted extensive field surveys dealing with the activities of the migrants that were returning from Mexico. We collected a number of males and females and saw that there was an obvious difference in their appearance. The wings of the males were badly faded and tattered, while those of the females were only slightly faded and not at all tattered. This physiological difference is correlated with mating and egg laying. After mating has taken place, either at the overwintering site or along the migratory route, the males lose body water, their wings become dry and brittle, and they die. The females continue on the northward migration, laying eggs along the route. When the complete complement of eggs has been deposited, the females also lose body water and their wings become dry and brittle.

We noted that the females flew close to the ground, searching for milkweed plants on which to deposit eggs, while the males flew about the tree blossoms. The flight of the females was rather leisurely; they paused to examine various plants, and when a milkweed was located they deposited eggs on it. No larvae and relatively few eggs were found during this period (April). This leisurely flight and oviposition observed in Texas is in marked contrast to that observed in the more northern reaches where flight is much more rapid, a type of flight I have termed "speed." Approaching a building that could be circumnavigated, the migrant females, without hesitation, flew over the building so as to continue on a direct line of flight to the northeast. This difference in flight activity in the southern and northern regions may be explained as follows. When the monarchs leave the over-wintering site, the females' reproductive organs are just beginning to develop and hence no eggs are deposited for the first part of the migration. As the ovaries develop and eggs begin to appear in the oviducts, oviposition begins, though relatively few eggs are ready to be deposited. As the females journey northward, the rate of development of the eggs increases, resulting in more rapid oviposition. The females fly more swiftly as they continue northward searching for milkweed plants. This results in the monarch butterfly population being spread over a wide area from south to north. Around Toronto, Ontario, monarch butterflies are often scarce during June and yet abundant in the regions north of Lake Superior, due to the rapid flight of the ovipositing females.

It has been suggested that the spring migrants travel northward but a short distance, deposit their eggs, and die. The resulting generation then proceeds northward, and so on. If such were the case, we would expect to find a large population of larvae in the southern parts of the continent in early spring and fresh, brightly colored butterflies in the central and northern parts of the continent in spring and early summer. This is not the case. Only a few larvae occur in southern localities, particularly southern Texas, in spring, and the adults found in central and northern localities in May and early June are obviously old and worn. Like those found in the overwintering sites in late winter, their wings are faded and slightly frayed. I have concluded that some, if not most, of the overwintering females return to the northern breeding grounds in spring and early summer; they are followed by their offspring in June and early July. Thus, in a particular area from the central to the more northern regions of the breeding grounds, one will find a mixture of tattered and faded migrants along with fresh, brightly colored, untattered ones, the first and second generations produced along the migratory route.

By mid-June females with tattered wings are seen fluttering feebly from one milkweed plant to another, endeavoring to deposit the last of their eggs before death concludes their remarkable journey across the continent. As I watch the early spring migrants visiting the milkweed plants in my yard, I find it difficult to believe that these seemingly frail travelers have journeyed to my garden all the way from Mexico.

PART 7

Range Extension

The monarch butterfly, an international traveler, has established colonies in many parts of the world. For over a hundred years, from 1849 to the present time, naturalists and biologists have recorded the presence of monarchs on islands of the South Pacific. This probably resulted from shipping trade between California (where large clusters of monarch butterflies form on trees during the fall and winter periods) and Hawaii, Tahiti, Samoa, New Zealand, and Australia. Once transported to these centers of trade from which other shipping activities took place, the monarchs soon spread to Fiji, the Solomons, Micronesia, Melanesia, Indonesia, and the Philippines. Small to comparatively large residential colonies were established on many of the islands where species of milkweed had been introduced or, in some cases, were indigenous.

Two factors in the life cycle of the monarch butterfly made possible its transference from North America across the thousands of miles of ocean. During fall migration, the monarch butterfly enters a reproductive dormancy period that lasts for several months and prolongs its active life span. Other species of butterflies also enter a dormancy period, termed a diapause, but, unlike the monarch, they become comatose and are not capable of active flight. Such species as the mourning cloak remain beneath forest or field litter to await the return of warm spring weather. The monarch butterflies overwintering along the coast of California at times are swept out over the ocean by strong offshore winds. They may alight on an ocean-going vessel and are thus carried to one of the distant islands. Overwintering monarch butterflies even form small clusters on the rigging of vessels lying in the harbors in San Francisco Bay, California.

Reports of monarch butterflies landing on ships after the ships leave port are not unusual. To investigate this possibility, one of my associates arranged to liberate at sea one hundred overwintering monarch butterflies that had been collected in California. This was done when the vessel was five hundred miles from the coast of California. The captain who liberated the butterflies reported that as a result of the strong winds, together with the speed of the vessel, none of the butterflies was able to land, although some attempted to do so. This experiment would indicate that monarch butterflies that have been blown out over the ocean are unable to attach themselves to ocean-going vessels and hence are not carried to distant lands in this manner. It is possible, however, that the butterflies might seek shelter from storms on vessels lying in port, there to remain throughout the voyage.

A second factor aiding in the dissemination of the monarch butterfly relates to the period of pupation, which may last for two or three weeks. Larvae search for suitable places on which to pupate, and often choose crates and boxes near the milkweed plants on which they are feeding, especially at railway depots. The boxes are transferred by rail to dockyards and placed on ships destined for the islands of the South Pacific.

On the map on page 175, I have recorded the years when monarch butterflies were first reported in the more easterly islands. Such reports occurred, for the most part, between the years 1840 and 1870, a period during which there was increased shipping trade between the islands and North America. The first published record does not mean, however, that the monarch butterflies were not present prior to such dates. The date given for the Marquesas, 1883, is no doubt a late recording, the actual date of arrival in this area being between 1840 and 1850.

If monarch butterflies were introduced into islands where species of milkweed were absent, then, of course, the butterflies would not survive. However, on a number of islands, species of milkweed, particularly *Asclepias currassavica,* had been introduced as a garden plant by missionaries in the early days of colonization. In addition, there are records of mattresses filled with milkweed down being taken to the islands, and the down stuffing would contain a few seeds. Milkweed soon spread to adjacent islands as a garden plant and as a result of windblown seeds, which may be carried for considerable distances by winds or by ships.

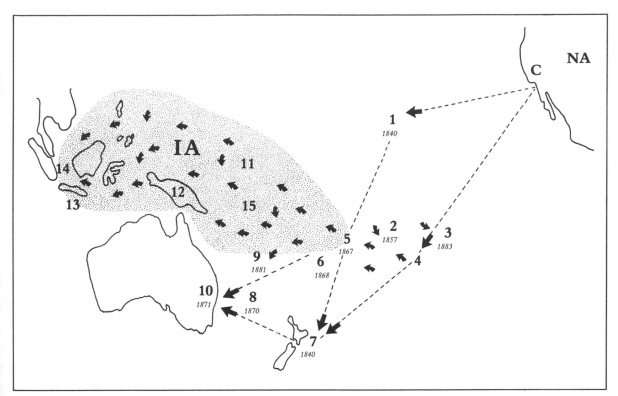

The dispersal of the monarch butterfly through the islands of the South Pacific was initiated by the shipping trade from California (C) to the islands of Hawaii (1), Tahiti (4), Samoa (5), New Zealand (7), and Australia (10). The presence of monarchs in the islands of Caroline (2), Marquesas (3), Tonga (6), Lord Howe (8), and New Caledonia (9) was recorded in the scientific literature between 1840 and 1870. The monarchs spread by ship and wind westward. Individuals were later reported on the islands of Ponape (11), Solomon (15), New Guinea (12), Java (13), and Sumatra (14). It is quite possible that eventually this intrepid traveler will be found around the globe between latitudes 45°N and 45°S.

The North American monarch butterfly has now spread across the islands of the South Pacific as far west as New Guinea and Java. I predict that eventually this species, which has been referred to as the "traveling butterfly" in popular literature, will spread across Eurasia and Africa. Colonies are now established off the coast of Africa in Madeira and the Canary Islands, thus completing a global dispersal between latitudes 45°N and 45°S.

An entomologist interested in the butterflies of New Zealand reported that the native Maoris had seen monarch butterflies, which they referred to as *kakahu,* prior to the advent of white men. The Maoris stated that the larvae fed on the pollen of a gourd that the natives cultivated, a most unusual and uncorroborated food habit. I am of the opinion that this is an erroneous identification. Several species of butterflies superficially resemble the monarch, hence wrong identifications easily can be made, especially by one not acquainted with the various species.

Three species of the genus *Asclepias* have been reported in New Zealand: *curassavica, semilunata,* and *tuberosa.* Larvae have also been reported feeding on three species of *Gomphocarpus,* a close relative of the genus *Asclepias: arborescens, physocarpus,* and *fruticosus. A. fruticosus* is referred to as the "swan plant" because its seed pod resembles a swan; it is grown in many gardens, often for the expressed purpose of attracting monarch butterflies.

The populations of monarch butterflies on the various islands are comparatively small due, for the most part, to a lack of sufficient milkweed plants. In addition, the monarchs are preyed upon by a number of species of birds during the overwintering period; their wings are found on the ground beneath the roosting clusters, as I described for the Mexican site. They also suffer from attacks by virus and bacteria and fall prey to many species of insect parasites and predators. Since these populations are rather small to begin with, such diseases and predators have a much more drastic effect than they would on the much larger populations in North America.

I have often been asked if the monarchs in the South Pacific migrate. Prior to carrying out field investigations on the flight habits of the monarchs in New Zealand and Australia, I thought that a migration pattern might have been established that, being in the Southern Hemisphere, would be the mirror image of the pattern in North America. To obtain data that would support or negate this idea, I established an alar-tagging program on North Island and South Island, New Zealand. Dr. Wise of the Auckland Institute and Museum carried out an excellent research program and published the results (see the references). Over a period of five years, thousands of monarch butterflies were tagged and released, and many were recaptured.

The data obtained indicated that, where temperatures fall below 10°C (50°F), there occurred adults in the reproductive dormancy phase. These individuals formed clusters in overwintering loci near the breeding areas. Individuals tagged and recaptured showed longevity in excess of eight months from fall tagging to spring recapture (which in the Southern Hemisphere means between April and October), a condition the same as that occurring in North America. However, there was no indication of a unilateral migratory pattern. I believe that, at the conclusion of the overwintering period, the individuals of the clusters simply disperse over the adjacent breeding grounds. Unfortunately, none of the specimens tagged on the overwintering loci were recaptured. They apparently dispersed to areas of sparse human habitation. (A similar situation occurred in California where the monarchs left the overwintering loci never to be recaptured.)

In those areas of Australia and New Zealand where temperatures remained above 10°C throughout the year, monarch butterflies in all stages of development were found. These constituted "resident populations." Such populations occur on other islands, too, according to my colleagues and associates.

Up to now, I have received no reports of overwintering clusters in these areas except from certain parts of Australia and New Zealand. I doubt if such clusters occur because the continuous high temperatures on the islands throughout the year prevent the larvae from entering reproductive dormancy.

In North America, the original home of the monarch butterfly, an annual remigration pattern was established that I believe is related to the earth's magnetic lines of force (this idea was brought to my attention by the late Dr. Williams). If such is the case, then monarch butterflies transferred to the Southern Hemisphere, where such lines of force are different, would not have an annual remigration. Dispersal rather than migration from an overwintering site would take place. A possible experiment occurs to me: If one were to transfer overwintering monarch butterflies from Australia or New Zealand to Mexico, would they fly northeast, following the same pattern as the monarchs that overwintered in Mexico?

PART 8

Predators, Parasites, and Diseases

Like all species of animals, the monarch butterfly has its quota of predators, diseases, and parasites. It is most disappointing for students of primary and secondary schools to find a large fly or a bee in the rearing cage or jar instead of a monarch butterfly larva or pupa. What is still most alarming is to witness a larva or pupa turning black and exuding a foul-smelling, inky fluid. However, as a result of such apparent unfortunate occurrences, students learn a great deal about other groups of insects and their lives. The large fly is a tachinid, a member of the order Diptera to which the common housefly belongs; the bee belongs to the order Hymenoptera, which includes parasitic wasps, bumblebees, and the honeybee. The students also witness, at first hand, nature's methods of controlling population growth. When an insect species becomes overabundant, parasites and disease reduce the numbers in a particular area. This introduces students to the discipline of biological control of insect populations. In place of chemical control that is both harmful to the environment and indiscriminately kills beneficial insects, man uses parasites and disease to control agricultural pests. By rearing thousands of parasitic insects in the laboratory and liberating them in areas infested with a particular agricultural pest, the population of the undesirable insect is greatly reduced and, in some instances, completely eradicated. Parasitic fungi, bacteria, and viruses are also used as agents in biological control.

PREDATORS

Most of the monarch predators are species of spiders and other insects. Adult monarchs are often caught in the large orb webs of spiders, particularly the very large species, such as the black and orange garden spider that constructs a large web of exceedingly strong silk that is capable of holding large insects. On a number of occasions I have found larvae wrapped like an Egyptian mummy in spider silk, caught in a web of the garden spider that was constructed in a cluster of milkweed plants. Adults, too, are frequently trapped as they fly among the flowers in search of nectar.

The praying mantis will seize and devour both adults and larvae. I remember watching a praying mantis poised on the yellow flower of a goldenrod plant, awaiting the arrival of a meal. As I watched, a monarch butterfly landed on the flower and began feeding. The praying mantis swayed gently back and forth, as if measuring the distance to the unwary butterfly. Then, with amazing speed, its front legs shot forth and impaled its fluttering victim. I was tempted at first to grasp the butterfly and release it from its captor, but having read so much about the idea that monarch butterflies were distasteful, I continued to watch as the praying mantis snipped off the wings and casually gnawed away at the body, discarding the legs and head. Having completed the meal, the mantis proceeded to clean its mouth parts. One could imagine that it was saying to itself, "My that was a tasty meal!"

On another occasion I watched a white-faced hornet attack a monarch larva that was crawling up the side of a building. The hornet carried it off to feed to its young housed in a nearby paper nest.

Some ant species will, on occasion, attack larvae that have fallen to the ground, particularly large ants of the genus *Formica* that build mounds in pastures. The smaller ants that are seen crawling over milkweed plants in search of aphids (from which they derive a sugary substance that is the waste product of aphid digestion) do not, as far as I have observed, attack monarch butterfly larvae.

I have received a number of reports from my associates of larvae being eaten by frogs, toads, lizards, and snakes. Such observations are no doubt valid, although I have never witnessed such predation myself. One could make an interesting series of experiments concerning the possibility of amphibians and reptiles feeding on monarch larvae—to my knowledge such a study has not been carried out.

Shrews have been reported to feed on the larvae, and mice have been observed devouring pupae. Shrews apparently attack the adults that have emerged from pupae formed close to the ground. Often the butterflies escape but bear the evidence of such attacks—shredded wings and pale coloration along the torn margins, caused by the escaping body fluid.

PARASITES

Four species of flies belonging to the family *Tachinidae* have been reported to be parasites of the monarch butterfly. These tachinid flies resemble large, spiny houseflies. They deposit their eggs on the surface of the body of the larva. The eggs are oval in shape, creamy white in color, and approximately 4 millimeters in length. When a tachinid larva, called a maggot, hatches from the underside of the egg next to the monarch larva's skin, it bores a hole and enters the interior of the larva's body. There it feeds on the internal tissues and body fluid, but at this stage of its development it does not destroy nerve tissue. The larva of the monarch butterfly continues to eat and to pass through its various instars, often entering the pupa stage. When the tachinid larva reaches its full development, it bores a hole through the monarch larva's skin and drops to the ground, often producing a long string of a mucuslike substance to aid in its descent. It then burrows into the ground, there to enter its next stage of development, the puparium. The puparium consists of the pupa surrounded by the skin of the last maggot instar. It is brown in color, oval in shape, approximately 7 millimeters in length, and somewhat resembles a small nut.

Before burrowing through the monarch larva skin, the maggot destroys parts of the nerve tissue, causing monarch larva to form a mat of silk and to remain quiescent on it. This allows the parasite maggot to escape more easily, since the monarch larva can no longer crawl about. Why the larva spins a mat of silk and remains quiescent is not known. However, I am of the opinion that when the tachinid maggot destroys some of the nerve tissue, this brings about the response in the monarch butterfly larva that it must shed its skin, as if passing into another instar.

Ichneumon flies (parasitic wasps) are another common parasite of many species of butterfly larvae. However, I have collected only one species of ichneumon fly from one group of caged monarch butterflies. Members of this family of parasites have the following characteristics. The abdomen, which is usually yellowish brown in color, is laterally flattened, and the legs are long and slender. A long threadlike structure protrudes from the end of the abdomen; this is the ovipositor by means of which the ichneumon wasp makes a hole in the monarch larva's skin and deposits an egg within the body cavity. The complete life cycle of this parasite, from egg to adult, is passed within the host's body. The winged adult wasp gains access to the outside by chewing a hole in the larva's skin.

Occasionally you may find a number of minute, stout-bodied, winged, beelike parasites issuing from a pupa or, less frequently, from the larva. These parasites belong to the family *Braconidae* and are referred to as braconids. The female braconid lays only one egg within the body of a monarch larva, but from this egg as many as thirty-two adult braconids will develop. Since all thirty-two have arisen from one egg, they are all of the same sex, either male or female.

In my many years of collecting larvae and pupae in the field, I have never encountered more than a 5 percent parasitism. Hence, I conclude that parasites are not an important factor affecting the size of monarch butterfly populations, as is the case in many other species of insects. This small degree of parasitism may be related to the migratory habits of monarch butterflies. Since they do not remain in one area throughout the year, they do not experience the buildup of populations of parasites that takes place among other species of butterflies and of moths and accounts for rapid changes in population densities.

DISEASES

Of all the disease organisms known to attack at various stages in the development of the monarch butterfly, the most virulent is the polyhedrosis virus. Most affected are the larval and pupal stages. An infected larva, in the early stages of the development of the disease, becomes noticeably lethargic. The bright yellow and white stripes begin to fade and are replaced by a light brown pigment. Gradually the entire larva becomes dark brown and finally black. If, in this final stage, you attempt to pick the larva up, its skin ruptures, emitting a foul-smelling, black fluid. Similarly, an infected pupa turns from light green to straw color and then black. It also emits the characteristic inky fluid when handled.

When I first encountered this disease among my laboratory populations, I assumed that it was caused by a bacterium. Years later, when I was on the staff of the university, I attempted to culture the organism, but without success. It became obvious that it was a virus. After consulting the voluminous literature dealing with insect pathology and doing some investigating with the aid of an electron microscope, I was able to identify the virus as a member of the polyhedrosis group. Later, one of my colleagues was able to identify it as a nuclear polyhedrosis virus. As I mentioned in part 4, this virus is responsible for marked fluctuations in population density of the monarch butterfly in North America. These fluctuations are correlated with a balance between the occurrence of virus mutants and the immune response in a particular population.

Occasionally, a larva becomes rather sluggish and eventually immobile. The body turns pale in color and the skin begins to wrinkle. Finally, all that is left of the larva is a dried, wrinkled skin. One of my colleagues (a microbiologist) and I were able to culture the organisms involved. As a result of our investigations, a scientific paper was published in which fifty-two strains of bacteria were described. Five of these were found to be pathogens. I had witnessed on numerous occasions the deposition of a bright red fluid just prior to defecation by the larva. Whether or not this fluid contained bacterial spores was not investigated.

There are a number of entomophagous fungi (fungi that attack only insects), but infections are rare in the monarch butterfly. I have experienced the presence of what appeared to be a fungus disease on only one occasion. One of my rearing cages had been neglected for a few days, owing to circumstances that required my attention elsewhere. The cage was overcrowded; the milkweed was in a state of decay; the larval droppings were matted together and covered with mold. Two larvae, clinging to the sides of the cage, exhibited a white mat of fungous hyphae surrounding their dead bodies. It is quite possible, however, that the fungus was not a pathogen but rather one living on the decaying bodies of the larvae. In all my many years of collecting monarch larvae and pupae in nature I have never encountered a specimen showing evidence of a fungus disease.

This large topographic map hung on my office wall for many years. When a recaptured monarch was reported, the place of tagging and the place of recapture were indicated on the map and a black thread was used to join the two points. The line of flight thus indicated is referred to as a "release-recapture line." As a result of constructing such lines for many recaptured tagged monarchs over a number of years, I was able to follow the fall migrations of the monarchs and to discover their overwintering locus in Mexico. Although most of the migrants moved in a southwestward direction, some moved southeastward to the Atlantic coast. This I refer to as an "aberrant migration route," which is discussed in more detail in the text.

PLATE 9

To alar tag a migrant monarch butterfly, remove the scales from a section of the upper and lower surfaces of the front wing as close to the base of the wing as possible. The tag, which has a pressure adhesive backing, is folded in half, placed over the leading edge of the wing, and pressed firmly against the wing membrane from which the scales have been removed.

The Neovolcanic Plateau, or Cross Mountain Range, extends across Mexico between latitudes 19° and 20° from the Gulf of Mexico to the Pacific Ocean. Many small towns and villages as well as large cities nestle in the mountains and the lush valleys fed by clear mountain streams. Mountain heights range from 2,700 m to over 5,500 m. Monarch butterflies overwinter in various loci at heights of 2,700 m to 5,000 m.

PLATE 10

During the fall migration, migrants form clusters on the branches of trees located along the migratory routes. Unlike the dense clusters that form on the trees at overwintering sites, these temporary clusters are much smaller, they are scattered, and they contain varying numbers of butterflies, from as few as ten to as many as three hundred. The monarchs tend to choose trees located on a high spot of land.

At dawn, when the sun rises above the horizon, each migrant spreads its wings, exposing its thorax and abdomen, which are covered with a dense coat of black scales and hairs that absorb the warm rays.

PLATE 11

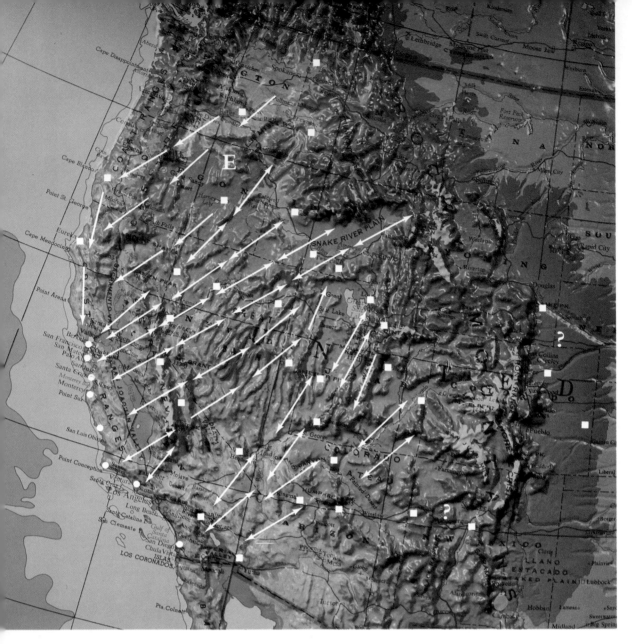

California is the overwintering site of the Western Population of monarchs. From field observations and recaptures of alar-tagged specimens in various areas (■) over a period of thirty years, the migratory routes to and from breeding grounds and overwintering loci (●) were charted (↔) . A general southwest-northeast pattern can be seen with slight deviations caused by intervening deserts, mountains, and valleys, particularly in the southwest. Occasional migrants in the northwest (E) reach the coast and move southward to the overwintering loci. The final destination of migrants from Wyoming, eastern Colorado, and New Mexico is unknown (?). The Sierra Madre mountains of Northern Mexico have been suggested.

PLATE 12

Monarchs overwinter on the pine and eucalyptus trees of California. Nine loci have been located from Muir Beach in the north to Ventura in the south. The number of monarchs in each locus varies from fewer than fifty to many thousands.

The arrival of the overwintering monarch butterflies on the Monterey Peninsula is so important to the local economy that a special day is set aside each fall to celebrate the event. Dressed in a variety of colorful costumes, some representing monarch butterflies, school children parade through the streets of Pacific Grove. Residents and visitors alike are not allowed to collect monarchs or to disturb the clusters.

PLATE 13

While sitting under a spruce tree alar tagging overwintering migrants, I heard a sharp cracking sound. The branch above me broke suddenly and thousands of monarchs fluttered to the ground. As I gazed at the mass of butterflies, I saw one bearing a white label — it was an alar-tagged monarch that had flown here from some distant breeding ground in the north.

The author and his wife, Norah, are surrounded by overwintering monarch butterflies as they place alar tags on the wings of the migrants. When such alar-tagged specimens are recaptured on their spring migration to various breeding grounds, their routes can be charted.

PLATE 14

Along the margins of the forest, the monarch butterflies swarm over bushes, vines, and tree stumps. Some creep along the ground seeking any upright support, including members of our field party. Here, field assistant Cathy Bruger poses beside a pillar of butterflies.

Contrary to the hypothesis of Batesian Mimicry, which suggests that butterflies are distasteful to birds, hundreds of wings and partly consumed bodies of monarchs litter the ground, attesting to predation by insectivorous birds.

PLATE 15

The tree branches, loaded with monarch butterflies, bend precariously toward the ground. I estimated there were thirty-five hundred butterflies on one small branch. Here, field assistant Cathy Bruger peers at me beneath a heavily laden branch.

The ground beneath the forest trees was carpeted with monarch butterflies. Members of our field party worked only on the margins of the forest where relatively few butterflies littered the ground. Otherwise, thousands of monarchs would have been crushed underfoot.

PLATE 16

Toward the end of the overwintering period, the roosting monarch butterflies grow restless. As if on cue, the clusters break up. The monarchs flow down the branches of the trees in a colorful cascade before taking wing and filling the air with brilliant orange. The sound of the fluttering of thousands of wings is like that of a distant waterfall.

PLATE 17

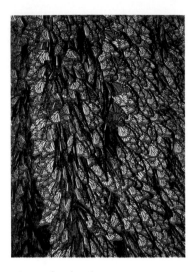

Not only do the overwintering monarch butterflies cling in large clusters to the branches of the mountain trees, but they also cover the trunks of the trees in such numbers as to completely cover the bark beneath.

What appear to be autumn leaves, golden in the setting sun, are thousands of overwintering monarch butterflies. The ground is carpeted with fluttering masses of the orange butterflies that have been dislodged from the trees by strong mountain winds. Mexican cattle, allowed to roam the mountainsides, pause to feed on a few butterflies while searching for green pastures.

PLATE 18

For many years I have collected monarch butterflies in the Toronto, Ontario, area from May to October. Monarchs collected in the early summer (shown in the first three rows) are faded and often have tattered wings. These are migrants that have traveled all the way from Mexico. In midsummer, brighter but still slightly faded specimens appear (fourth and fifth rows). These are the first generation resulting from eggs deposited by the migrants from Mexico along their path north. By late summer, only fresh, brightly colored monarchs are found (bottom row). These are the resident population, many of which will join in the fall migration south. Thus, throughout the summer there occurs a mixture of migrants from Mexico, generations produced on the path north, and one or two generations from the breeding area.

PLATE 19

1.

3.

2.

1. *Polyhedrosis, one of the most virulent and devastating diseases of the monarch butterfly, is caused by a virus. Afflicted larvae and pupae turn black; when ruptured, an inky, malodorous fluid is discharged. Occasionally, the virus is passed on to the adult and causes abdominal swelling (clubed abdomen). This disease is the principal cause of the fluctuations in numbers of monarchs from year to year.*

2. *More than fifty strains of bacteria have been identified in the monarch larva; of these, fifteen are considered to be pathogenic. Infected larvae become noticeably sluggish and shrunken; eventually only the skin remains. Rare in nature, infected larvae are most prevalent in populations reared in small jars or cages.*

3. *A number of beelike insects attack larvae and pupae. Of these, the small braconid bees are the most common. The female braconid deposits an egg inside the larva by means of her piercing ovipositor. From this single egg, a number of individuals are produced. They usually emerge from the pupa, but some species emerge during the larval stage. These are characterized by the formation of small, white cocoons attached to the skin of the infected larva.*

PLATE 20

a.

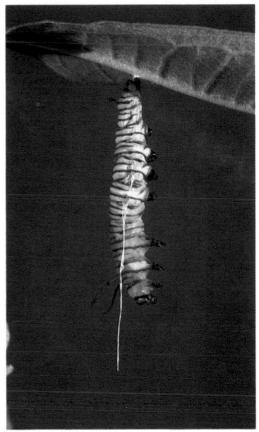

b.

c.

The most ubiquitous parasites of the monarch butterfly are the tachinid flies, the various species belonging to the family Tachinidae. Of these species, five are known to attack the larvae of the monarch. The adult fly resembles a large, hairy housefly (a). The female deposits her oval white eggs on the body of the larva. The maggots that hatch from the eggs burrow through the larval skin and feed on the internal tissues. When mature, the maggots drop to the ground, at times suspended from a string of tissue extending from the exit hole in the larval skin (b). After burrowing into the ground, each maggot forms a puparium—a pupa within the maggot skin. The puparium is oval in shape and light or dark brown in color (c). Such puparia may sometimes be found on the bottom of rearing jars or cages.

PLATE 21

The New World relatives (Danaus) *of the monarch butterfly from southern North America and South America. Top row: left,* D. gilippus gilippus *(♂♀); right,* D. gilippus gilippus *(♂♀). Second row: left,* D. gilippus cleothera *(♂♀); right,* D. gilippus nivosus *(♂♀). Third row: left,* D. gilippus berenice *(♂♀); right,* D. erisimus erisimus *(♂♀). Fourth row: left,* D. erisimus tethys *(♂♀); right,* D. erisimus montezuma *(♂♀). Fifth row: left,* D. cleophile *(♂♀); right,* D. jamaicensis *(♂♀). Sixth row: left,* D. erisimus erginus *(♂); right,* D. erippus *(♂♀).

PLATE 22

Color variations of male monarch butterflies from various parts of South America, Central America, and islands of the South Atlantic showing hybridization between megalippe *and* plexippus. *Top row: (left to right) Panama Canal; Dominican Republic; Dominican Republic. Second row: Virgin Islands; Nassau (Bahamas); Venezuela. Third row: Colombia. Fourth row: Puerto Rico; northern Brazil; Peru. Fifth row: Ontario, Canada.*

Following page: In order to test whether or not the diversity of wing color I found among specimens of monarch butterflies occurring on various islands of the South Atlantic, in South America, and in Central America was due to hybridization, I crossed male plexippus *with female* megalippe, *and female* plexippus *with male* megalippe. *The resulting adult offspring showed the same degree of color diversity as that found in nature. Some of the hybrids resembled the parents, but the majority exhibited wide variations.*

PLATE 23

PLATE 24

PART 9

Monarch-Viceroy Mimicry
and Bird Predation
—Fact or Fiction?

Much has been written about the superficial resemblance of the monarch to the viceroy butterfly. It has been suggested that the viceroy gains protection from bird predation because it resembles the monarch. Is this hypothesis supported by field observations?

The hypothesis known as Batesian Mimicry was named after its proposer, H. W. Bates, and it grew out of his observations while collecting butterflies in the Amazon regions of Brazil in 1862. He suggested that where a butterfly palatable to birds resembled one that was unpalatable, the tasty one was thus protected because it resembled the bitter one. Bates apparently never saw birds attempting to feed on butterflies, or at least he does not mention seeing them do so in his observations, nor did he carry out any experiments on the subject. The hypothesis assumes that birds attempt to eat the bitter variety and, one supposes, after a few such attempts, decide not to add this morsel to their future menu.

Meanwhile, flying among these unpalatable butterflies are other lookalike butterflies that probably are tasty to birds. We must assume, of course, that the birds take a few nibbles of these tastier varieties as well as the bitter ones. The birds thus become confused about which ones are bitter and which are sweet, since the two look alike. The theory behind Batesian Mimicry is that birds decide not to eat any of the butterflies, thus protecting the good-tasting ones. Carrying this proposal further, one must also assume that the thousands of fledgling birds that appear year after year must go through the process of tasting the butterflies and learning which ones are bitter and which sweet, much to the detriment of both types of butterflies.

Batesian Mimicry was proposed at the time that Darwinism was sweeping the scientific world. Darwin's theory of the origin of species, now recognized as a law, was based on numerous observations in nature. From observation ideas are formulated that may or may not stand the test of more observations and, in some cases, of experimentation. Irving Stone in his delightful book *The Origin,* published by Doubleday in 1980, relates the following conversation between Wallace and Darwin:

> "My difficulty [states Darwin] is, why are caterpillars sometimes beautifully and artistically coloured, seeing that so many species are coloured to escape danger. . . ?"
>
> "May I suggest [replies Wallace] that conspicuous caterpillars and other insects which are distasteful to birds are thereby easily recognized and avoided."
>
> Charles beamed with joy.
>
> "Wallace [replies Darwin], I never heard anything more ingenious."

From an idea may develop fact or fiction. But all too often one may be so imbued with an idea that one clings to it tenaciously, even though observations in nature indicate that it may be fiction.

Entomologists and others impressed with the idea of Batesian Mimicry began comparing butterflies and noting variations within a species or genus that would give protection and thus favor the perpetuation of certain colors—a dark form being more protected than a light one, or vice versa. When two species belonging to two different families appear to resemble each other (to the human eye, not to a bird's eye), such as the viceroy and the monarch butterflies, the researcher then turned his attention to the role played by birds in deciding which butterfly was bitter and which sweet. The idea so impressed some members of the scientific community and the lay public that literally hundreds of articles appeared in the scientific literature, and the idea spread to school textbooks and popular magazines. But in all of this there was a complete lack of Darwinian-type observation. The conclusion was simply that since the two species look alike, there must be some protection offered to one of them—as one researcher put it, "They are members of the look-alike club."

This hypothesis, as it applies to birds as predators of the viceroy and monarch butterflies, has puzzled me for many years. As a young lad involved in collecting insects as a hobby, I read a great deal about the ways that insects are protected from their predators by resembling various objects in nature. Some insects look like the twigs of bushes, some look like the foliage of trees, and others resemble the bark of trees. Such protective resemblances are indeed real and can be classified as "protective resemblance." I also read about the viceroy butterfly being protected from being eaten by birds because it resembled the monarch butterfly, which was considered to be bitter tasting to birds. I accepted this since it was quite obvious that the viceroy did indeed superficially look like the monarch butterfly. But as the years passed, and I became involved in studies of the monarch butterfly, I became aware of the fact that birds did *not* attempt to eat monarch butterflies. How could birds learn that monarch butterflies are bitter to taste if they did not taste them? I wondered.

Although Norah and I have watched thousands of monarch butterflies in nature, and have seen them being attacked by a bird only under unusual circumstances, we have, on numerous occasions, witnessed monarch butterflies chasing birds! Chipping sparrows and song sparrows that happen to fly into the territory of a male monarch butterfly are sometimes pursued by the butterfly—is this a case of Batesian Mimicry in reverse?

Yet, Batesian mimicry, as it applies to birds as predators of butterflies, continues to be an appealing concept. To demonstrate such blind faith, I recount the following incident. While I was arranging my collection of monarch and viceroy butterflies in my study, an entomologist of our zoology department happened to drop in.

"Do you believe in this idea of Batesian Mimicry as it applies to birds as predators bringing about the resemblance between the viceroy and the monarch butterfly?" I asked.

"Of course," came his quick response.

I removed a tray containing a collection of viceroy butterflies and placed it beside the tray of monarchs.

"Can you see any differences between these two butterflies?" I asked.

"They are quite different—anyone can see that," he replied.

"Don't you think a bird, with its amazing eyesight, could tell the difference?" I asked.

I outlined my field observations, and he agreed that he had never seen a bird attempt to eat a butterfly (he was an avid student of nature and had collected insects ever since boyhood).

"I agree with what you say," he responded, "but I have grown up with the idea that the monarch butterfly is distasteful to birds and thereby the viceroy is protected; I find it difficult to overlook such a close resemblance."

This appears to be the consensus of biologists and laymen.

The concept of Batesian Mimicry as it applies to the monarch butterfly has become accepted to such an extent that references are made in the literature to the idea that the monarch butterfly is "bitter to taste"—the reference to birds is omitted. This means that it tastes bitter to man, thus lending support to its tasting bitter to birds. In regard to this, I present the following experience.

At a meeting of the American Association for the Advancement of Science, the chairman of a group that I attended stated, in his introductory remarks about a paper to be read dealing with Batesian Mimicry, that a friend of his had actually tasted a monarch butterfly and had found it very bitter, the statement being made with much grimacing. I found this interesting since Norah and I had tasted monarch butterflies as an experiment and, much to our surprise, we found that they were not bitter. I enlisted some of my colleagues and students to make the test. All agreed that the monarch butterfly did not taste bitter, as far as human taste buds were concerned.

The researcher presenting the paper suggested that the reason why the monarch butterfly was distasteful was because the larvae fed on the leaves of the milkweed plant, which contained a bitter substance that was passed on to the butterfly, thus introducing the idea that milkweed leaves are bitter to the taste. But what animal finds milkweed leaves bitter to the taste? It must be man. This also bothered me because I had tasted the tender leaves of young milkweed plants of *A. syriaca* and found them to be far from bitter, though the leaves of the old plants, like old lettuce leaves, are somewhat bitter. (I pointed out in part 1 that the pods of the milkweed plant are a delicacy.)

One researcher, experimenting with caged Florida brush jays, came to the conclusion that, after a few attempts at eating the monarch butterflies, the birds rejected the viceroy butterfly "on sight." But viceroy and monarch butterflies were introduced into the cage in a stunned condition; they were not free flying, and therefore this was not a test that would show how the jays would react to the butterflies in nature.

Later, the same researcher, now working with blue jays, found that *some* of the monarch butterflies were not "unpalatable" to his experimental birds.

The researcher concluded that perhaps there was a difference in various species of milkweed as to their possession of a substance that gave a bad taste to the monarchs. To overcome this experimental aberration, the researcher, still insisting that birds were the predators responsible for the mimicry hypothesis, invented the term "automimicry" to describe a situation where the monarch butterflies mimic each other. The birds must learn by tasting different monarchs to distinguish not only unpalatable monarch butterflies from viceroys but also unpalatable monarch butterflies from tasty monarchs.

Other experiments have been carried out in which ground-up monarch butterflies were placed in medicinal capsules and forced down the throats of blue jays. Of course, the capsules were regurgitated—not because they contained monarch butterflies but because force-feeding a jay will cause such a reaction. So the experiment simply showed that blue jays do not like to have capsules thrust down their throats.

I was rather intrigued by one article, which appeared in a popular magazine, that showed a photograph, in beautiful color, of a blue jay holding a monarch butterfly in its beak, followed by a second photograph, presumably the same bird, regurgitating a substance that was supposed to be the monarch butterfly. However, on close inspection I found that the exudate issuing from the bird's beak contained no trace of any particulate matter; obviously the bird was not regurgitating the body of a monarch butterfly. Possibly it was the contents of a capsule.

I find it most difficult to understand why Florida brush jays and blue jays—neither of which is strictly insectivorous—were chosen as experimental birds in view of the fact that both birds are known to fill their crops with food, especially seeds, to be regurgitated later in order to remove the husks and thus obtain kernels, a fact known to all who have maintained bird-feeding stations. One would expect, therefore, that such birds would more readily regurgitate any foreign object. The research would have been much more meaningful if the researcher had chosen truly insectivorous birds, for example flycatchers (Tyrannidae), or species of amphibians and reptiles, rather than birds. Bear in mind that species of birds that habitually feed upon insects are mostly small, belonging to the families of sparrows and warblers. These birds are too small to attempt to capture a viceroy or a monarch butterfly. If there is anything in the hypothesis of birds preying on butterflies, it would be concerned with insectivorous birds, not blue jays and brush jays.

In recent years, researchers have found substances known as "cardenolides" (cardiac glycosides) in milkweed plants. These substances are related to digitalis, which is used to treat heart disease and is derived from the foxglove plant, *Digitalis pupurea.* In the field of medicine, these cardenolides are referred to as "cardiotonic glycosides," with special reference to digitoxin and digoxin. Because of this relationship to digitalis, some researchers and writers of popular articles have erroneously referred to cardenolides as "heart poisons," the word *poison* being used in order to emphasize its effect on birds that attempt to eat the monarch butterfly. In humans, such substances increase the force of muscular contractions in the heart. The conclusion is that such substances are responsible for monarch butterflies being unpalatable to birds. One wonders whether a bird might die of a heart attack after eating a monarch butterfly containing the so-called heart poison. I do not intend this statement to be facetious in view of the fact that one researcher is studying the effect of these substances on the heart of the pigeon, but I fail to understand why one would conclude that cardenolides are necessarily unpalatable substances. Perhaps there are other unpalatable substances in a monarch butterfly's body that might deter insectivorous animals, but not necessarily only birds.

Researchers studying other species of *Danaus,* the genus to which the monarch butterfly belongs, observed that they "suck withered leaves, stems, and seed-pods of certain species of Asteraceae." Substances known as "pyrrolizidine alkaloids" have been extracted from these plants and are considered by some to be the chemical substances that, transferred to the monarch butterflies, cause them to be unpalatable to birds. On summing up this research, one author states: "Such investigations should not only consider cardiac glycosides but also other compounds, since it is most probable that danaids are protected by a whole set of toxins, plant-derived substances like cardiac glycosides and pyrrolizidine alkaloids, and others." This researcher, along with all the others, fails to observe the reactions of birds to monarch butterflies in nature, thus making interpretation of the research results pure speculation.

The scientific literature abounds with attempts to justify the mimicry theory as it applies to birds feeding on butterflies. These papers contain an impressive array of tables, charts, and graphs resulting from experiments carried out in the crowded confines of cages in a laboratory. By the use of abstruse terminology the research assumes an aura of highly qualified investigations, but, when carefully analyzed, contains nothing of real value and no meaningful conclusions. Whether or not a milkweed plant contains heart poisons or any other chemical substances that are ingested by the larvae and passed on to the adults is irrelevant. The question is, Do birds attempt to eat viceroy and monarch butterflies in nature?

Having read research papers dealing with various experiments carried out by investigators using caged birds and monarch butterflies in the laboratory, I suggested to one of my graduate students that he might test out the results presented by other researchers. The student carried out the following experiment. A large flight cage was erected in the greenhouse. Fifty fledgling starlings, captured by a mink rancher in one of his traps, were introduced into the cage. The fledglings were obtained before monarch butterflies had arrived in the area, so none had tasted a monarch. After the birds became acclimatized to their caged conditions, live, active monarch butterflies (not stunned ones) were released into the cage, and recently killed monarchs were placed on the floor of the cage. (The larvae of the butterflies used in this experiment had been reared on four different species of milkweed. One of these species was reputed to contain cardenolides.)

The live butterflies fluttered against the sides of the cage. Attracted by the movement, the starlings immediately left their perches, grasped the fluttering insects, returned to their roosts, and proceeded to remove the wings and devour the bodies of the butterflies. The freshly killed butterflies lying on the bottom of the cage were not attacked. This whole experiment was repeated a number of times with the same results.

Duplicating the experiments of another researcher, the student made pellets of ground-up monarch butterflies, including the wings, and offered this fare to the starlings. The pellets were readily consumed and were not regurgitated. The student then mixed ground-up butterflies with some grain and, with this as the only food, produced a flock of healthy birds.

The experiments indicate that if birds were attracted to monarch butterflies as part of their diet, they would find them quite nutritious. The key word is *attracted*. Birds are attracted by the fluttering motion of the monarchs' wings. This is followed by attack and consumption.

When Norah and I were involved in alar tagging fall migrants in northern Florida in mid-December, we came across a cluster of monarch butterflies roosting on a group of pine trees at Alligator Point on the coast of the Gulf of Mexico. A cold frontal depression had passed through the area, lowering the temperature to near freezing. By shaking the limbs of the trees, we could dislodge the roosting migrants, which then fell to the ground like so many dead leaves. We gathered the fallen monarchs and placed them in paper bags, which were put in the shade beneath the trees to prevent the sun from warming the butterflies and thus causing them to flutter against the sides of the bags. The tagged monarchs were placed on a patch of sand where they were warmed by the rays of the sun. As they recovered from their stupor caused by the low temperatures, they began to flutter their wings in a shivering motion. This action attracted a rather large, dark-colored bird that grasped the butterflies and flew off with them to a neighboring bush.

After returning to the university, I wrote to a colleague living in Atlanta, Georgia, and asked him to investigate the same area to find out if many of the tagged butterflies had been attacked, and, if possible, to identify the bird involved. My colleague sent a photograph showing a number of monarch butterfly wings under the very bush to which we had observed the bird taking the captured specimens, and he was able to identify the bird as the black-billed cuckoo. This observation indicates that the cuckoo was attracted by the fluttering of the monarch butterfly; consuming it followed. Similar attacks take place at the overwintering sites (as I described in part 6), where low temperatures cause this shivering motion of the wings to take place.

Since I had never observed free-flying monarch or viceroy butterflies being attacked by birds in nature, it occurred to me that perhaps ornithologists who spent a considerable amount of time watching birds might have seen such interaction. I wrote letters to fifty-two members of the American Audubon Society asking them if they had ever seen a bird attack a monarch butterfly and, if so, the species of bird involved. I received twenty-eight replies, only two of which reported a bird attempting to capture a monarch butterfly; the birds involved were the scissor-tailed flycatcher and the western chickadee.

In the more northern parts of North America—the Yukon, the Northwest Territories, and Alaska—viceroy butterflies are ubiquitous in the southern portions, where there is an abundant supply of willow on which the larvae feed. Monarch butterflies do not occur in these northern areas. I wonder how the viceroys survive the onslaught of the thousands of migrating insectivorous birds—warblers and sparrows—that inhabit these regions during the breeding season.

In perusing the voluminous literature dealing with the subject of mimicry, I was not surprised to find that there were a number of scholars who did not agree with the Batesian Mimicry concept of birds eating butterflies. These naturalists based their conclusions on observations in nature rather than on the behavior of confined birds in a laboratory. I present a few of these—the publications from which the quotations have been taken are listed in the Selected References.

> The supporters of the theory regard birds as the main selective agent. At the outset we are met with the fact that relatively few birds have been observed to prey habitually on butterflies, while

some at any rate of those that do so show no discrimination between what should be theoretically pleasant to eat and what
should not be pleasant. Even if birds are the postulated enemies it
must be further shown that they exercise the postulated
discrimination. Looked at critically in the light of what we now
know about heredity and variation, the mimicry hypothesis
is an unsatisfactory explanation of the way in which these remarkable resemblances between different species of butterflies
have been brought about. Sometimes this is admitted by those
who nevertheless embrace the theory with a mild aloofness.
(R. C. Punnett)

Now, birds certainly feed very largely on caterpillars, while they
are but rarely seen to eat butterflies. If, therefore, the aim and object of these special resemblances is the protection of the species,
we should expect to see them in a nearly perfect state in caterpillars, on which birds feed very largely, and poorly developed in
butterflies, which do not appear to be greatly preyed upon by
birds. . . . As a matter of fact, the most striking cases of resemblance to inanimate objects are seen among butterflies, which
seem to stand least in need of them. (D. Dewar and F. Finn)

The little evidence available shows that young Ceylon birds imitate their parents in their choice of food; but as regards butterflies, the fact that there is no discrimination shown by adults
leads one to conclude either that few or no tasting experiments
were undertaken in youth, or, what is more probable, that their
taste with regards to them is indifferent. (N. Manders)

Researchers eager to prove the existence of mimicry under caged conditions
have, for the most part, completely neglected field observations or, if they
have made field observations, failed to record them along with their experimental data. That experiments using caged specimens produced no
meaningful results has been voiced by a number of authors; the following
are two examples.

It has been demonstrated that behaviour of captive animals
towards food is not a reliable indication of what wild individuals
of the same species would do in the presence of the same food. In
other words, since the feeding habits of an animal in captivity
may vary widely from its known habits in the natural state, there

is no avoiding the conclusion that the results obtained under experimental conditions do not indicate the part the animal plays in natural selection. (W. L. McAtee)

I am extremely doubtful as to any real value accruing from experiments on caged birds, whether nestlings or adult. No one, I imagine, believes that all butterflies taste alike; no doubt some are more tasty than others, and caged birds fed upon butterflies even with other insect food would no doubt learn in time to distinguish the different kinds; but this procedure to my mind begs the question, as it assumes that butterflies are an ordinary article of food in the wild state, a proposition regarding which the evidence here brought forward does not altogether support. (N. Manders)

Bird predation of monarch butterflies is of rare occurrence and usually takes place only when the butterflies exhibit a fluttering or shivering wing motion at low temperatures or under caged conditions. This predation should not be considered as having an effect on the survival of a species such as the viceroy simply because, to the human eye, it somewhat resembles the monarch butterfly, which is postulated to be unpalatable to birds. Therefore, all attempts to prove a mimicry hypothesis based on bird predation carried out under caged conditions should be discounted. If one desires an explanation for the close similarity in the appearance of viceroy and monarch butterflies, a simpler and more exact one is that of convergent evolution brought about by similar environmental factors operating on the two species over time.

I have come to the conclusion that the reason experimenters working with birds as the suspected predators have been unable to formulate worthwhile conclusions is simply because birds are not the predators involved. Insects have an extremely long palaeontological history dating back to the Cambrian epoch. Throughout these millions of years, various environmental changes took place, including the advent of numerous additional species of animals, from amphibians and reptiles (including birds) to mammals. Butterflies living in the same geological era were subjected to changes in the environment impinging on their survival. The characteristics of size, shape, and color that we now see in different species of butterflies were indelibly fixed in the hereditary gene complex millions of years ago and have persisted to the present time.

Protective resemblance to escape predator detection is undoubtedly of survival value. For example, there are insects that closely resemble twigs, the bark of trees, and the foliage of plants. I believe that such camouflage developed mostly during the late Palaeozoic and Mesozoic eras, when there existed a tremendous number of arboreal amphibians and lizards, predators that respond to motion and would not be attracted to insects remaining quiescent and resembling some object in nature such as plant parts. If you place a dead insect in front of a toad, the toad does not respond. If you touch the dead insect with a piece of fine wire so that it moves, there is an immediate response by the toad, and it will consume the insect. I have carried out many such experiments with lizards with the same results.

Many species of insects are undoubtedly distasteful to the various animals that might eat them. I believe that the evolution of bad-smelling or bad-tasting substances in the bodies of insects to repel predators developed not to ward off birds but amphibians and reptiles. If you offer an offensive insect to a toad or frog, it will immediately remove the insect from its mouth, often allowing the insect to crawl away unharmed. Hence, the substance has true survival value. But by the time a bird has pecked at an insect, or swallowed it so that it reaches the taste receptor cells at the back of the bird's throat, the insect is so damaged that it will not survive. Hence, the chemical repellant has little survival value.

It is interesting to note that insects that appear to possess some distasteful substance are often brightly colored (although there are numerous exceptions, such as dull brown bugs and black beetles that also appear to possess such substances). This has led to the theory of "warning coloration." However, many brightly colored insects do not apparently possess such distasteful substances. Not enough experimental studies have been carried out to come to an adequate conclusion on this issue. I do not believe that the orange coloration of the monarch butterfly belongs in the category of protective coloration against predators.

Formulate your own conclusions. I recall a statement given by one of my professors, the late Dr. H. G. Huntsman, when I was a student. He was dealing with a similar hypothesis concerning mimicry in species of fish and said: "Don't naively accept the opinions of others, with respect to a controversial subject, as gospel truth, as qualified as it may appear on paper; formulate your own conclusions based upon your own experiences."

In order to formulate your own conclusions, make observations in nature and answer the question: How often does a bird attempt to capture a viceroy or monarch butterfly?

New World Relatives
of the Monarch Butterfly

MEGALIPPE, PLEXIPPUS,
AND HYBRIDIZATION

The color patterns of monarch butterflies are fairly constant throughout North America. However, the occasional specimen is very dark, especially the black band along the leading edge of the hind wings. In some females, the band almost completely obliterates the two rows of white spots. Some monarchs possess very light spots at the apical portions of their front wings. Not only is this color variation present in adults, but larvae are occasionally collected in which the black band is large, almost obliterating the light yellow and white bands, thus imparting a dark color to the entire body.

Upon examining my collection of specimens from various islands of the South Atlantic and the Caribbean, northern areas of South America, and Central America, I noted a wide variation in the dark band of the hind pair of wings and a lack of color in the spots at the apex of the front pair of wings. This is most noticeable in males.

Upon receiving specimens of monarch butterflies from Montserrat in the Leeward Islands, I realized that they represented the dark form, which has been given the subspecies name *megalippe*. Comparing these to the specimens from Puerto Rico, I concluded that there was a degree of hybridization between *plexippus* from North America and *megalippe* from the islands. In order to investigate this possibility, Norah and I made frequent field trips to the islands of Montserrat and Antigua in the Leeward Islands of the Lesser Antilles, as well as to Trinidad and Tobago off the northeast coast of Venezuela, where we collected specimens of adults and larvae of *megalippe*.

The larvae of *megalippe* are very dark in color; the narrow black band found among the larvae in North America is expanded so as to obliterate most of the yellow band and, except for light streaks, all of the white band. I obtained hundreds of eggs from *megalippe* females and reared them to the adult stage. Of the first-generation specimens, all showed only the characteristics of *megalippe*. I then crossed them with the North America *plexippus* and obtained 320 hybrids in the first generation. The extent of the black band varied: 140 had no white band and were identical to *megalippe;* 103 showed streaks of white in the center of the black band; 55 had distinct but narrow white bands; and 22 had complete white bands similar to those of *plexippus*. I also found a wide range of variation in the color of the hybrid larvae. Some had little or no white band and a greatly reduced yellow band typical of the larvae of *megalippe*. Others had well-developed yellow and white bands identical to those of *plexippus*. The majority exhibited marked variation in the size of the black band. This experiment in crossing the two subspecies explained the range of variation in monarch butterfly coloration in the islands of the Caribbean, in Central America, and in North America.

Refer to color plate 24. The upper two specimens are *megalippe* from the island of Antigua. Note the dark band without any light spots along the margin of the hind wings of the male and the faint white spots in that of the female. Also note the lighter color of the spots on the apical portions of the front wings. I found these characteristics to be uniform throughout the population in Montserrat, Antigua, Trinidad, and Tobago. Comparing these with specimens from North America, shown in the second row, one notes the following: the white spots of *megalippe* are buff in *plexippus;* the white spots on the margin of the hind wings of *plexippus* are arranged in two distinct rows, but are absent in the females and faint or partly obliterated in the males of *megalippe*. The specimens shown in the second and third rows are hybrids. Note the slight buff color of the spots on the front wings and the marked variation in the dark band of the hind wings, varying from almost complete obliteration of the white spots to two complete rows of distinct spots.

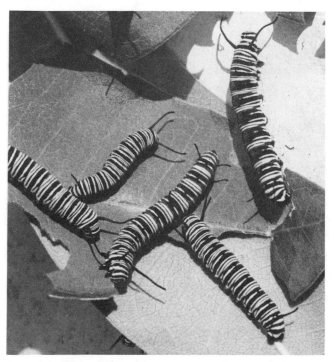

Larval hybrids resulting from crossing plexippus plexippus *from North America with the dark form, or subspecies,* plexippus megalippe, *which occurs in the islands of the South Atlantic and the Caribbean and in South and Central America, show the range of variation in the extent of the black band. In the typical* megalippe, *the dark band completely obliterates the white band and much of the yellow. Specimens from the Greater Antilles, Central America, and Yucatan exhibit the same variation. The occasional dark hybrid occurs in North America; I have a number of examples in my collection from the vicinity of Toronto, Ontario.*

South of the Brazilian forest occurs a true species, *Danaus erippus,* shown in plate 22, in which the black band seen in *plexippus* along the rear margin of the front wings is absent. In addition to this marked difference, the male genitalia are remarkably different from that of *Danaus plexippus.* This species apparently migrates in a manner similar to that of *plexippus* in North America, although no in-depth studies have been made to confirm such reports.

Thus, there are two distinct species of monarch butterflies in the New World: *Danaus plexippus* and *Danaus erippus,* with a melanistic form, *megalippe,* in the former, together with a wide range of variation due to hybridization between *plexippus* and *megalippe.*

QUEENS

In addition to the true monarch butterflies of the species *Danaus plexippus* and *D. erippus,* there are two other decidedly similar species: *D. gilippus* and *D. erisimus.* These two species are about three-quarters the size of the monarch butterfly. The alar gland of the male is much larger and much more conspicuous; the light spots on the front wings are smaller, more numerous, and white in color rather than buff. The general ground color of the wing varies from light to dark brown with a slight tinge of orange. Larvae possess three pairs of fleshy filaments instead of the two found in the monarch butterfly. Because of the variation in the number and arrangement of the light spots on the front wings, a number of subspecies have been proposed, many of which, I am certain, are hybrids resulting from the crossing of pure strains. These diminutive members of the royal family have been given the popular name "queens."

Since queen butterflies occur commonly in the southern parts of North America, I have included a color plate of the various species and subspecies for identification, along with the South American monarch butterfly, *Danaus erippus.*

In addition to the species and subspecies of the genus *Danaus* occurring in North America, there are numerous other species and subspecies found in other parts of the world, especially in Indonesia. Very little is known of their biology and habits.

Do Other Species
of Butterflies Migrate?

If we accept the definition of *migration* as a movement from one locality to another, then the answer to the question, Do other species of butterflies migrate? is yes. A number of species move en masse apparently in one direction, although alar-tagging experiments similar to those discussed in this book have not been carried out. While following the migratory route of the monarch butterfly along the coast of the Gulf of Mexico, I observed, year after year, mass movements of three species of butterflies: gulf fritillary, long-tailed skipper, and cloudless sulphur. These three species moved in the same westward direction as the monarch butterfly, at times in considerable numbers.

In order to obtain data on the movements of other species of butterflies, my associates and I, working in various parts of the United States over a period of ten years, alar tagged a number of species representing four families. They are:

1. Papilionidae (swallowtails): black swallowtail *(Papilio polyxenes asterias);* giant swallowtail *(Papilio cresphontes);* tiger swallowtail *(Papilio glaucus);* spicebush swallowtail *(Papilio troilus);* zebra

swallowtail *(Graphium marcellus)*; Baird's swallowtail *(Papilio bairdii)*; polydamus swallowtail *(Papilio polydamus)*.

2. Nymphalidae (brush-footed butterflies): hackberry *(Asterocampa celtis)*; tawny emperor *(Asterocampa clyton)*; viceroy *(Limenitis archippus)*; painted lady *(Vanessa cardui)*; buckeye *(Junonia coenia)*; mourning cloak *(Nymphalis antiopa)*; question mark *(Polygonia interrogationis)*; comma *(Polygonia comma)*; great spangled fritillary *(Speyeria cybele)*; tortoise shell *(Nymphalis milberti)*; white admiral *(Limenitis arthemis)*.

3. Pieridae (whites and sulphurs): cabbage *(Pieris rapae)*; orange clover *(Colias eurytheme)*; yellow clover *(Colias philodice)*; cloudless sulphur *(Phoebis sennae eubule)*; orange-barred sulphur *(Phoebis philea)*.

4. Hisperidae (skippers): silver-spotted *(Epargyreus clarus)*; Brazilian *(Calpodes ethlius)*.

The recapture data for these tagged species show that they did not move in any particular direction, either in fall or in spring, with the exception of the three species mentioned for the coast of the Gulf of Mexico. I would classify them as "nomads." Or perhaps they represent a dispersal from a breeding center, rather than a migration. Although some of the alar-tagged specimens were recaptured at considerable distances, such as the spicebush swallowtail that traveled 156 kilometers and a mourning cloak that traveled 103 kilometers, most returns showed distances traveled of less than 16 kilometers. The direction of movement was variable throughout the summer. In addition to the dispersal nature of the movements, none of the butterflies formed overnight roosting clusters.

I tentatively conclude, in the absence of more exact data, that the monarch butterfly is the only species that is an "annual remigrant." Ornithologists would consider the monarch butterfly a true migrant, using this term as I use the term remigrant.

Milkweed Species of North America

This list of *Asclepias* species is based on specimens I have collected and those sent to me, collections in colleges and universities, and records in the literature. Few species exist in the provinces of Canada with the exception of Ontario. The greatest number are found in Mexico. This leads me to believe that perhaps the aboriginal home of the monarch was Mexico. However, in the distant past, species of milkweed were confined to the eastern parts of the continent and later spread westward. This would indicate that the eastern breeding areas were the aboriginal home. (See part 5.)

CANADA

British Columbia (1 species)
  speciosa

Manitoba (6 species)

incarnata	*ovalifolia*	*speciosa*
verticillata	*syriaca*	*viridiflora*

New Brunswick (1 species)
syriaca

Nova Scotia (1 species)
incarnata

Ontario (10 species)

incarnata	*quadrifolia*	*hirtella*
verticillata	*syriaca*	*viridiflora*
tuberosa	*sullivantii*	
exaltata (phytolaccoides)	*purpurascens*	

Quebec (2 species)
incarnata
syriaca

Saskatchewan (2 species)
ovalifolia
speciosa

UNITED STATES

Alabama (14 species)

perennis	*amplexicaulis*	*obovata*
verticillata	*quadrifolia*	*longifolia*
tuberosa	*humistrata*	*viridiflora*
rubra	*variegata*	*viridis*
lanceolata	*michauxii*	

Arizona (26 species)

angustifolia	*macrosperma*	*brachystephana*
subverticillata	*macrotis*	*cutleri*
tuberosa	*lemmoni*	*viridiflora*
quinquedentata	*latifolia*	*cryptoceras*
hypoleuca	*erosa*	*rusbyi*
linaria	*albicans*	*engelmanniana*
hallii	*nummularia*	*elata*
speciosa	*subulata*	*asperula*
involucrata	*nyctaginifolia*	

Arkansas (12 species)

incarnata

perennis

verticillata

tuberosa

amplexicaulis

quadrifolia

variegata

purpurascens

hirtella

viridiflora

stenophylla

viridis

California (17 species)

cuarassavica

fascicularis

tuberosa

linaria

speciosa

latifolia

erosa

eriocarpa

albicans

vestita

subulata

nyctaginifolia

cordifolia

californica

cryptoceras

solanoana

asperula

Colorado (16 species)

incarnata

subverticillata

pumila

tuberosa

hallii

speciosa

involucrata

macrotis

arenaria

latifolia

uncialis

viridiflora

cryptoceras

stenophylla

engelmanniana

asperula

Connecticut (10 species)

incarnata

verticillata

tuberosa

exaltata

amplexicaulis

quadrifolia

syriaca

variegata

purpurascens

viridiflora

Delaware (12 species)

incarnata

verticillata

tuberosa

rubra

lanceolata

exaltata

amplexicaulis

syriaca

variegata

purpurascens

longifolia

viridiflora

District of Columbia (2 species)

incarnata

purpurascens

Florida (20 species)

incarnata	viridula	connivens
perennis	humistrata	cinerea
curassavica	variegata	feayi
verticillata	curtissii	longifolia
tuberosa	michauxii	viridis
lanceolata	tomentosa	pedicellata
amplexicaulis	obovata	

Georgia (20 species)

incarnata	amplexicaulis	connivens
perennis	quadrifolia	cinerea
verticillata	syriaca	longifolia
tuberosa	humistrata	viridiflora
rubra	variegata	viridis
lanceolata	michauxii	pedicellata
exaltata	obovata	

Idaho (5 species)

fascicularis	speciosa	asperula
subverticillata	cryptoceras	

Illinois (17 species)

incarnata	quadrifolia	purpurascens
perennis	ovalifolia	hirtella
verticillata	syriaca	viridiflora
tuberosa	meadii	nuttalliana
exaltata	sullivantii	viridis
amplexicaulis	variegata	

Indiana (13 species)

incarnata	amplexicaulis	purpurascens
perennis	quadrifolia	hirtella
verticillata	syriaca	viridiflora
tuberosa	sullivantii	
exaltata	variegata	

Iowa (15 species)

incarnata	quadrifolia	purpurascens
verticillata	ovalifolia	speciosa
tuberosa	syriaca	hirtella
exaltata	meadii	viridiflora
amplexicaulis	sullivantii	nuttalliana

Kansas (21 species)

incarnata	meadii	hirtella
verticillata	sullivantii	viridiflora
pumila	purpurascens	nuttalliana
tuberosa	speciosa	stenophylla
amplexicaulis	involucrata	engelmanniana
quadrifolia	arenaria	viridis
syriaca	latifolia	asperula

Kentucky (13 species)

incarnata	amplexicaulis	hirtella
perennis	quadrifolia	viridiflora
verticillata	syriaca	viridis
tuberosa	variegata	
exaltata	purpurascens	

Louisiana (15 species)

incarnata	rubra	michauxii
perennis	lanceolata	obovata
curassavica	amplexicaulis	longifolia
verticillata	humistrata	viridiflora
tuberosa	variegata	viridis

Maine (3 species)

incarnata	exaltata	syriaca

Maryland (7 species)

incarnata	rubra	viridiflora
verticillata	amplexicaulis	
tuberosa	variegata	

Massachusetts (8 species)

incarnata	exaltata	syriaca
verticillata	amplexicaulis	purpurascens
tuberosa	quadrifolia	

Michigan (9 species)

incarnata	exaltata	purpurascens
verticillata	amplexicaulis	hirtella
tuberosa	syriaca	viridiflora

North Carolina (14 species)

incarnata	amplexicaulis	tomentosa
verticillata	quadrifolia	longifolia
tuberosa	syriaca	viridiflora
lanceolata	humistrata	pedicellata
exaltata	variegata	

North Dakota (9 species)

incarnata	ovalifolia	speciosa
verticillata	syriaca	viridiflora
pumila	sullivantii	nuttalliana

Ohio (13 species)

incarnata	quadrifolia	hirtella
verticillata	syriaca	viridiflora
tuberosa	sullivantii	viridis
exaltata	variegata	
amplexicaulis	purpurascens	

Oklahoma (19 species)

incarnata	variegata	viridiflora
verticillata	purpurascens	stenophylla
tuberosa	speciosa	engelmanniana
amplexicaulis	macrotis	viridis
quadrifolia	arenaria	asperula
syriaca	latifolia	
sullivantii	hirtella	

Oregon (5 species)

fascicularis	speciosa	cryptoceras
syriaca	cordifolia	

Pennsylvania (10 species)

incarnata	amplexicaulis	purpurascens
verticillata	quadrifolia	viridiflora
tuberosa	syriaca	
exaltata	variegata	

Rhode Island (8 species)

incarnata	exaltata	syriaca
verticillata	amplexicaulis	purpurascens
tuberosa	quadrifolia	

South Carolina (16 species)

incarnata	quadrifolia	cinerea
perennis	humistrata	longifolia
verticillata	variegata	viridiflora
tuberosa	michauxii	pedicellata
lanceolata	tomentosa	
amplexicaulis	obovata	

South Dakota (10 species)

incarnata	syriaca	nuttalliana
verticillata	speciosa	stenophylla
tuberosa	arenaria	
ovafolia	viridiflora	

Minnesota (12 species)

incarnata	amplexicaulis	speciosa
verticillata	ovalifolia	hirtella
tuberosa	syriaca	viridiflora
exaltata	sullivantii	nuttalliana

Mississippi (10 species)

perennis	humistrata	longifolia
verticillata	variegata	viridis
tuberosa	michauxii	
lanceolata	obovata	

Missouri (16 species)

incarnata	quadrifolia	hirtella
perennis	syriaca	viridiflora
curassavica	meadii	stenophylla
verticillata	sullivantii	viridis
tuberosa	variegata	
amplexicaulis	purpurascens	

Montana (3 species)

syriaca	speciosa	viridiflora

Nebraska (15 species)

incarnata	syriaca	viridiflora
verticillata	sullivantii	nuttalliana
pumila	speciosa	stenophylla
tuberosa	arenaria	engelmanniana
amplexicaulis	latifolia	viridis

Nevada (9 species)

fascicularis	*erosa*	*cordifolia*
hallii	*subulata*	*cryptoceras*
speciosa	*ruthiae*	*asperula*

New Hampshire (6 species)

incarnata	*exaltata*	*syriaca*
tuberosa	*amplexicaulis*	*purpurascens*

New Jersey (12 species)

incarnata	*lanceolata*	*syriaca*
verticillata	*exaltata*	*variegata*
tuberosa	*amplexicaulis*	*purpurascens*
rubra	*quadrifolia*	*viridiflora*

New Mexico (21 species)

incarnata	*hallii*	*oenotheroides*
subverticillata	*speciosa*	*brachystephana*
pumila	*involucrata*	*uncialis*
tuberosa	*macrotis*	*viridiflora*
quinquedentata	*arenaria*	*engelmanniana*
scaposa	*latifolia*	*elata*
hypoleuca	*nyctaginifolia*	*aseperula*

New York (10 species)

incarnata	*amplexicaulis*	*purpurascens*
verticillata	*quadrifolia*	*viridiflora*
tuberosa	*syriaca*	
exaltata	*variegata*	

Tennessee (12 species)

incarnata	*exaltata*	*variegata*
perennis	*amplexicaulis*	*hirtella*
verticillata	*quadrifolia*	*viridiflora*
tuberosa	*syriaca*	*viridis*

Texas (30 species)

incarnata	lanceolata	oenotheroides
texana	amplexicaulis	emoryi
perennis	variegata	brachystephana
linearis	speciosa	viridiflora
curassavica	macrotis	stenophylla
subverticillata	tomentosa	engelmanniana
verticillata	arenaria	elata
pumila	latifolia	sperryi
tuberosa	obovata	viridis
rubra	nummularia	asperula

Utah (15 species)

incarnata	speciosa	ruthiae
fascicularis	involucrata	cutleri
subverticillata	macrosperma	cryptoceras
tuberosa	latifolia	rusbyi
hallii	labriformis	asperula

Vermont (6 species)

incarnata	exaltata	quadrifolia
tuberosa	amplexicaulis	syriaca

Virginia (12 species)

incarnata	exaltata	variegata
verticillata	amplexicaulis	purpurascens
tuberosa	quadrifolia	longifolia
lanceolata	syriaca	viridiflora

Washington (2 species)

fascicularis
speciosa

West Virginia (10 species)

incarnata	amplexicaulis	hirtella
verticillata	quadrifolia	viridiflora
tuberosa	syriaca	
exaltata	variegata	

Wisconsin (12 species)

incarnata	amplexicaulis	sullivantii
verticillata	ovalifolia	hirtella
tuberosa	syriaca	viridiflora
exaltata	meadii	nuttalliana

Wyoming (5 species)

pumila	speciosa	cryptoceras
hallii	viridiflora	

MEXICO (59 SPECIES)

texana	glaucescens	rosea
woodsoniana	pellucida	auriculata
pseudorubricaulis	hypoleuca	subulata
curassavica	pringlei	oenotheroides
augustifolia	pratensis	emoryi
fascicularis	linaria	standleyi
subverticillata	lanuginosa	brachystephana
mexicana	euphorbiaefolia	vinosa
leptopus	conzattii	viridiflora
gentryi	involucrata	engelmanniana
tuberosa	puberula	elata
ovata	macrotis	mirifica
similis	lemmoni	fournieri
contrayerba	laxiflora	zanthodacryon
coulteri	arenaria	sperryi
quinquedentata	eriocarpa	asperula
virletii	masonii	circinalis
scaposa	subaphylla	mcvaughii
crocea	albicans	atroviolacea
grandiflora	nummularia	

CENTRAL AMERICA (10 SPECIES)

woodsoniana	glaucescens	oenotheroides
curassavica	pellucida	elata
similis	rosea	
contrayerba	auriculata	

GREATER ANTILLES (2 SPECIES)

curassavica
nivea

Rearing
Monarch Butterflies

During the past thirty-two years, Norah and I have worked cooperatively with over four thousand volunteer research associates, including members of clubs and school classes. In order to obtain specimens for study and for alar tagging, our associates have used a variety of rearing methods. School children have raised monarch butterflies in jars, shoeboxes and milk cartons. The more enthusiastic naturalists have constructed cages of various sizes. The following will be of assistance to you if you wish to pursue the study of the monarch butterfly as a hobby, as a classroom project, or for experimental purposes.

EGGS AND YOUNG LARVAE

Since milkweed leaves on which eggs have been deposited will become dry or, if placed in a closed container, will rot, it is necessary to remove the eggs from the leaf and place them in a suitable container. I remove the eggs by cutting out a small portion of the leaf as close to the egg as possible. These leaf sections containing eggs are then placed in petri dishes (any shallow dish such as a saucer that can be covered with plastic wrap may be used). Keep the eggs well separated since newly emerged larvae will devour other eggs.

When the larvae emerge from the eggs, remove them from the dish, and place them in small jars containing milkweed leaves (small, tender leaves taken from young plants are best). Remove the larvae from the dish by means of a fine artist's brush, slightly moistened so as to cause the larvae to adhere to the bristles. Do not attempt to pick up the hatchlings with your fingers since they can be readily squashed.

As the larvae grow larger, transfer them to larger containers and eventually to rearing cages.

LARVAL CAGES

Although there are many types of containers that may be used for rearing the larvae, I have found the following to be most successful.

LARGE CAGES

These are used not only for rearing large numbers of larvae but also as flight cages for the adults. My cages measure 70 × 70 × 100 centimeters (2 × 2 × 3 feet). The frame of the cage is covered on four sides by glass screen, leaving the top and bottom of the cage open. Being open at the bottom, the cage can be placed over a cluster of milkweed plants. When rearing is carried out indoors, the cage can be placed over sheets of paper, thus allowing for easy removal of larval droppings. A piece of plywood, or stiff cardboard if used indoors, is placed over the open top; this allows one to introduce fresh milkweed plants and remove the old ones. Having a removable top also facilitates collecting suspended pupae.

SMALL TIERED CAGES

Smaller cages—mine measure 50 × 50 × 30 centimeters (20 × 8 × 12 inches)—are constructed in the same manner as the flight cages and can be placed one on top of the other. This allows for expansion of space when needed and for the removal of the adults that, on emerging from the pupae, tend to fly to the top cage, which can then be removed.

AQUARIA AND JARS

For observational purposes, especially for class demonstrations, aquaria and large glass jars have been used successfully. The difficulty in using such containers is that of removing the old plants and introducing fresh material, as well as the difficulty of removing the droppings. Usually, larvae can be transferred to clean jars and the dirty ones cleaned for the next transfer.

BUTTERFLY CAGES

For housing adults, I use cages that are the same size as those for rearing larvae, but I cover the sides with cheesecloth rather than glass screen. Cloth reduces the amount of damage to a butterfly's wings when the butterfly flies against the sides of the cage. A small hole in one or two of the upper corners allows for the insertion of a cloth soaked in a honey or sugar solution. I make the solution fresh every second day—one teaspoon of honey to a cup of water. The area around the wet cloth becomes dampened with the honey solution, thus increasing the feeding area. (It is interesting to note that the honey solution around the cloth eventually ferments, and females deposit eggs on it for reasons that I have never been able to discover.)

I have tried various modifications of this feeding method, such as suspending a dampened cloth—a strip about 4 centimeters wide and 24 centimeters long—through a hole in the top of the cage. A small vessel placed beneath the cloth collects the excess solution as it drips from the end. This method has the advantage that more solution can be added to the cloth without removing it. I use a medicine dropper to add more solution. I have also used small sponges soaked in the honey solution; these hold the solution without dripping. Cloth and sponges should be cleaned frequently.

If you wish to obtain eggs from egg-laying females collected in the field, place milkweed plants in the cage. Lean the plants against the sides of the cage so as to allow the females to more easily deposit their eggs. The plants can be readily removed and fresh material added by lifting the cage, since the bottom has been left open.

REMOVING PUPAE FROM CONTAINERS

To remove a pupa from a surface, first liberally moisten the silk mat that surrounds the button. Then, using a razor blade or sharp paring knife, gradually and carefully scrape the silk mat from its support. Place the pupa in a box or other container to allow the silk mat to dry. When dry, the silk mat will resemble a cord. To make a realistic suspension of the pupa, place a drop of a quick-drying glue on the silk mat and apply it to a small twig or other object suitable for your purpose. The silk mat must be held in place with a small piece of thread until the glue has set. The thread can be removed if you wish to take photographs.

A second and simpler method is to place the dry silk mat between the folds of a piece of adhesive tape. A pin or needle inserted through the tape allows you to attach the pupa to a piece of wood or cardboard. The disadvantage of this method compared to the use of glue, however, is the presence of the adhesive tape, especially if you intend to record your observations by taking photographs of each step in the pupal development.

TREATMENT OF
NEWLY EMERGED BUTTERFLIES

When a monarch butterfly first emerges from its pupa and while its wings are expanding, it is very soft and can be easily damaged. Therefore, the pupa should be suspended in a location free from the possibility of accidental jarring, which might cause the butterfly to fall to the floor. Newly emerged adults should not be handled. If you wish to transfer a specimen to some other location, do so by allowing it to cling to your finger or some object. At least twenty-four hours are required for the wings to become sufficiently hardened to allow for prolonged flight. At least two days should elapse before you attempt to apply an alar tag or kill a specimen for display purposes.

KEEPING MONARCH BUTTERFLIES
DURING THE WINTER MONTHS

By rearing monarch butterflies indoors in a room with temperatures at or above 21°C, it is possible to have live monarch butterflies available throughout the winter months. Collect specimens during the breeding season. If they are collected in the fall during the fall migration, mating will not take place, since the butterflies are in reproductive dormancy. Large flight cages are essential if the adults are to mate. If the monarchs will not mate, it is possible to "force mate" by placing the tip of the abdomen of a male against that of a female; the male will eventually grasp the female with his chitinous claspers and remain attached for several hours. However, in my laboratory I had no difficulty with mating so long as the flight cages were of a large size.

One of the difficulties of maintaining a breeding population during the winter months is having an adequate supply of milkweed leaves available for the larvae. If you have the use of a greenhouse, plants can be grown throughout the winter, or, as some teachers have done for classroom purposes, the plants may be grown in pots on the ledge of a well-lighted window. However, I have found that the simplest method is to use frozen milkweed leaves. Each year I gather a supply of leaves in the early summer, when the leaves are most tender and free of aphid infestation. I stack the leaves like a deck of cards, one upon the other, and place them in small bundles in plastic bags, which are then placed in a freezer. When leaves are required, a bundle is removed from its plastic envelope, the necessary number of leaves are removed and thawed, and the remainder are replaced in the freezer. Once thawed, the leaves decay rapidly, so it is necessary to replace them each day.

Various artificial diets have been used for rearing different species of butterflies and moths. They require fifteen different substances, many of them difficult to procure, together with a solution of eight different vitamins. I have used these artificial diets with some of my laboratory populations and have found that they are inconvenient and result in a much reduced growth rate.

If you wish to keep live monarch butterflies without rearing them, it is possible to do so by the use of periods of low temperatures. However, monarch butterflies that have entered the reproductive dormancy state, such as those involved in the fall migration, must be used—those in breeding condition will not survive. What you want to do is duplicate the conditions at the overwintering site, where temperatures are low and humidity high. High humidity is most important in whatever method is used.

Place specimens in plastic envelopes in which you have inserted a small piece of cotton soaked in water to maintain high humidity. The envelopes are then completely sealed—they contain sufficient oxygen to maintain life for short periods of time—and placed in a cool room at 4°C. Every two or three weeks the butterflies must be removed from the envelopes in a warm room in order to feed. This is done by holding a butterfly by the wings and bringing the tarsi of the legs into contact with a honey solution. Upon coming into contact with the solution, the butterfly's proboscis will extend and feeding will take place. Then return the butterfly to the envelope and place it once again in the cool room.

In my laboratory I had the use of three "growth chambers," which allowed for controlled conditions. The temperature could be lowered to bring about dormancy and raised for feeding. The humidity was kept high at all times.

One of my associates in New Zealand was able to keep two monarch butterflies, one male and one female, throughout the winter months by allowing them to fly free through the rooms of the house for brief periods for flight and feeding and then placing them in a cage to be stored in a cool room. The cage was constructed of mosquito netting and was sprayed each day with water to maintain a high humidity. The specimens were maintained for eight months under these conditions.

By rearing the monarch butterflies from eggs through to the adult stage, much can be learned, not only about the monarchs but also about insects in general. From the point of view of students, particularly those in elementary and secondary schools, I know of no more interesting and inspiring method of introducing the subject of entomology (the study of insects) and the role insects play in our economy and the world of living organisms. By collecting the larvae and eggs outdoors, students become aware of the interrelationships of insects and plants and, what is most important, they learn that there are very few insects that can be rightly labeled "pests." The vast majority of insects are beneficial and play an important role in the intricate network of dependency.

Selected References

GENERAL INFORMATION

A General Textbook of Entomology, by A. D. Imms and later revised by O. W. Richards and R. G. Davies (London: Butler and Tanner Ltd., 1973), is a book for the professional entomologist. It is a source book of encyclopedic proportions for information about insects in all their aspects. This book has been my constant companion since publication of the first edition in 1925.

The Butterfly Garden, by Miriam Rothchild and Clives Farrell (London: Michael Joseph Ltd., 1983), is directed primarily to those wishing to raise butterflies outdoors or in a greenhouse. It is well illustrated with numerous drawings and a few excellent photographs in color.

Introducing the Insect, by Fred Urquhart (London: Clarke, Irwin and Company Ltd., 1949), was intended as an introduction to the study of insect identification and habits. It contains numerous drawings by E. B. S. Logier. A second edition of the book was published in 1965 by Frederick Warne and Company, Ltd., London.

The Life of Insects, by V. B. Wigglesworth (London: Weidenfeld and Nicolson, 1964), is a readable presentation of various aspects of insect life, such as diet, growth, color, defense, vision, and so on. It is illustrated with excellent drawings and photographs.

SPECIFICALLY ABOUT THE MONARCH BUTTERFLY

Wings in the Meadow, by Jo Brewer (Boston, Mass.: Houghton Mifflin, 1967), deals with the life of the monarch butterfly, including its migration, told in a delightful manner and with personal anecdotes.

Monarch Butterflies, by Alice L. Hopf (New York: Thomas Y. Crowell, 1965), is intended for the young reader and deals primarily with methods of raising monarchs.

The Travels of Monarch X, by Ross E. Hutchins (Chicago, Ill.: Rand McNally, 1966), is about the adventures of one of my alar-tagged specimens as it journeys across the continent to its overwintering site in Mexico.

The Monarch Butterfly, by Fred Urquhart (Toronto: University of Toronto Press, 1960), presents a great deal of scientific data that is not in the present book, including a section on the external anatomy of the adult monarch butterfly.

SOUTH PACIFIC ISLANDS

New Zealand Butterflies, by George W. Gibbs (London: Collins, 1980). Of all the books on butterflies in my library and numerous others I have consulted over the years, this book is the most delightful contribution. Although written in a scholarly fashion, it is easy to read and contains a wealth of information, not only about the species found in New Zealand but also about the details of life cycles and the introduction of butterflies from other lands. Much of the information is presented in the first person, thus keeping the book from being too academic, which plagues so many scholarly publications.

When I began my studies of the monarch butterflies in New Zealand, I was unaware of the activities of Dr. K. A. S. Wise, curator of insects at the Auckland Institute and Museum, who was alar tagging the monarchs using my method as given to him by one of our associates, Dr. Smithers of Australia. Dr. Wise presented his research data in 1980 in a publication of the Auckland Institute. Since my research added nothing to what Dr. Wise had accomplished, I did not submit my data to a science journal. For those interested in Wise's data, a copy of his paper may be obtained by writing to the Auckland Institute (or to Dr. Wise).

Data concerning the distribution of the monarch butterfly on the islands of the South Pacific are contained in articles in a number of different journals, which I have summarized in this book.

MIMICRY

A great many scientific papers on Batesian and Muhlerian mimicry have been published—I have 826 references in my own file. Much of the data is based on laboratory experiments and is fraught with anthropomorphic conclusions and interpretations. It would serve no purpose to list even a representative number of these. However, for those who might wish to read some of these papers, I suggest the following from which further references may be obtained.

"Heart poisons in the monarch butterfly," by Reichstein, Parsons, and Rothchild. *Science*, vol. 161, 1968.

"Ecological Chemistry," by L. P. Brower. *Scientific American*, 1969. This semi-popular article deals with the possibility of the monarch being distasteful to birds based on the reactions of blue jays.

"Some adaptations between *Danaus plexippus* and its food plant, with notes on *Danaus chrysippus* and *Euploea core*," by Erickson, Kellett, and Rothchild. *London Journal of Zoology*, vol. 185, 1978.

SCIENTIFIC PAPERS QUOTED IN TEXT

"Some breeding experiments on *Catopsilia pyranthe* and notes on the migration of butterflies in Ceylon." *Transactions of the Entomological Society of London*, 1904.

"An investigation into the validity of Mullerean and other forms of mimicry." *Proceeding of the Zoological Society of London*, 1911.

"Mimicry in butterflies," by R. C. Punnett. Cambridge University Press, 1915.

"The making of species," by Douglas Dewar and Frank Finn. John Lane Co., New York, 1919.

"Effectiveness in nature of the so-called adaptations in the animal kingdom," by W. L. McAtee. Written in 1932 and published in the Smithsonian Miscellaneous Collection, no. 85.

W. B. McAtee's answers to criticisms of his paper with respect to protective adaptation of insects. *Proceedings of the Royal Entomological Society of London,* 1932.

"The integumental anatomy of the monarch butterfly, *Danaus plexippus L.,*" by Paul R. Ehrlich. *University of Kansas Scientific Bulletin,* no. 38, 1958. This publication defines in minute detail the complicated arrangement of the various parts of the external anatomy of the adult monarch butterfly.

MORE SCIENTIFIC PAPERS

The following are a few of my articles that have appeared in various scientific journals and have formed the basis for this book. I list them mainly for researchers interested in following up some of the items contained in them as well as references to the publications of other researchers in the same field.

"Virus-caused epizootic as a factor in population fluctuations of the monarch butterfly." *Journal of Invertebrate Pathology,* vol. 8, 1966.

"Fluctuation in numbers of the monarch butterfly in North America." *Atalanta* (West Germany), vol. 3, 1970.

"Functions of the prismatic pigmented maculae (PPM) of the pupa of *Danaus p. plexippus." Annales Zoologica Fennici,* vol. 9, 1972.

"Epidermal cells of the PPM of the pupa of the monarch butterfly." *Journal of the Lepidoptera Society,* vol. 26, 1972.

"The overwintering site of the eastern population of the monarch butterfly in southern Mexico." *Journal of the Lepidoptera Society,* vol. 30, 1976.

"Found at last: The monarch's winter home." *National Geographic,* Aug. 1976.

"Autumnal migration routes of the eastern population of the monarch butterfly in North America." *Canadian Journal of Zoology,* vol. 56, 1978.

"Vernal migration of the monarch butterfly in North America." *Canadian Entomologist,* vol. 3, 1979.

"Aberrant autumnal migration of the eastern population of the monarch butterfly." *Canadian Entomologist,* vol. 3, 1979.

Index